The Woman Who Spilled Words All over Herself

Other Books by Rosemary Daniell

The Woman Who Spilled Words All Over Herself

Writing and Living the Zona Rosa Way

ROSEMARY DANIELL

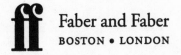

Faber and Faber
BOSTON • LONDON

Copyright © 1997 by Rosemary Daniell
This paperback edition first published in 1998.

Library of Congress Cataloging-in-Publication Data

Daniell, Rosemary.
    The woman who spilled words all over herself : writing and living
  the Zona Rosa way / Rosemary Daniell.
        p.   cm.
    ISBN 0-571-19935-6 (paper)
    1. Authorship. 2. Creative writing. 3. Women authors.
  4. Women and literature. I. Title.
  PN471.D36   1997
  808'.02–dc20   96-43624
                                                        CIP

Cover design by Janet M. Clesse
Printed in the United States of America

... without sweets, or a mouth,
                or a thicket of roses,
you come flying.
                    —PABLO NERUDA

Stay at your table and listen.
Don't even listen, just wait.
Don't even wait, be completely quiet and alone.
The world will offer itself to you to be unmasked ...
in raptures, it will writhe before you.
                                —FRANZ KAFKA

I speak to the highest that is in you.
                    —NAVAJO SAYING.

*For my mother, Melissa Ruth Connell, a beautiful southern
woman who was also a talented writer who thought
she didn't have the right to be one*

Acknowledgments

With gratitude to every woman and man who has been a part of Zona Rosa, and thus my life, especially Lenore, Ruby, Jane Ann, and Joan, who left this world—and us—too soon. Always, you have inspired me.

With special thanks to Mrs. Brown, my seventh-grade teacher—wherever you may be—for helping me realize that yes, I could write.

With thanks, too, to Danielle Alexander for sharing her copyediting expertise; to Robin Banks for smoothing the bumps along the way; to Caitlin McRae for her willingness to help with the mundane; and to Charlotte Harrell, Lois Knight, Sarah Rakes, and Patricia Von Schlegal for their artistic imput.

With thanks also to Pat Conroy, Bruce Feiler, and Carol Polsgrove (especially Carol, for her invaluable advice on this book), writers and friends who have supported me in my own writing goals, and the goal of helping others to write. Thanks, too, to the many friends at a distance who have supported and inspired me—especially Florence King, Joyce Maynard, and Erica Jong.

With thanks to my editor, Dan Weaver, and the several other fine editors who have supported me along the way. With appreciation, too, to the Corporation of Yaddo, with whose support much of this manuscript was completed. Appreciation and affection also to Wendy Weil, my longtime agent and friend.

And as always, thanks to my husband, Zane; my sister, Anne; my son, Laurens; and my two daughters, Laura and Darcy, for their continued patience, interest, and love.

Contents

As a young mother of three children under five, I swung my feet to the floor from my bed one morning thinking that—much like Peter O'Toole, playing Lawrence of Arabia in the movie I had recently seen—I was about to trudge across a vast desert beneath an endless beating sun. Though far removed from my suburban world—the diapers waiting to be washed, the bowls of cereal to be dished up—this image sustained me through that and other days, giving me courage before I had seriously imagined that I might make writing—the making of metaphors—the center of my life. Yet in a way, that desert I imagined trudging could also have been a word picture of the adventure on which I would soon embark: putting one foot—or in this case, word—in front of another, creating those faint, oft-tediously sustained lines in the sand. For it would be a path that, like motherhood, would require infinite patience, but would also offer exquisite and subtle ecstasies. This is the story of how I learned to follow both paths as well as a third path of teaching others how they might follow them, too. In the meantime, my mother, a gifted yet unrealized writer, would commit suicide; for a long while, all I wanted was a life as different from hers as possible. It would be twenty years before her inspiration would culminate in the mission I call Zona Rosa. Yet what happened along the way became a spiritual quest as well as an aesthetic one: an unexpected rainbow, a journey of the heart.

< ONE >

The Lady Who Spilled
Poetry All over Herself

*Everything I needed to know about teaching
creative writing. Or what I learned in high school,
grammar school, and kindergarten.*

It was 1971, I was thirty-five years old, and the time was the
Greening of America. Fortunately for me and other struggling
poets, the Poetry in the Schools program, inspired by Kenneth
Koch's work with public school children in New York City, sponsored by the National Endowment for the Arts and state arts
councils, was stimulating kids and giving jobs to artists throughout the country. When I became involved in Georgia (and later
in South Carolina and Wyoming), it just seemed like a conven-
ient—if difficult—means of making a minimal living while
going on with my own writing.

Without knowing it, and long before the term was coined, I
was about to get an education in connecting with "the child
within." Without education courses or having heard of Attention Deficit Disorder, as it's now trendily designated, I would
soon be cast adrift within rooms full of angry girls in detention
centers and among unwed teenage mothers for whom school
was simply a holding cell. I would be plunged headfirst and
alone into classrooms of, say, forty spitball-throwing fourth-
graders, or thirty-five surly high school sophomores named

things like Toyota, Fresca, and Hare Krishna by teenage mothers with a bent for novelty. And I would quickly realize that I had to find an immediate means of not just communicating with them, but stimulating them.

Since I had taken a Rousseau-like attitude toward my own children, believing them basically good at heart and in little need of discipline, I had to learn to keep the attention of large groups who at first had little interest in what I had to say (though first-graders might be *very* interested in what I had in my pocket-book). Before long I would know that second-graders, laboriously drawing large letters on paper with wide lines, could take a whole hour to write one sentence: it was far better to get them to say their lines aloud.

I would also discover that the teachers, even when present, were not always much help. ("I stopped writing them down after a while—I'm sorry they're not more *creative*," apologized the second-grade teacher who was supposed to have been transcribing the wonderful story—"And then the camel got out of the back of the pickup truck, and got in front with the driver, and was eating a pear . . ."—that I had been drawing line by line from her students.)

I would learn how to stare down disruptive high school jocks. ("Would you like to come sit up here beside me? Maybe we could even hold hands.") I would sweetly challenge the hulking presence in the back of the room who had been inciting his buddies to riot with what might have been called child abuse if directed toward a more vulnerable boy.

But the best way of connecting, I found, was by becoming a thirty-something teenager, or even a seven- or nine-year-old again. Among them, I was a much younger Rosemary, able to remember being teased by my classmates for wetting my pants in fourth grade, or proudly wearing the red glass ring from a Cracker Jack box, given me by my boyfriend Troy in the seventh.

I had not yet heard of neuro-linguistic programming and its theory of communicating through visual, auditory, and kines-

thetic mediums. But out of desperation I quickly discovered that
the senses were what worked. I learned to use little stories full of
visual imagery to illustrate quickly to a classroom full of recalci-
trant kids how the personal was appropriate for our poems.

One story was about a visiting poet who goes into a classroom, and says, "Today, we will talk about poetry." All the kids
but one wrote the word *poetry* at the top of their pages; one
wrote the word *pottery.* "No, no—that's not right," the teacher
protested, looking over the student's shoulder. "It's not *pottery*—
it's *poetry!*" "But poetry and pottery are not that different," the
poet interjected. "In pottery, we shape clay into a vase or a bowl,
to hold whatever we want it to hold. In poetry, we simply shape
words and sentences to hold our meaning."

Another story had to do with a fantasy fifth-grader who wrote
a letter to the editor of the local paper: "There's something very
strange happening! Some white things that look like popcorn are
popping out all over the trees!" The editor scoffed, "That's nothing new. That's just the dogwood that blooms every spring!" But
it was new to that fifth-grader, I told the kids, and no matter
how many times dogwood had bloomed before, it would still be
a good subject for him to write about in his poetry.

They liked the one about the poet who hitched a ride with a
truck driver down in Texas: "What're you carryin'?" the poet
asked. "Po-try," said the driver. Delighted, the poet rode all the
way to Iowa, thinking the back of truck was loaded with books.
But when they arrived at their destination, the driver unloaded a
truckload of chickens!

And then there was the way a nine-year-old described the
process through which ideas for writing came to her: "I may be
doing something normal, maybe walking down the driveway to
the mailbox. Then some words start swirling around inside my
head like the autumn leaves. Then, pop! Suddenly they come together in a poem!"

I said that I knew what she meant, because for me, a poem
growing inside me "feels like I am pregnant in the head."

I found that kids, closer to fantasy and dreams, understood certain kinds of things right away. "What is surrealism? It's just putting the real world and the imaginary world together," a fourth-grader said. Closer to birth, they were still closer to non-existence. "Brushing my hair, looking into the mirror, I wonder if I am really real," wrote another fourth-grader. I remembered how I, too, had experienced a sense of unreality about life before enough time had passed, and I had, by virtue of experience, "gotten used to it."

And wasn't this the way we adults lost our freshness—simply by "getting used to" the miracles of life, no longer seeing them in all their magic? The mystic who Jack Nicholson consults when he is turning into a wolf in the movie of that name says, "Life *is* mystical. We just get used to it." Like someone in a foreign country, the child sees everything afresh; to the child, what we consider ordinary is extraordinary, even frightening.

Indeed, there were fantasies common to each age: for example, kindergartners and first-graders had almost all fantasized a snake inside the toilet bowl, or being sucked down the bathtub drain; many fourth-graders imagined they could read minds. ("What? Don't you think I was normal?" my husband, Zane, answered, laughing, when I asked whether he had ever imagined such things.) And once I tapped into a group's fantasy level, I found I had it made.

When I searched out images to explain the elements of creative writing, the universe provided them for me, perhaps through a bit of conversation or a snip of something heard on the radio. It was easy to help the kids to understand unity in a piece of writing by describing the way concrete is poured into wooden forms, a steel cable down its middle, during the construction of a building. The steel cable, I told them, was the unity holding the whole thing together, much like the bones inside our skeletons, holding together our "1,000 parts" (as our bodies are described in a commercial for Lever Brothers soap). Explaining the way a long piece of writing may have a simple theme, I talked about the ground in a piece of music—the simple melodic structure to which more complex variations might attach. "You should be able to describe what you're writing about in one simple sentence," I told them, a bit of advice I would use throughout the years with much older students. "Those other things you add on—those little extras—are just like balls or tinsel on a Christmas tree." Time after time, the kids stunned me with their capacity to grasp abstract concepts, once they were stated simply enough.

But what surprised them most was when I confronted them with their own sense of isolation in the universe and their self-consciousness. While each was thinking that he or she was the only one in the room—indeed, the world!—with a particular set of feelings or problems, there were, I told them, probably at least a dozen others sitting nearby who felt exactly the same way. Drawing concentric circles on the board, using ideas from my readings in psychology, I described the ways we set boundaries:

"The outer part of the circle—SOCIAL—is the way we relate casually, say, when we say hi to someone we barely know in the hall, or greet an acquaintance at church. The next part of the circle—ACTIVITY SHARING—is when we share an activity with others who we may not know particularly well—such as sitting here in the classroom, or working on the school paper.

"But as we get further into the circle—PLAY—we are becoming more intimate. The people we choose to play with are our pals, people we might call and say, 'Let's go shoot some baskets,' or 'Let's check out the new nail polish colors at Woolworth's. Or the boys at the Dairy Queen.'

"But now, in the next level of the circle—FANTASY SHARING—we're becoming more intimate. The friends we share fantasies with are usually best friends, people we feel free with, the kind of girlfriend we'll tell about the crush we have on that cute boy we see in the hallway every day, but who hasn't even spoken to us yet." As we got deeper into the circle, the faces in the classroom filled with a half-embarrassed recognition. I had begun to recognize what their suppressed giggles meant—that we were getting close to the bone.

"And then, there's that one remaining part of the circle, like a bull's eye—the *I*—that part of us that is our deepest part, the part that only a few people will know during our lifetime." I paused, looking into their faces before tossing out my challenge. "We will write from that *I*, that center of the circle. Also from fantasy-sharing and play. Because those are the truest parts of ourselves."

"Have you ever noticed how we never look at one another for very long—how it's even considered rude?" I asked the class in preparation for a writing exercise. "In fact, if someone stares at you in the hall, you usually think something's wrong with you? Even if it's someone you like—someone you might have a crush on—you try not to let them see you staring, don't you? Yet, what is the most interesting thing in the world? Other *people!*" I talked about the way people of different cultures have a different tolerance for looking and seeing; for example, what might be rude or even unsafe in New York City would be considered natural in a small town in America, or in a village in Guatemala.

To show how hard it is to look, I picked two students—unlikely ones, a shy boy and a gorgeous girl—to stand at either side of the room. They were to look at each other steadily, taking turns making simple comments ("You have on a blue shirt". . . "Your shoelaces are tangled"), then take a step forward until their toes met in the middle of the room. If either looked away, he or she had to step back, which made the game last longer. As the pair blushed and struggled not to look away from each other, the classroom hooted and hollered like an audience at a Pearl Jam concert.

Next, I assigned each student a partner, choosing for them instead of letting them choose a friend. Each was to interview his or her partner for three minutes, as though they had never met before, asking the things they had never dared ask; the shorter partner would begin, the taller partner would follow. They were required to answer, though they could lie.

Then—this was the hard part—they were to look at each other, without speaking and without looking away, memorizing the other's appearance, for three minutes. "You will look at this person as though you've never seen a person before!" I instructed. "Memorize her ears, her shirt, her shoes—and if anyone looks away, more time will be added!"

After three minutes of giggles and blushes, I asked them to return to their desks to write a "partner" poem, written from a "you" point of view, as though addressing the partner. They could add associations about themselves ("Looking at the blue waves on your shirt made me think of the time I went to the ocean with my grandparents when I was four, and saw the waves for the first time"), and they were to end the piece with one line describing how he or she felt during the exercise ("Looking at you, I felt like jumping through the window" . . . "Looking into your eyes, I felt like a marshmallow melting in a cup of hot chocolate," and so on). Breaking through social barriers in this way prepared them to write about what was even harder: themselves.

Sometimes, even during first period, the students seem weighted by a languor one could cut with a knife. ("It was then that I became a sex addict," Zane joked. "Forced as I was by boredom into looking at the girls' legs, or up their dresses.")

"How many people felt like coming to school this morning?" I ask. Usually, only one or two students raises a hand to my question. At eight in the morning, a number of students already have their heads on their desks; in an afternoon class, most will move drowsy eyes toward the windows, prisoners dreaming of escape.

"Good!" I respond, chalking the word FEELINGS on the board. "Because that shows how we often don't get to go by our feelings—and feelings are one of the main things we have that we can put into our poems.

"Sometimes we might be mad at our parents or a teacher, and not be able express it. Or sometimes we might really like someone, and not be able to go by our feelings because we're too shy to tell them." I go on, exploring other situations in which we might act at odds with our emotions.

"Now, how many people have ever daydreamed in class?" This time, most of the kids' arms shoot up.

"Oh, good! I love people to daydream in my classes! Because what are you doing when you're daydreaming? You're having—"

"Fantasies!" someone replies, and I write that word on the board. This is a good place to ask whether some of those who raised their hands might be willing to share his or her fantasies—the kinds of daydreams they have in class. The high school students blush furiously, making what they fantasize obvious, but a second-grader pipes up, "I was thinking that the fence around the school is really monkeys holding hands." The younger the students are, the freer their flights. "This morning, I thought the sun looked just like a red-hot octopus up in the sky!" a dreamy third-grader declares.

"And what are fantasies you have at night, while you're asleep?" By now I have their attention. "Dreams!" they cry in unison. In fact, so many volunteer to tell their recent dreams that we have to desist in order to go on.

"And what is your mind full of, like raisins in a fruitcake, unless you have amnesia?" I ask.

"Memories!" someone says from the back of the room, and I inscribe this on our list. "Memories are like a well—the more you dip your bucket down into it, the more will come up for you, giving you more stuff to put into your writing," I tell them.

"And what are you having every moment of every day, even if it seems like you're not—even if you're bored, or so on?"

They look a bit more puzzled at this one, until somebody gets it. "Experiences!" she shouts triumphantly, as I chalk her realization up with the rest.

"And have you ever had something just come to you, like a lightbulb suddenly coming on in your head?"

"Ideas!"

"These are all things we have inside us. And then there's one last thing." THE WORLD AROUND US, I write on the board. "How does the world around us get *inside* us? How do I know, for instance, that Jimmy has on a red shirt, or that Janice has blue eyes?"

"Because you can *see* them!" somebody yells, as though I'm a dummy.

"And what are the other four senses, the other way the world around us gets inside us? And unless you're Helen Keller, you've got all of these!"

Now, listing SEE, HEAR, TOUCH, TASTE, and SMELL on the board beneath THE WORLD AROUND US, I have them right where I want them, and the board looks something like this:

```
FEELINGS                    "Perfection
FANTASIES                   is terrible; it
DREAMS                      cannot have
EXPERIENCES                 children."
IDEAS                       —Sylvia Plath
MEMORIES
                and
      THE WORLD AROUND US
                    ∨
                   see
                   hear
                   touch
                   taste
                   smell
                    ∨
Immediacy comes from the use of: concrete images
                    ∨
                  WORDS
```

"Is there anyone in this room who doesn't have feelings, fantasies, dreams, ideas, experiences, or all his or her five senses? And is there anyone in here who doesn't know any *words*?" I add when they fall silent: "Good! Because these are our raw materials for writing, and writing is just putting these things into *words*. Now I know that every person in this room has everything he or she needs to write a poem!"

"And what do you think that line from the poet Sylvia Plath means?" I ask next. "Don't you think she's saying that if we're too perfect, we can't be creative?"

Later I would tell them about *layering*—about how the more raw materials—feelings, fantasies, dreams, memories, ideas, and experiences—and the more senses—seeing, hearing, smelling, tasting, and touching—we brought into our writing, the richer and more dimensional it would be.

But there were two other requests I discovered that immediately resulted in better writing. One was the request, if we were writing poetry, to forgo rhyming. Unfortunately, many of the students still thought that was what a poem was—a piece of writing that rhymed. "But what are you doing if you're writing something that must rhyme?" I asked. "Aren't you thinking more about the word for the end of your line—about making your poem 'perfect,' rather than what you want to say?" Using the kind of language with which I hoped they could identify, I described, in a way that would surely make my more academic peers cringe, the difference in a poem and a piece of prose: "A poem is like a Hershey bar; a work of prose is like a whole chocolate cake. . . ."

The other request was that they confine their writing to concrete imagery. "Concrete imagery is just putting those ways we get the world around us inside us—through seeing, hearing, touching, tasting, and smelling—into *words*."

But in order to understand what concrete imagery was, we first had to understand its opposite: "Those things that make us want to write—feelings—are often described by words that are abstract. For example, if I say the word *love*, do you see the word *love* hanging up here on a string?" I asked, acting as though I were holding an imaginary sign up in front of them. "No? Well, what does come into your mind? Would anyone be willing to share the picture that comes into his or her mind when she hears the word *love*?" Murmurs of embarrassment, especially if the group are high-schoolers. Then one admitted to a mental image: "It's my boyfriend, when I see him in the hall." Or, "A mother, cuddling her newborn baby." Again, the age group dictated the kind of imagery: the younger kids were natural anarchists, while the teenagers were at first arch conformists.

"Well, I noticed that you didn't even need to use the word *love*: what was in your mind was a picture. And all you have to do to express love in your writing is to paint that picture with words. You never even need to use the word *love* at all, because if you paint the picture well enough, we'll *know* what you mean." After going through a few more words describing feelings—fear, serenity, happiness, excitement—they understand what abstract nouns are, and I'm able to ask them to avoid them.

"What color is it when I clap my hands like this?" I would ask, suddenly slapping my palms together sharply. "Red!" several people would reply. Emotions could be described by colors, I suggested. "What color is excitement? fear? peacefulness?" "Orange!" "Fuchsia!" "Green!" And so could the senses: "What color is the smell of Vick's Vapo-Rub?" "Blue!" comes the inevitable answer.

But I want them to understand even more viscerally the power of concrete imagery. "This afternoon after school we'll be getting on a bus to go to the Holiday Inn, where we will dive into a swimming pool filled with red Jell-O," I would tell them. Then ask, "How many people had a picture come into your mind when you heard those words?" When just about everyone raises a hand, we further discuss what flavor the Jell-O will be, whether it will have nuts and fruit cocktail in it, whether it will be jumbled up or smooth, how it will taste, smell, feel on the skin, and so on.

Depending on the grade level, my imagery varies—for a fourth-grade class I might use the notion of a spaceship that looks like a giant marshmallow on legs landing on the playground, and small green marshmallow-shaped men walk out. But whatever imagery we use, the students understand immediately: I made those pictures come into their heads by using a certain set of words. It's as good a device as a magic ring ordered from the back of a comic book, or a pamphlet on *How to Talk to Girls*!

"Poetry is a cool dude walking down the hall with six girls," wrote a high school jock, once he learned the power of metaphor.

Yet prior to that awareness always came a deluge of pre-imagistic writing, usually in the form of love poems, beginning something like "I love my boyfriend / he is so cute . . ." To which I would respond that I knew little more about the boyfriend than I had before; was it the little blond curls on the back of his neck she liked, or what?

But after I asked the kids to stick to concrete images, they came up with lines like these:

> *Your eyes are as blue as the sky.*
> *Your hair is like golden brown wheat.*
> *Your lips are like red cherries.*
> *Your face reminds me of a lemon meringue pie.*
> *When I'm with you*
>   *I feel like a worm in rich dirt.*

And:

> *He came into the room*
> *and I felt like a stick of margarine*
> *in a pot of boiling fudge.*

Or, depending on the age:

> *Kissing a girl is like drinking a gallon of prune juice.*
> *And holding her hand is like holding*
> *a piece of Kentucky Fried Chicken.*

Or this by a fifth-grade boy:

> *Girls are like bugers— they take up space.*

And one even illustrated his venom:

T u r n i P
G r e e n S

G i r L S   A r e
l i K e   T u r n i P
G r e e n s   —
T h e y
S T y i n k

B Y   a   5 y r   o l d

But the girls, incipient ten-year-old feminists, got their revenge:

> *Boys are like chopped-up frogs*
> *Or smushed prunes on the floor.*

What I was discovering was that to get the kids to write the good stuff, they first had to be allowed to write, as did this fifth-grader: *Dan and Lamar / dooing it / dooing it / Dan and Lamar / eating it / eating it / think it is candy / but it's not / it's a big fat buger / with a cherry on top. . . .*

A favorite poem at every grade level was "Eggs," by New York poet ("and belly dancer," I told them) Daniela Gioseffi, in which the poet does everything imaginable with raw eggs, finally stepping into a bathtub full of twelve hundred of them, a moment at which the classroom was inevitably filled with gasps. "That's *nasty*," protested one girl as I read each succeeding line. As I read it a second time, I requested that she say "nasty" at the end of

each line as a kind of chorus or coda, because another small secret I had discovered was that of incorporating, even exaggerat-
ing, the kids' natural feelings and reactions.

The poem was so chocked full of sensory imagery that it was a
perfect example of how a poet could make the reader have a certain experience through the choice of language. "Can't you just see
those eggs, taste them, feel them on your skin?" I would ask above
their moans. "And even hear them—as in when she '*plopped* them
into the tub,' until they '*popped* in the visceral mass?'" Ms. Gioseffi
had used onomatopoeia in a way that made the term easy to explain, even to a second-grader. "But there was one sense she left
out—what was that?" I asked, until someone finally came up with
it: smell. "But we can imagine what all those eggs would smell
like, can't we?" Next came the debate on whether she had actually
done the things cited in the poem. "You did everything right in
that poem on the eggs," a fourth-grade boy wrote Gioseffi in a
letter, "but you forgot to put the stopper in the bathtub drain!"

The visual arts had always stimulated me, helping me leap over
tall buildings in the psyche. Once, driving down Fifth Avenue
with the novelist Blanche Boyd, we approached the cowboy bar
at the corner of Fifth Avenue and 12th Street where she was to
interview the editor of *Country Music* magazine. I had been to
the bar once before, but now, like a vision from *King Kong*, I saw
rising above us, atop the building's second floor, a huge green
iguana. Was I hallucinating, I wondered, dizzied by the sights
and sounds of Manhattan, not to speak of the toke we had
shared on the way downtown?

It was a controversial piece of sculpture, I learned in a saner
moment, created by Bob Wade, the same Texas sculptor who had
designed a 42-foot-high pair of cowboy boots, made to resemble
ostrich skin with phony calf uppers, for a site in Washington,
D.C. And each sculpture was exactly the sort of thing to stimulate the kids. After telling them about these works, I went on

to describe the Cadillac Ranch, a series of up-ended Cadillacs
planted by Texas millionaire Stanley God Bless America Marsh 3,
on his ranch near Amarillo. I talked about Claes Oldenburg's
huge stuffed sculptures—a toilet, an electric fan, a six-foot ash-
tray complete with stuffed cigarette butts, as well as a giant lipstick sculpture for a site at Yale University. I described the ham-
burger bed a New York sculptor had created for himself: a round
mattress, its round headboard against the wall, complete with
tomato slice and lettuce leaf spreads, and two pickle pillows. We
looked at pictures of the paintings of Rene Magritte—the man
with a birdcage complete with bird instead of a head, two people
kissing through cloths over their faces, a man with a boulder suspended just above him ("Like the future, only he can't see it!"
said a fourth-grader).

After we had discussed Andy Warhol's famous Campbell
soup cans and Brillo soap pad boxes, I asked, "Why do you think
these artists took these ordinary things and showed them in such
unusual ways?" "To get famous?" "To make money?" So people
would put them on TV?" they would shout, ever sponges of cultural values. But that was not what I was getting at.

"What if you came into this classroom and saw a stick of margarine or a Snickers bar hanging from a string from the ceiling.
Would you notice it?" "Yeah! Of course!" they would respond,
looking at me as though I'm crazy. "Why?" I asked innocently.
"Those are just ordinary things, aren't they?" "Because it's not
s'posed to be there—it's out of place!" "Yes, and don't you think
maybe that's why this artist made these works of art, to make us
look at ordinary things in a new way?!"

Now they were totally receptive to talking about something as
abstract as context (or as Carlos Castenada put it, our "gloss on reality") and how, in our poems or stories, we are free to play around
with context, to help our readers or listeners see things afresh.

It was hard for them to believe that I had lived B.T., or Before
Television, but this, too, became a ploy: didn't they know that
television, and every other invention, from automobiles to cas-

sette players, had come from that same part of the brain with which I was asking them to come up with poems and stories? Or at times, I challenged them, promising a prize to anyone who could go the whole week—honor system—without watching TV. "To clear the mind," I said, as they looked at me as though I had suggested a trip to Mars or, worse, a week of evenings spent reading the plays of Shakespeare.

Privately, I thought of my method as orgasmic: foreplay, plateau, and release, when each student finally came up with a piece of writing. MTV, horror movies, even Stephen King. I was shameless in bringing up anything that worked. If I had described my method to the kids that sexy way, it might have been called child abuse. But in action, it worked.

"The two sexiest places in the world: high schools & Army posts," I had once written in a poem. They are also among the funniest. I had learned during my marriage to Zane that soldiers have their own kind of zany humor; in the high schools, I learned that students did, too.

When I began reading a poem in Appalachia that began with the line "I throwed a chicken . . ." the whole class broke up as I struggled to keep a straight face. But didn't I have only myself to blame, since I had asked them to write a poem with the word *chicken* in every line? And who knew? Maybe the author would grow up to be a country-western songwriter.

Or there was the class of high school seniors in South Georgia, some of them hulking nineteen- or twenty-year-olds, with whom I had just created a series of similes. As they shouted them out, I had chalked them on the board. "Now we will read these lines together," I instructed, meaning that I would read the lines in sequence, as one poem. Instead, the whole classroom began intoning in unison, a bizarre chorus: "Close-Up toothpaste is like a tick's blood, after it has sucked your arm . . . Eating broccoli is like sliding down a razor blade into a vat of alcohol. . . ."

Many were the moments when my adult, more literal, vision clashed with their teenage, and thus more melodramatic, one, and I lost it. As I read aloud a poem by a fourteen-year-old in which she and her boyfriend "go up in flames," I assumed the piece was describing an imaginary car crash; instead, the author, a plump girl in jeans and flowered top, confessed that it was about the feelings they had had while necking in the backseat. When she explained this, I laughed so hard that I bumped my purse over, and from it, to my blushing chagrin and the students' delight, a chorus line of tampons rolled down the aisle between their feet.

And then in middle Georgia there was the black tenth-grader who danced to her poems on the auditorium stage, unself-consciously gyrating her buxom body before the whole school, just as she danced each Sunday in her sanctified church:

> *Go-to-Hel-lo Monica Child!*
> *Let me tell you 'bout this*
> *microglycerous, super duper*
> *dyn-o-mite full developed*
> *strong out J. T. that I met the*
> *other night. Chile the dude's*
> *name was Plenty. And when he*
> *said Plenty I said, "Plenty of what?"*
> *He said, "Hey! Fox don't you see*
> *all this on me. I'm neat to*
> *the teat, decked to death, well put*
> *together, extraordinary in these*
> *clothes." He was a Bad Bad*
> *Mister in them skin-tight britches.*
> *He was sort of fine you know.*

"What is fat? / Fat is excess love / given in a seven-layer / piece of cake. Fat / is something special / chocolate cookies with choco-late sauce on top. / Fat is cute. Fat is / something people hate. /

Fat is a chicken. Fat." My daughter Darcy, still afflicted with baby fat, wrote this at nine. When in seventh grade she started to slim down and would ask how she looked, I would say, "Just like Raquel Welch!" "Raquel Welch is too fat!" she would snap back. Nothing I could say at the time would console her. But hearing her poem and her story seemed to soothe the kids in my classes who were also living through a time of lumpy bodies and out-of-sync psyches.

Given awareness and permission, and my promise that, but for obscene words ("This *is* a school, and I want to keep my job!"), I would not censor them, the kids would, slowly at first, then in a rush, write as fast as they could. To their amazement, nothing bad happened, and they still got dates. (Except perhaps in the case of the good-looking football star who wrote so honestly about his abuse of the girls he dated. All the girls in the class who had gone out with him hooted in agreement.) They burst forth with poems about divorce, about child abuse, about being teased, about feeling fat or otherwise defective, even about grief and loss, and the fear of death. As Natalie Angier theorized in the *New York Times*, they wrote and talked about all the things that we adults no longer discuss in polite company, even if we still care about them

In fact, all I had to do to know what would affect them was to recall what it was like to be a teenager. I remembered my own fears of death, my nausea at the idea of the galaxies and all that endless space, and my terror that, because of the atomic bomb, I wouldn't live past thirty. At eight and nine, between the reels of Claudette Colbert in *Since You Went Away*, or Greer Garson in *Mrs. Miniver*, I had watched the newsreels, with their photos of the bodies of the Holocaust victims, piled high like cordwood, jutting hands and hipbones. When I was twelve, I heard, first over the radio, then via newsprint, of the Winecoff Hotel fire, only miles from where I lived in Atlanta, with people jumping from the windows to their deaths, across the street from Davison's Department Store, where Mother had taken me just the week before to shop for socks or underwear. It was easy to recall how imprinted I had been; how the images had clung, emerging in my dreams at night.

I learned that when I read to the students from certain works, they became quiet, remembering experiences from their own lives. Theodore Roethke's poem "The Meadow Mouse" was one of these. In it he describes finding a small mouse, "wriggling like a minuscule puppy," and taking it to his back porch to safety, to love and feed from a "bottle cap watering-trough," only to find it gone the next morning. Every child had at least fantasized rescuing and making a pet of a small wild animal. Another favorite was Anne Sexton's "Grief for a Daughter," in which she describes the way she realizes she cannot go through her daughter's pain for her after a horse has stood on the girl's foot: "Three toenails swirled like shells . . . left to float in blood in her riding boot. . . ."

The process of separating from parents was an ongoing theme for each of my students. But I also knew that one of the things that kept them from gaining confidence in their own writing was that, like many aspiring adult writers, they felt discouraged when their first-draft efforts fell short of the stories they enjoyed in books or magazines. I explained that every published piece of writing was written by a professional writer who more than likely had revised the piece time after time.

Even better was reading from something written by someone their own age—and by the time I had been working in the schools for several years, I had many such pieces. Donna White, a high school senior in Camden, South Carolina, had written about being fat and teased so much about it—"listening to them *oink* and call *pig* and *fatso*," and finally, even spit on by "the Rock Boy . . . in front of everybody"—that she had gone home and burned the pretty dress her mother had made for her, "until there were only the ashes left. I had thought it was a pretty dress, too." This prose poem evoked intense feeling; holding up their hands, almost everyone admitted to having been either teasee or teaser. Some of the best works written after this reading were by older boys, popular football players or hunks, who, perhaps for the first time, reflected back with regret over the times they had teased someone smaller or weaker.

But the more poignant were by those who had suffered the pangs of such persecution. "Like going home and dying, or eating a whole pie," wrote a sixth-grade boy, pinkly miserable in his overweight, of how he felt after such tauntings. When we wrote our next poems, he wrote a piece for which I praised him: "The cucumber with eyes lives in a garden, / eats sunshine & water. / When you come to pick him, / he looks up at you. / When you start to cut him, / he cries."

Another lesson for me was the realization that even a student who appeared totally uninterested might be absorbing what was going on after all—that, in fact, all of us have different listening styles. In a rural high school in middle Georgia, a gangly ninth-grade boy read a newspaper during my whole presentation. Then I gave an assignment, based on a suggestion by the poet Kenneth Koch, that each student write a poem with a lie in every line. While the others wrote at their desks, the boy continued reading. But the next morning, he turned in a piece that, using the metaphor of deer hunting, acutely described a young man's attempt to break with his mother's control, whether real or imagined, and the way that control was killing his spirit. Reading it, I could almost feel the taut and painful reach of a virtual umbilical cord: each couplet in the poem included one line about the deer hunt, another about "Mama," and his thoughts of what she's doing back at the house, concluding with this, after the shooting of the deer: "[You] start to drag him to the pickup but you don't get that far. / Because somebody shoots you in the back. / Mama's got a headache."

Their simplicity of vision was an inspiration: "I hit my friend on the shoulder to relieve the pain inside myself," wrote a second-grader. Or as a sixth-grader wrote on the same theme, "My bike is red. / I like my bike. / I ride my bike / to hide my feelings." The clarity for which we adults must sometimes struggle rose effortlessly from their less cluttered minds, often expressing their sheer joy at being alive: "I get that feeling / oh ye / It's in my head / oh ye / a loaf of bread / oh ye."

And then there was the poem written by a senior at a small south Georgia high school, an ordinary student on an ordinary day:

> *Entirely without consideration for mitigating*
> *circumstances we rush along though life . . .*
> *bundling up the kids and the dog and trading in*
> *the car and mowing the lawn and seeding*
> *the flowerbed but it dies because you*
> *don't water it 'cause you're traveling*
> *to Miami to a convention of office workers*
> *then you type up your report and run*
> *down to the post office and miss the*
> *picnic and wish it wouldn't rain but*
> *but the next time it does you don't care you*
> *you have to change the oil in the car at the*
> *garage and pay bills and suddenly*
> *it's over . . .*
> *Entirely without consideration for mitigating*
> *circumstances we rush along through life and*
> *time like a wound-up clock . . .*

And wasn't that the fate we were all seeking to avoid—to momentarily stop mortality with our words? To give meaning to our hurdling through time and space?

In the small community near Boone, North Carolina, where Zane's parents had grown up, folks spoke a near-Elizabethan English, and the curious, or was it the suspicious, came out on the porches of their wooden houses, or stopped their work in the fields, to look at us as we drove by on our way to the small rocky cemetery where some of Zane's forebears were buried. He had told me about his Uncle Ben, a baseball fanatic who had lived in those hills, and who had made his own baseball field as well as architectural marvels from the native stones that would probably today be termed "outsider" art.

As we walked over the grassy knolls, looking at the names on the gravestones, several brown horses gazed at us over a log fence, as curious, it seemed, as the locals. Near where we found his grandmother and an aunt was a fresh grave commemorating a common event of small-town life in the deep South: yet another high school senior had met his death while hurtling down country roads; his round young face shone out at us from a full-color photo encased in a heart-shaped Plexiglas frame, attached to a headstone still surrounded by fresh flowers.

In Appalachia, at a school atop Lookout Mountain, Tennessee, the kids told stories of ghosts and strange "natural" phenomena ("A snake'll go down a baby's throat 'n drink the milk," "If you kill some kinds of snakes, you'll drop dead on the spot"). To class, they brought snake and animal skins, lemons to suck, hunks of homemade cornbread or cake to supplement the beans and cornbread variations we ate every day in the lunchroom. One brought me a cigar box ingenuously covered in sequins and matchsticks, made by "an ole man down the road a piece." The girls wore homemade feedsack dresses, the boys bib overalls, and were often barefoot. Rusted car carcasses lay in their yards; outhouses stood behind the gray wood shacks they lived in, sometimes with as many as eleven brothers and sisters.

"Mountain Men Are Free Men," declared a school poster, and while none of these kids dared dream of college, the creeks, trees, and animal life provided an education of another kind. While a student down the mountain from the wealthy Dalton carpet industry community, destined for prep school and Yale or Princeton, or at the very least Chapel Hill, might write, "I wish I was a trillionaire, or owned a munitions plant," a boy from the Appalachian school might write wistfully, almost as though for the moon, "I wish I had $25 to go to 4-H camp." Mothers at the wealthy end of the mountain, I was told, bought the quilts made by the Appalachian women, selling them at much higher prices to Saks Fifth Avenue and other New York stores.

Yet self-pity was unknown to these kids. Despite their poverty, they were proud young people, earthy and tough-minded. When a beautiful curly haired fifth-grader pulled up her shirt to show me the tube that had been in her kidney since infancy, the others kids looked on without curiosity, murmuring, "Yeah, she kin even go swimmin' with it. I seen it down at the creek plenty a times." The girl with the tube brought me a gospel record made by her mother and father, accompanied by a signed picture of her whole family, with the names and ages of each member inscribed on the back.

I was sure that a shy boy wearing horn-rims, who went home loaded down with library books each day and said that his family didn't own a TV, must be from a more intellectually inclined background than the other kids. Instead he turned out to live deep in the woods, in a tarpaper shack, which he couldn't leave when it rained because the creek rose, making him miss school for days at a time, and had a father who couldn't work and a mother who walked for miles in bobby socks to pick up their monthly welfare check.

At the school at the Georgia State Mental Hospital, a nine-year-old black boy, with a dreamy wistful grin and an IQ (I was told) of 60, wrote a line that haunted me: "I wish I was the water waves that roll down the hills." Sometimes, such children seemed to live in a world of dreams, dreams perhaps more accessible to them than to those who have learned more easily to live in the world.

In Macon, there was the quiet fourth-grader, dying before our eyes of scleroderma, her pale freckled skin stretched painfully, cracking over her skinny pink arms. She lived in the Holiday Inn, where her father was the night manager, next to the cheaper Days Inn where I had lived during my stay. I would never again pass a Holiday Inn without thinking of her, her head bent shyly over her desk, her industry as she poured forth her poems expressing her feelings about the short life that was left to her.

It was in the schools that I learned never to underestimate the creativity inherent in human beings, nor to predict where it might occur. My students opened my eyes, helping me realize that creativity was everywhere, and that while writing is a special profession (just as special as I had imagined it during the afternoons I read and daydreamed away in the children's room of Atlanta's Carnegie Library), it is not just for the privileged, or the few.

Indeed, it was from the kids that I learned everything I would later use in teaching adults. It was their clear sight that makes me pray, each day, for a childlike mind.

When a Scottish friend's mother visited Savannah from Glasgow, she commented that the black people who populated the streets and porches seemed to be having more fun than anyone else. She didn't know that they stayed outside in the heat because, unlike their white neighbors, they couldn't afford air conditioning or, in some cases, electricity.

A lot of the kids I met, especially those in training schools and the special schools for unwed mothers, say, in Macon or Milledgeville, were angry—often without even knowing it. After all, they had been born black, poor, and stuck in the welfare system, probably without a book in the house, in the deep South. These girls had never heard of *The Secret Garden*, had never had the Beatrix Potter stories or *Winnie the Pooh* read to them as kids, and neither had their mothers or fathers (when there *were* fathers). They had never played the flute or been given piano lessons. The domestic arts of interior decoration—not to speak of art on the walls—and gourmet cooking were unknown to them (middle-class people may forget that even special cooking requires that bit of extra money to buy herbs, spices, and trendy ingredients.) All they knew were the soaps, featuring the pseudo-miseries of middle-class white people; mothers who were on drugs or who worked as maids for a low wage; and brothers—forerunners of the youths who now sport Rolexes and gold chains with pistol charms—who wandered the streets at night, possibly becoming shooting victims. At a black club in Savannah, someone had removed a numeral from a sign beside the door, making it read "Must Be 8 to Enter." Despite their tender ages, motherhood seemed to be a primary source of self-esteem, an immediate entree into adulthood as surely mutilating to their futures as female circumcision rites are to women's bodies.

Fifteen years later, Nell, who taught remedial classes at an inner-city middle school in Savannah, would tell me about the kids there: in the hallway and in the lunchroom, they glared at her, a middle-aged thin white woman in proper shoes, as though she were the enemy. Though most were black, many had never even heard of slavery or the Civil War. On the other hand, they imagined Africa—events in Rwanda and other hot spots virtually unknown to them—to be a golden land where, if they were suddenly deposited there, they would find themselves wearing gold chains, new jackets, and Reeboks. Through a thin partition, she could hear her male co-teacher, a Black Muslim, relating every aspect of American history to Islam. Among the rest of the staff, also mostly black, the most glamorous teacher sold home decorations on the side—the most popular was a set of brass fans to hang on the wall—and brought chitlins from home for lunch. In the teacher's lounge, a colleague asked her whether Lee Harvey Oswald had shot Martin Luther King; once, the principal had asked the faculty to "conjugate" in another room for a meeting.

At a training school for girls from thirteen to seventeen, I was told that the young women had been detained largely for being "unmanageable"; that is, for using drugs, for promiscuity, and for running away from home, but rarely for such "serious offenses as shoplifting"—though I learned that Monicka, a six-foot girl a with huge Afro who wore miniskirts and African jewelry, had been arrested for "molesting little children." (Ironically, the boys in the training schools had mostly been incarcerated for more serious crimes—burglary, car theft, and assault; sleeping around and running away was apparently considered ordinary behavior for young males.) Several of the girls had infants at home; Sandra, a fourteen-year-old who turned out to be the best poet in the class, was the mother of a two-year-old.

Yet how could I fault these young women? Wasn't what I thought of as culture, *white* people's culture? Most of the girls were romantics, believing that if only they met the right boy, all their past lacks could be obliterated in a perfect love. But hadn't I entertained the same fantasies, back in Tucker, Georgia? And hadn't I, too, sought to escape the limitations of my life through marriage, motherhood, and rebellion, at nearly as young an age? Mother and I may have expected a man to take care of us, while they may have depended on the system. And what was the difference, really?

As my stereotyped expectations diminished, stamped out by the impossibility of my changing these girls, I began to realize that beneath their flamboyant surfaces lay an incredible creativity, corralled into too narrow confines. Hairstyles, dress, jewelry were among their few outlets: hair was frizzed, twisted, or topped by blond wigs; fake and real tattoos blossomed; worn jeans were embroidered and reembroidered. Those who sported removable gold caps on their teeth, especially the ones with an initial, wore them with the pride a middle-class deb might sport a Tiffany solitaire. Every day, it seemed, they changed identity through their inventiveness.

Since none of my usual ploys were working, I sat at the wooden school table with them, listening to their conversations. They talked about boyfriends and beauty culture, sexual experiences and abortions and childbirth; about LSD trips and running away from home; about their families and the feeling of being locked up. They had little vocabulary, grammar, or handwriting skills. But they did have a storytelling tradition and an oral creativity that amazed me.

As Monicka vigorously chewed gum and leaned back in her chair, describing her own funeral, I started, almost without thought, to take down what she said. The next day, I brought her speech in, neatly typed, and rhythmically read it back to the class as an oral poem:

> *I want to be buried*
> *in black velvet hot pants*
> *& black suede boots*
> *over my knees—*
> *I'll be in a jeweled coffin*
> *& leave my diary to Mrs. Daniell*
> *(it has $18,000 in it!)*
> *my mini-bike to that girl named Mary*
> *& my hot pants to Toni*
> *& my costume jewelry to Marchelle*
> *& be buried in my real jewelry.*
> *I want Sellars Funeral Home*
> *to have my body. . . .*

By the end of the week, through the same method, these five "remedial" girls had produced a number of truly amazing works. That I appreciated their colloquialism and native wit thrilled them. But the poem that touched me most was one in which Sandra, the fourteen-year-old mother, came up with a metaphorical portrait of her life:

> *Once there was a girl named Sandra.*
> *She would go to the show*
> *pick popcorn off the floor—*
> *she would eat all the leftovers.*
> *She would slip into the store and steal popcorn.*
> *But finally she got a big box—*
> *the man in the store gave it to her.*

Years later, reading Robert Hughes's "The Complaints of Multiculturalism," in his *A Culture of Complaint*, I wondered if he had ever sat in with such a group. "It's the difference between thinking your life is hopeless and *knowing* it is," author Dorothy Allison said, speaking of another disenfranchised group, in "White Trash" in *New York* magazine. When I heard the food writer Betty Fussell read from an essay in which she described washing out hog entrails in the bathtub of her New York apartment in order to cook them as chitlins, I thought of the blacks I knew down South who really ate them—not as an exotic delicacy, but because they were cheap. (At hog-slaughtering time on Grandmother Carroll's farm, she had rendered fat for soap, had made homemade sausages and smoked the choicer meats, but had given the intestines to the black workers.) And I thought again of those girls, possibly grandmothers by now, making do with what they had, a culture that didn't honor them.

> *I like a cup of coffee when I first get up in the morning*
> *Now I have to wait until the coffee's lukewarm. . . .*
> *I used to have a nightcap before I went to bed*
> *But now I take aspirin instead. . . .*

"We can let you work in the prisons," the director for the Georgia State Council for the Arts had announced, as though I was no longer fit for any company but that of convicted felons when my first book, *A Sexual Tour of the Deep South*, a collection of poems replete with an unladylike anger and sexuality, was published. At the time, I had protested, insisting that I continue working in the schools as well.

But now, as I listened to Doris read from her poems at a prison-wide poetry reading, the culmination of the six-week poetry workshop I had just conducted in the Georgia state prison for women during late August and September of 1975, I was excited. Here I had seen firsthand the similarities among women from different backgrounds. Here, my bonding with dispossessed women had jelled. Indeed, the experience was one that would mark me, impelling my desire to work with women who wanted—not just wanted, but *needed*—to write long before *Zona Rosa,* my future writing group for women, was even an idea.

> *Yes I lost my freedom & it's all my fault*
> *it's just like being locked in a vault—*
> *a time for this & a time for that.*
> *Will I ever get my freedom back?*

As Doris continued, her melancholy voice echoed through the huge, dimly lit gymnasium, a rapt sea of mostly black female faces, toward the white male prison guards, standing arms crossed, legs apart, at the rear of the room. I remembered when I had first met her, her story of being railroaded into prison by the white police officer who was the father of five of her six illegitimate children: fat and depressed looking, she had worn scuffed purple velour bedroom slippers and clutched a copy of *The Upper Room,* the same Methodist tract in which my mother had searched for strength.

My mind spun with images of the others as well—of fifty-five-year-old Jewell's dream of "stayin' in one a them motels, jes' onc't"; of Chain Gang Candy's tale of throwing Clorox into her faithless husband's eyes. Of Queenie, who, adorned in an elegant Muslim headdress, holding out a slender hand as though she were at tea in a palace, saying, "I'm a kleptomaniac, but I want to start a charm class." Of Easter Sunday, who could have passed for an average teenager, with her jeans embroidered with the names of boyfriends, each of her toenails painted a different color, had she not told us how she had left a party, gone home for her daddy's shotgun, and come back to shoot the rival for her man over the punch bowl.

I thought of Frankie, fair, with long brown hair, who had been to Georgia State University for a year before she had been shot in the stomach during a raid on her drug-dealer boyfriend. I recalled Peggy's story of how she had come to be there: "I heard 'bout muh

husban' bein' with thet other woman, so I went to the fact'ry
where they wuz workin' 'n *tore* thet place up. Thet night I went
down to the river 'n wuz drinkin' wine 'n feelin' fine—till I got
home. 'N there he wuz, hidin' behin' the porch swing. 'N 'fore I
could get holda muh gun, he's pulled his out 'n shot me in the leg,
'n thet's the las' I saw of thet son of a bitch! I don't know why they
put me in here," she mused, "since *I* wuz thuh one thet got shot."

And then there was the most disturbing member of the group,
Sheba, a caramel beauty from Detroit who had followed a lover
down south with his new girlfriend; the most guarded, she had
never discussed her crime in the group, though she was said to
have repeatedly stabbed, then burned the girlfriend alive.

The time at the prison for me had been a poignant one for
other reasons: for a year, my mother, Melissa, had attended the
Georgia College for Women in the town of Milledgeville where
the prison was located. There, Mother, the year before the belle
of Atlanta, had been required to wear a stiff school uniform—
navy wool pleated skirt and white middy blouse. As a student at
Fulton High School, she had been so popular that she often had
four and five dates on a weekend. But here, she couldn't even entertain in the school parlor without Grandmother Carroll's written permission. When one of her many beaus had finally made
the 100-mile trek to sit for an hour on a straight-backed chair
under the severe gaze of a matron, he had promptly gone back to
the city to marry Mother's sister, Nancy, becoming my Uncle
Luther (a good thing, I would think later, as I watched Uncle
Luther pound his fist on the table at any infringement of good
manners by my cousin Lu Anne). That year, Mother grew rounder
and rounder on the starchy school food and cried herself to sleep
every night; at the end of it, she pleaded with Grandmother Carroll to let her return to Atlanta. She didn't know at that time that
her romantic fate, Daddy, had attended the nearby Georgia Military Academy, where he played his saxophone on the roof to at-
tract the girls.

The white-columned antebellum town was also the last home

of the novelist and short story writer Flannery O'Connor. She, too, had attended Georgia College for Women and, more feisty than Mother, had survived to go on to Iowa Writers' School, only to be struck down by lupus in her thirties. I imagined her loneliness when she came home to raise peacocks and be cared for by her mother, of her return to that town of pouffed hair and southern belles with brains as shallow as dried-up creek beds. I had visited the room set aside for her manuscripts at the college, now co-ed and renamed Georgia College at Milledgeville, and had even been asked by the English Department to give a reading—until the department head read my newly published book and called to cancel, citing my work as "too sensational."

During my stay at the John Milledge Motel, where I rented a room for $24.50 for a five-day week, I was also thinking about a less likely woman: Jayne Mansfield. Ms. Mansfield was said to have stayed for one night in the concrete block motel, and the image of her lying in one of the sprung beds, her bleached blond hair spread over the thin pillows, the white chenille spread, excited my imagination. That, plus a recent reading of a biography of her life in which she was cited as having an IQ of 150, that her sexual image had been a deliberate creation in order to promote her career. I had also heard of the way she was said to have died—decapitated by a wire that crossed the dark Mississippi road as she drove out of New Orleans with her third husband. She seemed to me to be a perfect metaphor for the way many women are split, mind and body, in their lives.

In addition, Alice Walker, not yet the author of *The Color Purple*, had grown up just down Highway 441 in Eatonton, Georgia. Though Alice had at first said she didn't think she could be friends with a white southern woman, she later relented. I had gone to meet her at *Ms.* magazine, where she worked, and where, still starry-eyed over the icons of the women's movement, I had been introduced to Gloria Steinem's feet in the ladies' room. Now, driving each week through Alice's hometown on my way to Milledgeville from Atlanta, I would think of Alice's timely escape from the South via scholarships, first to Spellman College, then Sarah Lawrence, of how her blackness had perhaps given her a clear sight about the region that I never had.

Each night as I drove back to the motel after my stint at the prison, the Spanish moss dripped like eerie ghosts from the great live oaks, and my mind was haunted by them all—by Alice, growing up on a tenant farm, in a town dominated by the white man; by Flannery, weird and Catholic, swollen by cortisone and struggling to write in her hospital bed; by Jayne, separated mind from body, in death as she had been in life; and by Mother, with her unshattered girlish dreams.

But it was the women from the prison who continued to fill my mind as, back at the motel room, I poured myself a shot of Black Jack, opened a can of bean dip to eat with Fritoes, then quickly turned on the color television set. As I lay waiting for the Black Jack and the *Tony Orlando and Dawn Show* to do their work, my thoughts would churn with the ways in which the women in prison and I were alike. Wasn't I a rebel, a female James Dean or Marlon Brando, and wasn't their rebelliousness why they were where they were? Hadn't I yearned to be a disturber of the peace, even if through ideas rather than acts? Just because I had not murdered, forged checks, or committed armed robbery didn't mean I hadn't experienced the same feelings.

The women at the prison were, in many ways, the grown-up versions of the young women in the training schools. They had acted out their rage, or else had passively accepted a fate prescribed for them by others. "In nature, there are no rewards or punishments; there are only consequences," I had read. It would be easy to say that they had ended up in prison because of the natural consequences of entropy, or the paths of least resistance. But they were also deeply acculturated, each taught to believe that the man in her life was more important than anything else, more important than their own feelings, talents, or intelligence. Almost all the women had ended up in prison because of something to do with a man, with pleasing a man, or about what they considered to be their roles as women. Several had killed the men who had abused them; Jewell, for example, had murdered the man who had married her when she was fifty, then had cheated her out of her meager savings and molested her teenage daughter. Others had been in armed robberies or had written bad checks in order to please a boyfriend. As I listened to their stories, I recalled all too painfully the times I, too, had mutilated myself because of a blocked love or hate for the men in my life, going back to the first man in my life, Daddy, who because of his drinking had often been as absent as though he had abandoned us in the flesh.

Indeed, I had had just enough dysfunction and tragedy in my own life to identify with theirs. But through blessings of accident and birth, I had also been given gifts—Daddy had loved poetry, and Mother had honored storytelling and everything to do with the written word. Despite everything that had happened in our little family, our agonies paled beside those of the women in prison, who, for the most part, had known nothing but poverty from their very beginnings; who, more often than not, had been born with the "disability" of being black in a white southern culture—who had little sense of their right to rage or a good life, and who had only the rawest means with which to express themselves.

Already, I was firm in my belief in the healing power of art. Richard Speck, I read, had begun painting in prison. Could the young nurses he murdered have been saved had he begun painting at an earlier age? And could some of these women have been saved from their fate via poetry, if they had had a means of self-expression other than acting out? As it was, their rage either turned inward, or outward, in ways that were antisocial. Yet I suspected many of them would have been saved from their self-destructive actions if they had had access to art. In fact, I felt that I was at last viewing evidence of my notion that writing could heal, or at the very least, *relieve* pain, even under the worst of circumstances.

I was now on the prisoners' side, against the administration and all the many ways we were kept from expressing ourselves. "Those women aren't interested in poetry!" scoffed the prune of a woman who taught the G.E.D. classes when I told her that the women in the workshop wanted to give a reading. When I asked the Georgia Department of Corrections to allocate funds to anthologize the women's poems, they refused, saying the poems had not been written in a manner that "could have been used as a crime-prevention tool." But I had encouraged the women to write honestly and openly of their experiences and feelings: I knew that they, like everyone else, wished to be known, to express themselves as they were.

The other discovery was the strength of their life force. Tonight, the sea of faces before us exploded with laughter, applause, and vindication as the audience heard, possibly for the first time, their real feelings formally expressed by women like themselves, inside the prison walls.

> *My body is shaped like a Co-Cola bottle . . .*
> *& when I walk I shake like jelly*
> *because jam don't shake like that . . .*

half-sang Chain Gang Candy, who was wearing her de rigueur short brown cotton dress (something like the Brownie uniform I had worn at eleven), heavy brown oxfords, and white socks. To her audience's delight, she gave her ample bottom a shake at the end of each line.

Next, Easter Sunday described her promise to herself about her future relationships with men:

> *When he says "hi"*
> *I'll say "good-bye." . . .*

Then Frankie, her light brown hair falling beside her freckled face as she looked down at a sheaf of notebook paper, began reading, her vowels flat with South Georgia rhythms, a group poem "by Doris, Tanya, Maybelle, Rosemary, and me," and the crowd went quiet:

Bein' white is like bein' dipped in bleach
It's like bein' a ku klux man's sheet. . . .
Being black is like goin' to the back of the cafe
when you were ten & wondering why. . . .
Bein' black is bein' a maid & always goin'
to the back door because that's what your grandmother
*   always did. . . .*
it's like takin' home the white women's leftovers. . . .

By the time Peggy read her poem, I noticed that the women
in the audience were sitting on the edges of their folding chairs.
Peggy could usually be counted on for a laugh. I would never forget her story of how "Once I wuz datin' a dude with no arms and
only one leg, 'n thet's why I stold his car—I knew he couldn't run
after me!" But now, as she began reading, I felt the kind of shiver
up the back of my arms that I only felt at something authentic:

Inside every human shell a person
inside every person an emotion—
each has the need to feel to express to share.
Let's not pretend because we really need each other. . . .

At this line, the women burst into applause. Peggy's poetry was
not great—hell, it wasn't even *good* poetry! But I could tell by the
rapt expressions of the women in the first rows that these were
feelings they needed to hear expressed, validated.

It is easier for me to relate to your sadness—
when you come to me with your problems .
When you need me
I become totally involved.
But when you share your happiness
I sometimes feel left out. . . .

When Sheba grasped the microphone, she began a poem
about growing up in Detroit, emphasizing each syllable in her
precise diction:

> *You're somewhere in the middle of seven other kids . . .*
> *Mama called her six little women "golden girls"*
> *& her man child "handsome" . . .*
> *No one ever mentioned black or poor . . .*
> *I'm a flower but all the beauty lovers*
> *are gone somewhere. . . .*

But as she began her next piece, her chiseled features tightened in a controlled rage. She was one of the more naturally talented writers in the group, a poet to whom a barbed irony came easily, bringing into focus a whole panorama of questions about the nature of evil. As she read, a Yankee edge to her tone, I wondered at the guts it had taken her to read it, and what the guards who shuffled in the shadows at the back of the room were feeling and thinking about her—just as, years later, I would wonder when I read in the *Savannah News-Press* that guards at the institution had been charged with sexual abuse, if Sheba was still a prisoner there:

> *The Man is a carpenter's vise*
> *squeezing the life & color from my body.*
> *The Man is a computer ignoring my humanity*
> *to feed his white—SOUTHERN—ancient ego.*
> *He is a leech attached to the comfort*
> *of degrading & humiliating the black intellect*
> *sucking the life & color from my body.*
> *The Man grins at the power he has*
> *over hundreds of women.*
> *The Man is a machine gone wild.*

But it was Doris, the mother of six, who, coming up to read again, was the star of our show. Doris waited until the women in the room had stopped stomping and hollering, then, pausing with the timing of a natural performer, holding the microphone close like a blues singer, she belted out her next poem in a deep, mournful voice. This one was about giving birth to one of her children in the town where she had lived; how, like mothers throughout history, she had done what she thought she had to do in order to protect her child:

> *In a small town in the South*
> *a small hospital stands*
> *a hospital with hard-hearted nurses.*
> *The doctor says someone has crossed the line.*
> *But I don't show my hurt*
> *my hate for these people*
> *of whom my baby will be a part*
> *because I have my baby to think of*
> *I have to love them instead*
> *(so) my baby growing up*
> *will think she was wanted*
> *even if her mother was degraded. . . .*

Yet it was Doris's last poem, one of identification with her own mother, that cut through me like a dull knife, striking at the heart of the constant pain which I knew to be Mother's legacy:

> *My mother she never cried.*
> *But her face held the lines of grief—*
> *I guess being hurt so much*
> *by love sets a pattern*
> *of not setting your heart free to love*
> *of keeping it from being shattered.*
> *I never did get to know my mother*
> *because she drifted so far away—*
> *she told my brothers & me*
> *she was going to another town to stay.*
> *Then the phone call one windy night—*
> *her worries were over at last—*
> *death had taken her away. . . .*

It was as though Doris had read the poem just for me. That night, when I got back to my room at the John Milledge Motel, the phone rang as I turned my key in the lock. I tossed my book bag on the bed, then picked up the receiver to hear my sister Anne saying that Mother had finally done what she had long threatened. She had overdosed on pills and was being taken by ambulance to the Crawford Long Hospital in Atlanta—could I meet her there?

I would never see Mother conscious again. Like Doris, I would almost be relieved to see, as she lay atop a table in a room in intensive care, the deep lines of some long-held inner tension finally airbrushed from her newly smooth cheeks.

Yet as Mother lay dying, something strong and alive of which I was not yet aware was moving out of her body and into mine, where it would grow like a spiritual pregnancy. What would emerge, alive and kicking, a half-dozen years later would be the desire to find a way and a place for women like her, like Doris, and all the rest to express ourselves, to be heard.

< TWO >

How I Wrote My Heart Out &
How You Can Too

My mother, Melissa, was a beautiful southern woman and a talented writer who thought she didn't have the right to be. My sister, Anne, and I had been told constantly by the women of our family that she was "the prettiest girl in Atlanta," as though that had been her highest value. (Indeed, a photo of her at eighteen, holding red roses, wearing a favorite black velvet dance dress, later graced the cover of the book I would write in my attempt to come to terms with her life and death.) "She could have had any boy in Atlanta," we were told, and she had chosen our charismatic and Valentino-handsome daddy, whose charms had only lasted until the full blossoming of her melancholia and his alcoholism. After Mother's suicide at sixty, Anne and I discovered that, ladylike to the end, she had destroyed her best and most personal pieces of writing. "To be a southern girl must be hard," the poet Maxine Kumin said to me once; to be one like Mother, a fragile belle who also was burdened with a brain, must have been hell.

Despite Mother's melancholy, Daddy's failures, their reverence for the creative had spilled over on me, becoming the best gift they ever gave me. Daddy treasured the little blue-paper-bound book of poems privately printed by his fraternity brother Claude. (He was also a stickler for proper English usage—Anne and I were not permitted to use the word *kids* in referring to our friends because, he said, it really meant "baby goats.") Mother cherished her volumes of *Vanity Fair*, left from her one year in college, not to speak of her dreams of becoming a writer herself. At Davison's Department Store on Peachtree Street she had bought a paperback, *Writing Made Simple*, for one dollar; the book had chapters on "How to Write a Short Story," "How to Write a Novel," "How to Write a Magazine Article," and so on. She kept it throughout the years, and when I began writing, I found that the book actually contained good advice. She referred with pride to my and Anne's great-grandparents on her father's side, a Methodist minister and his wife who had recited passages of Shakespeare and Milton at the dinner table. When she spoke of her favorite authors, a tremulous, worshipful note filled her voice. She also supported me in attending art classes downtown every Saturday when I was eleven, defending to my more prig- gish aunts the male nudes I had sketched from a statue.

And then there was the storytelling tradition in our family. I had heard so many times about the way Mother and Daddy had eloped that I felt I had been there; he in a fedora and fine wool overcoat, she in a satin-lined cloche and fitted coat, with stitched satin lapels to match; or of how Grandmother Carroll's mother- to-be had found her mother's best hand-painted butter dish in a gully on the side of the road, after the Yankee soldiers had gone through, scattering everything.

Thus, even as a child I had known that being an artist of some kind—a poet, a novelist, a painter—was the most fun one could have in life. I sensed that such a life meant being able to be a child forever, whatever forever meant. Such a person, I imag- ined, was one who was exempt from the mundane, who lived simply but well, surrounded by heady ideas, books, and interest- ing eclectic friends for whom she cooked up vast vats of soup or lasagna and who, unbound by convention, lived in strange places and had unusual love affairs. (And who sometimes dissi- pated themselves to good end: "$25 for food, $50 for booze, $100 for dope—and my rent's free because I'm squatting in the house I'm renovating," a writer friend said, describing his weekly budget.)

Mother and Daddy, children of the Depression, counting every penny, and made even poorer by Daddy's gambling and drinking, had to satisfy their cravings for adventure by buying guava jelly rather than apple at the Piggly Wiggly, and by being the first people on our street to have a black-and-white TV set, on which we watched Milton Berle every Saturday night. But fortunately, Mother had also given me the message that the worthwhile things are often hard to achieve. In a book she gave me, *Captain Perseverance,* the narrator steered his little boat through any waters, no matter how rough. Like him, I was determined to fulfill my dream of becoming an artist or a writer. The only thing I didn't understand was why *every*one didn't want such a life.

As a widely traveled Charleston friend said, when I asked whether she had ever considered living somewhere other than the South, "No—because the only alternative is living in the *North*!"

"Yes, but how did *you* become a writer?" someone in the audience inevitably asks after a reading.

The closer to the Northeast, to the groves of academe, the more persistent was the question, the more puzzled the tone. It was as if, southern, a high school dropout, with a failed if handsome alcoholic father, a suicidal southern-belle mother, I was from darkest Africa.

I was asked the question by college students, baffled as to how one would know what to read without a knowledgeable professor to guide them. I was questioned, sometimes crossly, by male peers, often creative writing professors who themselves may have gone to Yale or the Iowa Writers' Workshop. I was queried by well-educated women who were successful in other fields— MDs, attorneys, or professors—who often as not looked at me as though they couldn't imagine, as we say down south, that "I had a brain in my head." ("I can't believe *you* wrote that!" a woman psychotherapist said after the minister at our Unitarian Church read a poem I had penned as part of the service, bringing much of the congregation to tears.) And most frequently, I was asked how I had done it by otherwise traditional southern women my age who had dreamed for a lifetime of becoming writers themselves. All of them possibly asked the question for the same reason—how had a reasonably pretty, feminine-looking southern woman, who, like the latter group, had spent much of her life as a wife and mother, changing diapers and sheets, cooking up the requisite number of meals, ended up as a serious writer? Had I gone on to a lifetime of garden club committee work or Bible School teaching, none from these groups would have been surprised.

Nor had I by some fluke been placed in the proper schools, in juxtaposition to the proper influences. I had not lived my life in New York or London, informed by literary parents. Far from mine was the experience of Virginia Woolf, with her scholarly parents, her Cambridge-educated brothers. My history was also unlike, say, that of Alice Walker, a sister in southern heritage who had been sent north on fellowship, to have a famous writer-teacher pick up her early works, present them to a publisher. Instead, the most I had been encouraged to hope for was marriage to the "right"—that is, prosperous, or even just steadily working, non-drunken-or-abusive—man or a job as a clerk-typist or secretary.

Finally, when the question had been asked often enough, I began to wonder myself: How *did* this unlikely girl from the sticks—who had walked down a dirt road to a rural high school where shop and Home Ec were the most important subjects, who had heard the Bible Belt preacher shout against the sins of worldliness, but who had never, until her late twenties, met a living author, or heard one quoted outside the classroom or the dinner table, end up becoming a poet and a writer, a woman who loved books—good books—above all else? And how, through it all, had I protected—at first, like a fragile pregnancy, then like a growing fetus—that ephemeral bubble inside me that was my creative life?

Indeed, I had sidestepped the question myself in my first prose book, *Fatal Flowers*, an autobiographical account of growing up female and southern, and of Mother's life and death. "Keep references to yourself as a writer to a minimum," my editor had advised. "Otherwise, you distance the reader."

Sometimes I would answer by saying I started writing by carving my boyfriend Troy's name on my desk in sixth grade. At other times I said that I began when I was seven, writing poems that I illustrated with pictures of Mickey Mouse and Donald Duck, then tried to sell for a penny on Peachtree Street in my hometown of Atlanta. I had been inspired to believe I could write, I would claim, by a poem I had read in one of my mother's *Ladies' Home Journals*: as I read the complete verse, "We frogs / love bogs," I realized I could do that, too.

Or I would describe my first "book," written at nine during a time I cried about horses: how after seeing the movie version of *My Friend Flicka* I went home to write my own horse story on notebook paper tied together with shoelaces, illustrated with deformed-looking beasts, with a plot remarkably like that of Mary O'Hara's classic. It was a work marred only, in my view, by my spelling of *horse,* which I spelled "house" throughout the story. Then I might mention my second book, which I considered an equal success, a collection of totally untested recipes for such dishes as green grits and egg-shaped Jell-O ("Tap a hole in the ends of raw eggs, shake out the insides, fill them with Jell-O, then chill and peel"), again written on the ubiquitous notebook paper.

I might even recount a conversation I had had with a worldly New Yorker, the husband of a friend, early in my adult writing life, when I was still a young housewife. Earnestly, I had been discussing the stages in my poetry, citing the stages in Picasso's painting as an example. "*You* are comparing your*self* to Pi*cass*o?" he chortled. "Yes—why not?" I said, surprised at his reaction.

Around that same time, I would tell my questioners, I had taken my cat to the vet, where I picked *Cat* magazine off the waiting room table. Oh, maybe I can have a poem printed someday in *Cat* magazine! I thought to myself, reading in the back that they paid 50 cents a line. At that point, mere publication was still a tremulous dream.

But I knew even as I spoke that these were throwaway lines, a showwoman's way of evading a question that has a long and sometimes circuitous answer.

"Be careful what you want, you might get it!" was a saying I heard over and over as a child, in a southern rephrasing of Socrates. And while I may not always have been happy with the choices I made of, say, lovers or husbands, I rarely have been less than happy about my choice of writing. Though there have been detours along the way— some caused by fate, more by myself— I've never looked back.

The years I spent contentedly scribbling away in my five-year diary, or happily ensconced in one of the big stuffed green chairs in the children's room of Atlanta's Carnegie Library, imagining that I would read every book from A through Z; and that maybe someday one of my books might even be there on the shelves among them, was a dreamily prescient period, bearing out my present belief that each of us have a golden time—usually just before adolescence—during which our goals and interests are pure.

Later, more distracted, I would revise my goal of reading *every* book in the library, hoping that if I surrounded myself with enough of them, the books would go into my brain by osmosis. Decades before the recent research that shows that girls experience a drop in self-esteem at puberty, I was a perfect example of the phenomenon. Along with the development of feminine attributes, I was also infected with the impulses of almost every adult woman I have ever met, southern or not: to please, especially the opposite sex, and to find my salvation through others—in other words, by being "sweet and nice," as Mother and Grandmother Carroll had repeatedly put it. While I was having little success with this goal—the nicer I was on the outside, the meaner I felt inside—much of my energy now went in pursuit of it. Nor were matters helped by the craziness in our little family, or the fact that I was cradled—if not so gently—in the heart of the Bible Belt.

For one thing, I was soon boy crazy, my girlish ambitions sinking behind a new passion for whiskers, a masculine form, and mysterious protuberances. Mother and Daddy were really into their fights, and at the Baptist Church each Sunday morning, the handsome preacher, his black hair oiled back in dizzying, Elvis-like waves, railed against the two main sins, sex and drink. We sang hymns about the Blood of the Lamb and what worms we were. So what was I to think of myself—with my drunken daddy, my whining, miserable mother; my swelling breasts, and an animal in my newly furred pubis that came alive with each boy I kissed, tossing me into nightmares of hellfire and damnation? After a session spent necking in the living room while *Deep Purple* played on the record player (and having broken Mother's rule about having boys to the house when she wasn't there), I was tormented. To punish myself, I scratched my boyfriend Troy's initials inside my thigh with a safety pin, then whacked off my long brown pageboy with Mother's pinking shears and poured a bottle of peroxide over my head, turning my once-shining hair a dull orange. That the preacher would soon be convicted by the church deacons of sexual sins—he was seen kissing the plump old-maid church organist—did little to repeal my low estimate of myself.

Each weekday, I trudged down a dirt road to Tucker High School in the town of Tucker, Georgia, where we'd moved because of Daddy's gambling and drinking, and because Mother's parents, Grandmother and Granddaddy Carroll, lived nearby. They had helped provide us with the little house in which Anne, my "baby sister," as I still called her, and I slept on a rollaway bed in the kitchen. Though I was popular and a cheerleader, and owned a magical pink angora sweater that, if I wore it on a Thursday, guaranteed me a date for Friday night (Anne said she hated to follow me at the school because I had the reputation for having more dates than any girl who had ever gone there), I felt fat and as lowly as a slug, usually dressed as I was in a hand-me-down from Mother's sister, Aunt Betty.

Without knowing it then, I was probably also feeling the burden of my intelligence, the intelligence Mother had tried so hard to subdue in herself. She had planted a profusion of sweet peas—cream, vermilion, fuchsia—in the side yard, and otherwise spent her time trying to make ends meet. To support us, she was now hailing down the Greyhound bus on the highway each morning, going into Atlanta to work as a clerk-typist, a job for which her years as a belle had left her unprepared, then coming home exhausted each night to life with an alcoholic husband, a surly teenage daughter, and an anxious preteen one.

At Tucker High School, the few students who planned on going to college were considered weirdos. When the student body was given a school-wide IQ test, as I considered which circles to pencil, I sat feeling messier and fatter than usual, a thick cotton pad moist between my thighs—my menstruation reminding me even more vividly of my lowly female status, my limited future options. When another girl and I tied for the highest scores, I was offered a scholarship to the Dale Strebel School of Cosmetology, which was what the school thought a bright girl should do, and which Mother, in one of her moments of rare good sense—possibly because of her prejudice against pink-collar workers—made me turn down.

While I had been saved from a life as a hairstylist, no one had ever mentioned college. The only other future I saw for myself was hailing down the bus on the highway like Mother did and going downtown to type all day, or the one favored by the women of my family: "You are who you marry," Grandmother Carroll had told Anne and me over and over, in a more pragmatic version of St. Paul's "Marry or burn." Daddy was drinking more and more each night and, distracted from his rage at Mother by my burgeoning sexuality, was calling me "whore" and "slut." Some of my girlfriends had already married, at fourteen and fifteen; one girl had had three children by age eighteen. I, too, had begun dreaming of an escape via Octagon Soap and Electroluxes, a kind of nunnery à la Donna Reed. Marriage was obviously the way out.

And this, I set about—however unconsciously—to achieve. In fact, before it was all over, Grandmother Carroll, had she still been alive, would have had reason—given the number of my husbands—to believe I had fallen victim to multiple personality disorder.

Required to make a white Home Ec apron before she would be allowed to graduate from Georgia College for Women, the novelist Flannery O'Connor also made three tiny white aprons for three baby ducks that followed her around the campus. Yet, unlike O'Connor, who had had the good sense to make light of the feminine arts, I took to them with a vengeance, as much a true believer as Mother had been.

I participated in a charm course led by a skinny yet imperious ninth-grade mother who arrived at the school auditorium wearing pumps, thick pancake, and Maybelline. Feeling like a whale on stilts in the presence of such glamour, I walked, as directed, down an imaginary runway with my toes out.

In Home Ec, taught by a maiden lady named Miss Ina Mae Jones, I learned to bake biscuits like little chef's hats, made my white Home Ec apron, and even took on more ambitious sewing projects, dreaming of pretty clothes to wear on dates. During the summer I was fourteen, I made my masterpiece from a Vogue pattern, a pink waffle pique sundress with scallops around the bottom of the jacket and its sleeves, at the neckline, and around the hem. Each scallop was an engineering marvel, turned with a special little tool from Woolworth's. In fact, the dress turned out so well I began to think I had a career ahead as a seamstress, not knowing that from then on, as my life temporarily fell apart, my sewing would, too, becoming full of protruding seams and buttonholes that couldn't be fixed.

That summer I also baked a cake, a pie, or cookies each day while Mother was away at work. She had hired Precious, a fat black maid who wore a knife in her stocking top, to look after us. Every day, Anne, Precious, and I gobbled down the sweets, because I knew Mother would be angry if she knew I had been using supplies from the groceries that she shopped for each week, counting every penny. Otherwise, I hid the half-eaten pecan pies, the oatmeal cookies, beneath my bras and panties in the drawer of the dresser, which sat in the kitchen beside our rollaway bed. They would be crammed into my mouth when I came in from dates to the drive-in, made ravenous by some pimply faced boy's kisses and sexual urges that were yet to be fulfilled.

One day, as my girlfriend Ruby and I walked to the end of my driveway, carrying a pan of freshly made brownies that we intended to eat at her house, a blond Greek god of an "older" man—seventeen—who lived down the road, but who went to another high school, and who had never before deigned to speak, walked by. "I'm Junior," he said, seeing the brownies and introducing himself. He talked to us for as long as it took him to gouge all the brownies from the pan, eating them by the handful.

A few days later, I sat in a lawn chair, reading a Frank Yerby novel about ravished maidens and cruel blond swordsmen, when Junior appeared in my yard.

"Can you go out on dates yet?" Dry-mouthed, conscious of my heart beating, I nodded in assent.

"Are you busy Friday night?" the god continued. Now, certain that he was about to ask me for a date, my heart beat even faster, and I nodded again.

"Well, my cousin T.J. needs a blind date," he grinned, satisfied.

And that was how my cooking skills led to marriage, and how I came to wear the pink waffle pique dress on my first date with the boy who became my first husband.

I had two main boyfriends in high school, and I married them both.

I married the first at sixteen, the other at twenty. Paul was a college boy who—to the chagrin of my high school–age beaus—took me downtown to the Fox Theater in Atlanta, then to the Varsity for chiliburgers and "Varsity Oranges" (vanilla ice cream frothed into artificially flavored orange drink) in his daddy's big black Buick Riviera. But I found our dates tame, and Paul too easy to control. Though I didn't know it yet, an attraction to anarchy was already my hubris. T.J. was a sometime bricklayer and laborer a year out of high school who was known as one of the wildest boys in the county, and who, though we didn't know to call it rape then, had forced himself upon me on our second date, which took place a full year after the first. ("Are you a Christian?" he whispered in my ear on our first date, trying to look down the front of the pink pique dress in the backseat of Junior's clunker.) Since, at sixteen, I had already had sex with two other boys, each of whom I had also hoped to marry, I knew I was "ruined." Once they had their way with me, my former lovers confirmed my sense of myself: the first had told his buddies, then never called again; the second abandoned me when he found I wore falsies under my heavy wool cheerleading sweater. Thus, when T.J. and Paul made me choose between them, I naturally chose T.J., the wild and crazy one, who, driven by his own demons and hormonal imperatives, was willing to marry immediately.

T.J.'s reputation was not unfounded; besides driving junkers down two-lane country roads at ninety miles an hour, he was also, when crossed, given to physical rages. Three violent years followed, leaving me with a son, David; yet miraculously intact. Marriage—even marriage to a boy-man with problems of his own—agreed with me, giving me a degree of control over my life that I hadn't known before, and, as important—as I waited the long hours for him on the army posts where he was stationed—time to read (though many of the books and articles I read, such as "Can This Marriage Be Saved?" in the *Ladies' Home Journal* and Bishop Fulton Sheen's book on being a good Christian woman, were about how to be a better wife, how to stem the tide of my young husband's anger). The other army wives thought I was weird when I used part of our meager allotment of $140 a month to buy magazines and paperbacks and to pay a monthly installment on a "Finish High School at Home" course, ordered off the back of one of T.J.'s matchbooks. When I had mailed off the tiny coupon, a man in a dark rayon suit arrived, driving over the dusty roads to close the deal. As David sat damply on my lap, I signed the contract, and soon I was poring over the biology and civics texts that had begun arriving in the mail. While T.J. drank beer and complained, I cooked, supplementing our stores with the canned milk and Spam he had ripped off from the mess hall where he was a cook; worked at the exercises the magazines assured would flatten my stomach (my figure was better than ever, a fact that drove T.J. mad with jealousy), and studied, cleaned, and tended David. Sometimes, I lay wanly on the couch nursing the bruises inflicted by T.J.'s fists, as he cried and laid his head on my chest, begging forgiveness. As a southern girl, I was a tee-totaler, and knew what my role was: to be a sex object and a pseudo-mother, and to keep my errant man in line, even to pray for his soul if necessary. On Sundays, while T.J. slept off a hang-over, I went to the Baptist Church, just as I had back in Georgia. "Just as I am-m . . . With-out-ut one plea . . . but thet thy blood wuz shed . . . fo-er me-e-e" we would croon during the "Invita-tion," while the preacher coaxed us sinners to "Come on down

'n lay it ALL down on JEE-sus!" Twice a week, like the other en-
listed men's wives, I walked down the dirt road with David in the
stroller to the grocery store where we had military credit, or to
the laundromat, where the smell of ammonia fogged the air as
we washed our babies' urine-soaked diapers in wringer washing
machines.

Even then, I sensed that it was language that would save me.
Already, words and ideas provided a detachment that, like a bell
jar, shielded me during a situation that was becoming more and
more dangerous, a detachment that enabled me finally, back in
Georgia, to make my escape. Taking fifteen-month-old David, I
had fled to Tucker, to Grandmother Carroll's house, where we
lived with her and Granddaddy Carroll. Mother, who had divorced Daddy and had a breakdown and shock treatments, and
Anne, who was now in high school, lived there, too. Despite
Mother's hysteria—"Marriage is sacred," she would cry ner-
vously: I shouldn't leave my young husband, even if he *did* beat
me, strangle me, and hold pillows over my face, threatening to
smother me—it was not an unhappy time. Grandmother's farm-
house was old-fashioned and spacious, with high-ceilinged bed-
rooms (each with a fireplace), a huge wraparound verandah and
grounds, and chickens and peacocks in the yard. Every night,
Anne and I fought over who would get to sleep with David, hot
wet diapers and all.

It was 1955; I was nineteen years old. I didn't know what sexual harassment was—nobody did—and I had only murmured
polite replies to the Emory University personnel director's queries
as to whether I'd had sex with my husband before marriage, and
whether I wore a panty girdle under my straight skirts. Despite
my lack of education, I was being given the $40-a-week job as
secretary to the Director of Student Aid because of my high
score on the IQ test, he told me. Thus, I was soon doing exactly
as Mother had done, taking the Greyhound, plus a second bus,
into town each day. During the day, a black girl took care of
David for $15 a week. But somehow, I no longer felt trapped. In-

stead, I felt as though my life was just beginning. One day, as I stood brushing my long hair in the ladies' room, thinking how lucky I was, a message, like the voice of God, came to me: "As long as you have your mind, nothing bad can ever happen to you."

Despite my tribulations, I also felt pretty, prettier than I ever had in high school. I was thin and I knew I looked sexy in the curvy $17.95 dresses, the baby-doll high heels I had begun wearing to work. I had a chartreuse rayon linen suit that complemented my figure, and my long red-brown hair hung in Rita Hayworth waves down my back. There would be no time for casual dating, for frivolity: Mother, Grandmother, and my aunts were all giving me the same message—it was time to set my sights on marriage, again as a form of escape.

At twenty, I married Paul, who in the interim since I'd dated him in high school had gotten a master's degree and become an earnest young architect—"good husban' material," all my female clan agreed. He had given me a half-karat diamond in a Tiffany setting; a wedding followed in which, carrying a bouquet of cymbidian orchids, I marched down an aisle atop a satin aisle cloth wearing a ballerina-length dress in tiers of embroidered yellow organdy, a hundred tiny covered buttons up the back, a matching organdy-covered pillbox, and satin pumps dyed the same shade.

By twenty-three, I was middle class for the first time in my life and had all the things I had been taught would make me happy—three beautiful children, including two daughters, a professional husband, and a split-level house with built-in pink appliances. But something was wrong. I had suffered the first real grief in my life when David, age two, had been hit by a car before my eyes, just after Paul and I returned from our honeymoon. After a coma and months of therapy, David recovered. But some internal tension had made nursing Laura and my third baby, Darcy, painful; I had a depression after Darcy's birth, and though I had no name for the queasiness, the fear I was feeling, I had begun experiencing massive anxiety attacks. What was wrong with me? Was I dying of cancer, I wondered, seeing blood in my diaphragm, or gripped by abdominal cramps as the babies screamed in the morning?

We attended the Presbyterian church in which my new husband grew up, but I had begun questioning the Christianity I was taught as a child. "Do I really believe in Jesus anymore?" I found myself scribbling fearfully in the journals I had begun keeping in composition books. On the other hand, I remembered the parable of the talents, of how the Lord had blessed the servant who had multiplied his talents. But what were mine, and what was I supposed to do with them? When I found myself unable to recite the Apostle's Creed, the good-looking young minister who lived in our subdivision came to visit. "That doesn't matter—a *lot* of people don't believe it and say it anyway," he said when I told him about my difficulty. His answer made me feel that a religious solution to my problems was even more unlikely.

Gradually, I remembered how, in that golden time before sex had come to dominate my life, I had loved drawing and writing and inventing (though every time I had boiled wild flowers to make perfume, they had ended up smelling like turnip greens). One twilight, as Paul and I sat on the back stoop watching the children play on the swing set and run after lightning bugs, the sound of crickets had lulled me into a vision. As vague as a dream sequence in a movie, the colors nebulous and vague, a picture of myself came, doing something I couldn't make out. Something that was important, and which would make me travel, perhaps all over the world, and cause me to meet many exotic people.

But first, I had to explore *what*. With my young husband's blessings, I tried painting, attending art classes downtown at night at the Atlanta College of Art. "Like the woodcuts of Dürer," my instructor said solemnly of a tempera work I had done with a palette knife, depicting David, age four, and I walking away from storm clouds toward sunlight. But I didn't know who Dürer was, and figure painting, which I took next, was hard. When I worked on my paintings at home, down in the concrete-floored basement near the washer and dryer, the babies would get into the oil paints, smearing them everywhere. Still at a loss, I enrolled in a modern poetry class in the continuing education program at Emory University.

When I sat down in that dingy, fluorescent-lit classroom, I didn't know that my life was about to change forever. As a high school dropout, I was a literary virgin who had never heard of T. S. Eliot or Emily Dickinson. But when Professor H. E. Francis began reading from the modern poets, his face filled with obvious passion, I felt as though I might faint. His voice transported me in a way no Washed-in-the Blood preacher or Baptist hymn ever had. The syllables rolling from his tongue lifted me on high in an evangelical fervor that made me feel he was speaking not only in tongues but in private messages meant for me alone. At that moment, as surely as if I had fallen in love at first sight, I had fallen in love with modern poetry at first hearing. (Later, I would learn that this brilliant and articulate professor was a fine short story writer in his own right.)

My fervor continued through the poetry workshop I attended the next quarter, to which each week I brought the poems that had begun pouring from my brain (sometimes emerging in perfect meter). I was further enflamed as I listened for the first time to a live poet read from his works. As James Dickey, who had then published only one book, read from his works at a little art gallery on Peachtree Road in Atlanta, I felt as though (as we say down south) I had "died and gone to heaven." I was again filled with a near-religious ecstasy. I could not believe that words, mere words, could be put together in a way that caused me to feel the way I was feeling, but however they were put together, I wanted—perhaps more than I had ever wanted anything in my life—to learn how to do it.

Thus, my commitment was made, a commitment that has never failed. For the next twelve years I devoted myself to learning to write poetry. A new world had opened to me, a world in which the everyday events of my life—finding a dead bluebird in the backyard, or watching the kids on their swing set; even folding the laundry or baking a lemon meringue pie—took on new and mysterious meanings, meanings that revealed themselves in the poems that had begun bursting into my head like bubbles. Whereas life had before felt drab—as colorless as my children's books until they painted the pages with water to make color magically appear—color now sprang forth, juicy and plentiful.

Each week, I attended a poetry workshop at the homes of the members of a group who had formed out of our workshop at Emory. The other members were far more formally educated than I was—one had been our instructor at Emory, several had doctorates—but I was the star, the primitive natural who delighted them by pronouncing Oedipus, "O-ped-ee-ous," or saying, "I meant to put an ejaculation point," rather than an exclamation point, "at the end of this line." I copied the poems of the poets I admired in long hand, poems by Dickey and Theodore Roethke and Ted Hughes and Thom Gunn and Randall Jarrell, trying to get the feel of how they had been written, to analyze the way the poet had constructed them. (I hadn't yet noticed that the subjects of my admiration were all men.) I wrote poetry reviews without payment for the *Atlanta Journal-Constitution* in order to get free copies of new poetry collections, and to learn further by analyzing those poems as well. So intense was I in my passion that a schoolteacher warned, "You won't live past age thirty!"

When James Dickey came back to Atlanta from Italy where he and his family had been living on a Guggenheim Fellowship, he was on unemployment and agreed to meet with our group. Like Junior, the boy from down the road from my house in

Tucker, he was a blond god to me—a living poet whose works
had been published. We each paid him $2 apiece to critique our
poems, but I was so in awe of him I could barely speak, despite
the fact that he singled me and my poems out for his attention.
"You'll be a greater poet than I am someday," he said, laying his
big hand on my thigh. "The woman has never truly been known
in poetry. She either says too little or too much." Listening to my
master speak, I determined at that moment that I would be the
first woman to write a woman's true experience in poetry; of
course, I was planning to do so in a way that would please
Dickey and my male mentors.

Dickey also told me that 90 percent of poets died of alcoholism or suicide, but I quietly decided that I would not become
one of them; indeed, I felt that Mother's suffering had risen
more out of her *not* becoming the writer she was meant to be,
rather than from her creative nature. In fact, though I didn't
know it then, I may have been a perfect example of Carl Jung's
statement that "nothing influences the lives of the children more
than the unlived lives of the parents." It was as though Mother's
frustrated passion for writing had been born in me, fully formed.

But the world was changing, and so was I. Each night as I
watched the news on the little black-and-white TV set in my
kitchen as I cooked, I saw students not much younger than I
was, marching in Selma or protesting at Columbia University or
against the Vietnam War. Before long, with some equally avid
members of my poetry group, I was driving downtown to Atlanta to march myself, often as not taking the kids along. I felt
political for the first time in my life—quickly certain of which
side I was on—and it felt good. Soon, awash in the turbulent sea
of my own feelings, and a true believer in the new humanistic
psychology movement, I was in therapy. But most important
was something called the women's movement. I pored over the
works of Betty Friedan, Simone de Beauvoir, and Kate Millet,
reeling with the shock of recognition: was it really possible that a

woman might expect something other than self-denial for herself, maybe even something close to *satisfaction*?

After thirteen increasingly lonely years of marriage to Paul, who had suffered through the changes dictated by my newfound priorities—changes I considered positive, but which he considered less so—we divorced. After our separation, I got a job typing half-days in the dark basement of the Royal Typewriter Company on Peachtree Street. Then came the call from the land development company, offering me $600 a month to write copy—it was 1968, and I was suddenly rich enough to hire a maid to come in three afternoons a week to cook and tend the children. I had workmen come in to install the washer and dryer Paul had promised for years but had never provided, and for the first time I felt the thrill of self-sufficiency. In another, less successful act of liberation, I painted the kitchen floor fuchsia, but before I could apply the polyurethane, as suggested by *Glamour* magazine, the kids tracked through it, leaving footprints in what looked, until we moved, like a sea of wet bubble gum.

Also, I was more certain than ever that the distance provided by the requirements of literary production would save me from the violence, the chaos of my dysfunctional southern past; indeed, what could be more removed from that chaos than the reflection required to find the right word, or the ritualistic counting of syllables in search of the perfect meter? Each evening, Laura, Darcy, and I cooked together; after dinner, we cleaned the kitchen, then I sat at my desk in the dining room amid the TV set, the guinea pigs, and the Barbie doll fights, revising my poems, sending out manuscripts, or writing a review for the *Atlanta Journal-Constitution* until bedtime. "I dreamed the house was on fire, and you wouldn't save me because you were typing," Darcy told me tearfully at age nine. Gradually, the children grew used to the sight of me bent over the old upright manual Royal I had bought on time—$17 a month—from a local office supply store, or the cut-and-pasted papers spread out over the living room rug, and even the beds, where I placed them in order to read and compare the drafts. My youthful co-editors were accustomed to my mutterings, my asking which image or version was better, what they thought of a transition or a paragraph.

Within a couple of years, the job involuntarily ended, an event undoubtedly hastened by my presentation of an effete ad campaign—something poetic, about brown leaves and quail and the meaning of life, which probably belonged in a literary journal rather than on Atlanta billboards—to a rotund, cigar-smoking, diamond-flashing (read *important*) client of the firm. The situation had not been helped, either, by the cover piece I had written in my spare time on the women's movement for *Atlanta* magazine, an account that shocked by referring to masturbation. "Don't you know that's why we men work so hard—to keep women in little white gloves, not having to think about things like that!" my boss yelled at me when the piece hit the newsstands. (That piece was further publicized by an interview with me in the *Atlanta Journal-Constitution* for which I wore a very short skirt and said I didn't believe in marriage.) I didn't again bring up the fact that he had been paying the male "art director," younger and less experienced, more than me, even though I was the "creative director." ("They have a girl over at WGST who does *all* their copy for $500 a month," he stormed back at me the first time I mentioned it.) Instead, I packed my things with relief and headed, not the first time, for the unemployment office, sorry to leave my IBM Selectric and the Xerox machine, but glad to no longer be staring out the windows of an office building, writing poetry (as I'm sure my boss suspected) on company time.

In the meantime, I had also acquired a new husband. Ben was a Jewish prince from Boston, a Columbia-and-Yale-educated intellectual I had met at a writers' conference, who aspired to become a writer himself. Though the poets Richard Eberhardt and Alan Dugan had praised my poems during the conference while ignoring his, I knew that he was my superior because he told me so (he would also protect me, he said, from men like Eberhardt, who had placed his hand atop my breast during our private conference to discuss my work). Nine years my junior, he had written pamphlets for SDS and knew the Columbia students who had blown themselves up in the New York townhouse. A feminist, he insisted that I not shave my legs or under my arms ("I *hated* it when you wore sundresses back then," my sister Anne would confess later). Besides that, he was handsome: a kind of Jewish Robert Redford, his eyelashes lay long on his cheeks as he slept. We shared an absurdist sensibility: we placed a broken-down washing machine and an old manual typewriter atop a pile of pine logs in the backyard as pieces of sculpture, to be admired by the friends with whom we sat under the hundred-foot pines, sipping white wine and talking literature. For his birthday, I had given him a Baskin-Robbins ice cream cake iced with the Star of David in deference to his Judaism, plus a velveteen rug from Woolworth's, depicting Jesus walking across the waters, which he promptly hung on the dining room wall. I was on unemployment, and my house was full of cracks through which the roaches and slugs crawled at night. When I received a certified letter, I opened it excitedly, thinking I had won a literary prize; instead, it was from the housing authorities, saying that our Atlanta neighbors had complained that we didn't have screens on our windows, and that our yard was overgrown and full of junk. But the kids and I were cooking gourmet meals every night, and Ben claimed to be supportive of my goals.

When I began reading some new poets—Anne Sexton, Sylvia Plath—I was stunned by both their virtuosity and their accuracy. But when I told Dickey how much I liked these new poems, he was angry, saying, "They're just shrill, hysterical females who write about throwing their abortions in a gutter." And then I began to ask, who is Dickey—or any man—to say what is right about women's experiences? From that point forward my writing began to change. Whereas before I had been writing socially (and literarily) acceptable pieces on animals, nature, and family life (some of which had been published in little magazines; one had even appeared on *The Younger Poets Page* of *The Atlantic Monthly*), I now began to write directly out of my experience as a woman, including my experiences of anger and sexuality.

During the summer I rented a room away from the house in order to finish a manuscript at a white-hot pace—some of the poems pouring from my psyche frightened even me. But something, suddenly, had released me from the "if you can't say anything nice, don't say anything at all" imprint with which I had been brought up. My own rage (and Mother's, for whom I would later realize I had been a surrogate voice) flooded forth in a torrent of brutal images and language, held in control only through the reins of form.

At the same time, I began receiving messages that the poems were also meaningful to others. When I first read them in public, at the Callenwolde Arts Center in Atlanta in 1973, I walked into the hall still undecided as to whether I should read from the older, more acceptable poems, or risk the new material. Then two women friends in the lobby asked that I read from the new poems for them. As I read, my male peers on the writing committee looked down at the floor in what looked like chagrin, and some people walked out. But afterward women, and some men, swarmed around me, saying that the poems said exactly what they had felt but had been unable to say.

The poems, collected, would become my first published book, *A Sexual Tour of the Deep South*. I had the heady experience of having the collection accepted, even choosing between Doubleday and Holt, Rinehart and Winston (which I chose because of the quiet, intelligent feminism of my soon-to-be-editor, Jennifer Josephy). That year was made even more glorious when I received news of my first grant from the National Endowment for the Arts. That someone would actually give me money because of my writing was beyond my wildest dreams.

But not everyone appreciated my new work. When I left the manuscript with an editor at Liveright who had liked a first manuscript of my nature lyrics, he told me he would read it overnight, that I should call the next morning. When I did, he yelled at me over the phone: "I *hated* it! I felt like I'd fallen down a vaginal orifice!"

Ben, the one who had the literary credentials, didn't seem heartened by my unlikely success. His own play, which he had written after a former girlfriend who was sure that she had been responsible for the Vietnam War committed suicide by burning herself to death Buddhist-style, had been sent back to him by Robert Brustein of the Yale Drama School with a curt note. Before long, Ben would flee the South, saying he hoped never to see another azalea or southern belle for the rest of his life.

Despite my grief at that loss, I had reasons for happiness: twelve years after I had begun, my work had been accepted. My girlhood dreams were coming true, my twilight vision from the backyard had solidified. I would have my own book in the Atlanta Carnegie Library at last.

< THREE >

Writing in the Pink Zone
Or How I Became Zona Rosa

In 1981, after the publication of *Fatal Flowers*, I was teaching once-a-week, six-week courses in creative writing for the city of Savannah at the local science center. Speaking at a long table amid the snake cages and lifesize models of dinosaurs, I heard my voice repeating itself, covering again during each set of half-dozen sessions the initial ground of how I had become a writer and how they might, too. Despite this, I noticed that several, mostly middle-aged, women signed up again and again. Would they like to meet once a month, work in a more intensive workshop? I asked each of them.

Ruby, near seventy, had been coming to the classes in an effort to reduce her blood pressure through journal writing after learning that her husband of forty years had started writing to his old girlfriend. (Later, we would hear her stories of being held for two years in a tuberculosis sanitarium during her teens, watching patients sicken and die, before it turned out that she didn't have tuberculosis after all: she had merely been infected with hookworm from going barefoot on the farm.) Lenore, a petite black woman in her twenties who looked more like a teenager than an adult, was on disability and twice-a-week dialysis. ("Feel a this," she said to me proudly, holding out her skinny wrist in order for me to touch the vibrations in the shunt in the blood vessel just beneath the skin, giving the sense of her being kept alive only by a fragile power.) Gladys had a thick South Georgia accent and gave every appearance of being a conventional Baptist housewife— until one heard her speak, and felt the shock of delight at her dry, oft-radical irreverences. ("I think every young woman should read this book," she said of *Fatal Flowers*, explaining why she had recommended it to her daughter as the subject for a term paper, despite the fact that the book was considered so shocking that even the proprietor of the local bookstore was asking buyers, "Are you sure you want to *read this*?") Onetha was a midlife good ol' girl who was the city clerk married to the fire chief in the nearby army town of Hinesville. Her country-western song lyrics were sometimes performed at Bubba's, the local watering hole for GIs; she also wrote rhymed verses for friends, hand-decorating them with her own calligraphy.

We began casually, even carelessly, just we five women, meeting in my tiny Victorian upstairs apartment, and sometimes in someone else's inevitably more luxurious living room. At first, the gathering was just a chance to talk about what I loved most— writing—and to make a little pin money. I didn't expect it to last long.

But we had additions to the group. I found my walk-up flat becoming crowded as other women heard about us. Soon we had a core group, with one common denominator: each carried around inside her like pregnancies the stories she hadn't been able to tell.

Elsa was an Italian from Trieste, a former fashion model and once the roller-skating champion of Italy, who after becoming pregnant and being abandoned by an American soldier during World War II, then rejected by her aristocratic Catholic family, had married another American GI. She had come to America, keeping the secret of her son's birth—the son who had ultimately rejected her because of it, which led to a breakdown and the desire to tell her story.

Lila, the arts and entertainment editor of the *Savannah News-Press*, was Deborah Norville–gorgeous, and always fashion-model perfect in what seemed to be an endless array of stylish outfits.

"They look like they could give birth and never chip a nail!" a woman from New Jersey would gripe about a certain kind of southern woman, whose beauty seems unduplicated anywhere' else in the country. Lila was one of those. "If only I hadn't bought *all* those *clothes*," she would moan later, "I could have taken a year off to write!" She had come from a clan of happy, loving people. In fact, they were so happy and loving, so impossible to rebel against, that she was impeded from feeling any kind of real ambition for herself.

Susan was reserved and elegant-looking—silver hair pulled into a chignon, slender and fashionably dressed—a professor of English at a small local college who had, along with her husband, docked in Savannah after sailing their boat across the Atlantic. The daughter of a prominent and domineering Ohio attorney, she had long wanted to fulfill her dream of becoming a serious novelist but had somehow always felt blocked.

Abbie was an outspoken black woman with a Ph.D. who was obsessed by a story from her childhood, in which her mother had dared to register to vote in their small hometown, only to be tripped by an overalled white man as she stood at the top of the marble steps of the county courthouse, holding five-year-old Abbie's hand. She had fallen to the bottom of the steps, and that night, the Ku Klux Klan had burned a cross on their yard. Refusing to tell her husband why the Klan had come, she fled that night to Savannah with Abbie and her siblings.

Joan, too, was black and a scholar, the holder of a doctorate earned during time off from the forty years she had taught sociology at Savannah State College. Delicately pretty and fashionable at seventy-six, I thought of her as "The Last of the Black Southern Belles." She had lived off-campus in the same house for fifty years, and called the poetry that she got up in the middle of the night to write "my scratchin's." As a young woman she had worn the de rigueur hat and white gloves as she sat for examinations; she and her late husband, an integrationist of the 1940s who had lost his job as a history professor at the same college be-

cause of his "radical" views, had had to secretly go to the Savannah Beach at midnight because "Negroes" weren't allowed.

When we had been meeting for two years I decided the group
needed a name. After a trip to Mexico City, I labeled it *Zona
Rosa*, the Pink Zone, after what was once the brothel district, but
was now a tourist area full of shops and nightclubs. My daughter
Laura and I had eaten tiny salted fishes there, and had bought
bouquets of tightly coiled crepe paper rosebuds. The name had a
tongue-in-cheek quality since the women in the writing group
were nothing if not proper; it also made me think of an all-
female rock group. More important, the name would serve as a
reminder that this was the feminine zone.

My choice to keep the group to one sex was in part coinci-
dental—indeed, who fills such writing classes but women?—and
in part deliberate. I knew that southern women, especially white
middle-class southern women, are not a group likely to receive
much empathy from others. But I wanted these women to feel
free to be themselves, something I knew was hard for some
southern women in a mixed group, trained as we are to put men
and social and familial requirements first. Over martinis at a
Greenville country club, I had heard the misery in the voice of
a wealthy South Carolina banker's wife. Before marriage she was
a talented writer; at midlife this mother of four was perilously
near a breakdown, yet unable to break with the constraints of
her role. The following week, she told me bitterly, would be
spent searching out white leather gloves ("They have to be *over*
the elbow!") for her daughter's upcoming debutante ball. I remembered how the inmates at the Georgia prison had stomped,
screamed, and cheered at the reading of their peers' poetry, after
a G.E.D. teacher at the prison had scoffed to me that none of
them would be interested. I had heard, and heard of, the remarks
made by male creative writing professors to their young women
students ("When I asked for his critique, he said, 'With breasts

like that, why worry?'"). I recalled a similar group I had led in the North Georgia mountains, made up of feisty outspoken mountain women who had nonetheless seemed to lose their tongues and wills the moment a visiting male poet entered the room. If we had a male writer as a special guest, I decided, he would be invited for the very end of the afternoon, after we had read and discussed manuscripts and every woman had had a chance to have her say.

As the Zona Rosa ranks grew, we drank coffee, wine, and Coca-Cola, washing down refreshments that became more and more elaborate—special salads, the kinds of hors d'oeuvres that take hours to make, and homemade cakes from recipes handed down from somebody's grandmother ("The Goddesses of Excess," Nurse Pat, a death-and-dying counselor at a local hospital, suggested we call ourselves). We met one Saturday afternoon a month, afternoons that extended into evenings as we talked on and on about books, writing, and our lives. We talked about men and children and sex. "What are y'all talkin' about?" Joan insisted innocently as a contingent in the kitchen discussed whether women really enjoyed performing oral sex, including swallowing. We joked about our love-hate relationship with the other gender ("She said that two of her friends' husbands just up 'n left 'em. And I said, 'How did they get them to *do* that?'"). Some, newly single, loved my friend Nancy's advice on dating over fifty: "Always take off your knee-highs before taking off your skirt or slacks!" We talked about our roles as women, and about life and death. Eventually, we would share mortal illnesses and other tragedies. And despite—perhaps because of—this sharing, the women of Zona Rosa, not used to being taken seriously outside my living room, read manuscripts at a level that made no concessions to low standards.

At first I felt mostly my differences from the women in Zona Rosa. After all, I had long since deliberately distanced myself from patriarchy, fleeing middle-class roles as though chased by demons. By that point in my life, after seeing what had happened to Mother, I considered naïveté, not to mention any voluntary adherence to convention, as the most self-destructive character-istic a woman could have. Driven by an almost unseemly curios-ity (did I do the things I did because I was a writer, or was I a writer because I did the things I did?), plus my desire to lead a life as different from Mother's as possible, I had been married several times and had enjoyed (and had written about) a period of sexual novelty that included affairs with women and the de-liberate crossing of class barriers. (Indeed, my fourth husband, Zane, albeit a reader of J. M. Coetzee and Joseph Conrad, is from that delicious-looking blue-collar group with biceps devel-oped by actual physical work, a group of which many middle-class women allow themselves only surreptitious glances.) I had tried drugs, lived alone and supported myself, and had had ex-otic travel adventures, from dancing with a witch doctor in a jungle disco in Guatemala to living in a hotel-cum-brothel in Costa Rica, to working as one of the first women aboard an off-shore oil rig, barely escaping with my feminism intact. Perhaps most dangerously, I had survived affairs with two Famous South-ern Poets who were as well known for their sexism as for their writing. ("You always did go for those guys from the fishing camps!" teased my friend Pat Conroy.) Indeed, I had done all of these things as though driven. And while some of the members of Zona Rosa had known things I hadn't, such as happy child-hoods, supportive parents, the chance to get good educations, have long-lasting marriages, and financial security, I was the only one who had had these particular experiences.

But as time went on, I also felt how alike we were, remember-ing that my dreams had been much like theirs. Like many of them, I had grown up in the deep South during the 1950s, many of my dresses handmade by a grandmother who still read *Seven-teen* magazine when she was in her seventies. I was also the woman who at eleven had scribbled in my five-year diary my desire to get married at seventeen (to my seventh-grade sweetheart, Troy), wearing a baby blue satin wedding dress with six bridesmaids in blue net dresses; then have six children, bake perfect cakes in my perfect Betty Crocker kitchen—writing novels on the side while the cakes were baking in the oven. This bliss would take place, I was sure, in the dream house complete with round rooms and goldfish swimming beneath glass-floored hallways, as I had designed in my Blue Horse notebook.

I, too, had spent hours, even days, of my time as a young woman, shopping for the right earrings, the right blouse. (Indeed, Courtenay and I had spent so much time shopping at the same department store—Rich's, in Atlanta—that we often regaled each other with memories of lunches in the store's Magnolia Room, the times we left our young children in the store nursery, exact locations of the best sale tables in the famous Rich's basement.) For I knew, as that product of the '50s, I had to do all those other things first (and perfectly) before I could even begin to do what I wanted to do most.

And maybe because living in the South is like living in the '50s forever, our younger members were not so different, either; as in the fictional TV town of *Evening Shade*, everything in the small-town South seems to stay the same. Lila, beautiful, unmarried, and near forty, had always been the Good Daughter, unable to rebel against her kindly southern clan, especially the unspoken rule, impressed on her by her mother, that one always looked away from the dark side. As Lila talked about this imprint, how it kept her from delving deeper inside herself in her writing, I saw her perched on a limb of a flowering tree—a perch keeping her just a few short feet above her own full creativity and blossoming. I recalled the way my own aunts and cousins had judged one another on the basis of a new dress or hairdo—or whether, heavens forbid, one had worn white shoes after Labor Day. I remembered growing up in the same kind of small-town atmosphere, the Baptist preacher's promises of heaven to those who followed the rules (and, of course, hell to those who didn't) raining down on the suited or flower-hatted-and-white-gloved members of the congregation, and the way I had felt around the Sunday dinner table, with my aunts all talking about a recipe for a special Jell-O "salit," my stout uncles about "bidness," averting their eyes from Daddy's drunkenness, Mother's misery.

Indeed, these early imprints had deep roots, their filaments winding down into my unconscious long after I thought I had escaped. At a poetry festival at the University of Louisiana in Baton Rouge, the one female among five male poets, I easily withstood the hostility of my well-published male colleagues (whose comments, often drunken, ranged from "You just can't write like that," to "Wanna fuck, baby?"). I met with a caucus of young women to hear their protests about their male creative writing professors and gave a reading from poetry that broke every taboo with which I had been brought up, using words that my proper mother would have fainted to hear. But still, the night before I left home for the event, I had dreamed that I had to take pizza for refreshments because I was a woman.

Nor was it only, as I had believed, the southern women among us who were afflicted with this "disease," this other-directedness: Susan, from Chicago; Nancy, from Minneapolis; Jana, from New Jersey; and even more deeply, Elsa, from Trieste, had been imprinted with the same imperatives.

The women in the group who had moved to the Savannah area with their husbands—whether because of his job, or because he wanted to retire to a constant golf or tennis game—all seemed to suffer from a low-grade depression. The older women found themselves sports widows, or trapped with aging (even sick) men, cut off from the lives they had known. The younger ones simmered with a low-boiling rage at a decision that had not been theirs, one which may have taken them from careers in L.A. or Washington. Within the safety of the group we could admit to the loneliness a woman could feel even in a "good" marriage. (Even before the phrase "channel-surfing" had become a part of the vernacular, several women had written about their mates' addiction to the remote control.)

On the other hand, we could openly laud the pleasures of solitude. Everyone nodded when Melinda, a "professional" wife and mother, baking challah bread and rich desserts for her family, said her husband had taken her kids away over the holidays, and she had had "the best Thanksgiving I've ever had—painting the kitchen and eating a broiled chicken breast by myself." (Within five years, with her first novel near completion, Melinda would also, coincidentally, stop preparing the sweets and drop forty pounds.) When Joan, now 83, said that she wasn't sure she wanted to remarry despite an ardent gentleman suitor, but thought that maybe she should because she was having a hard time opening jar lids, I gave her a device to make the task easier—and we never heard about the boyfriend again.

And then there were the women who first found the freedom to blossom creatively after a divorce after thirty years of marriage. For some of us, the admission that we were actually happier or better off away from the ones to whom we had devoted our lives was the most subversive one we could make. Courtenay had spent many of her adult years playing the bridge and garden club member and law-partner's hostess-wife, as well as being a mother to three sons, one of whom had a chronic illness. But in her novel-in-progress, she found herself describing a character who like herself, had, at different times, been a student at a women's college, a resident at an artists' retreat, and an adult graduate student, living away from home and family, and realized that these had been the happiest times in her life.

Because of some built-in block against hypocrisy, a survival mechanism of my own, I had long been blessed with the capacity to recognize such truths—however dismaying they might be at the moment. I had also been blessed—or some might say cursed—with a kind of fearlessness (or what some would call a lack of common sense), allowing me to be more risk-taking, more daring than most. Taking to heart a therapist-friend's state-

ment that the two things we think we need, but which in fact we
don't, are security and defenses, I was the personification of
Melvin Konner's book title, *Why the Reckless Survive*. In regard to
my role as a woman, I was the traveler Paul Bowles describes in
The Sheltering Sky: "Another important difference between tourist and traveler is that the former accepts his own civilization
without question; not so the traveler, who compares it with the
others, and rejects those elements he finds not to his liking." Or
was it just that, given my desire to escape my dysfunctional past,
change my life, I had taken Simone de Beauvoir, Betty Friedan,
and Kate Millet to heart? That in addition to *Good Housekeeping*
and *The Ladies' Home Journal*, I had also read Jean Genet, Henry
Miller, and Anaïs Nin?

But in many ways, I was still like the women in Zona Rosa.
Indeed, I was beginning to realize that the same psyche-binding
of women was happening everywhere, making them appear, if
not always accurately, universally conservative. "I had exactly the
same experience growing up as you did," a woman wrote me
from Novia Scotia, after reading *Fatal Flowers*. The one idea
with which we had all been engraved, as deeply as though it were
tattooed, was that freedom, especially sexual (and thus social)
freedom for women led inevitably to destruction.

The other way that we were alike was that these were women
who, like me, yearned after creative fulfillment, an escape from the
mundane and from the emotional repression that is at the heart
of the lives of most—and perhaps especially, traditional southern
women. As we talked, we began to see the rules by which we had
been taught. And the shock of the truth, whether our own or
someone else's, was like a thrilling breeze, invigorating us.

.At the same time, these were women who still feared the
truth, who in a variation of the "hidden injuries of class," realized intuitively that they would become an aberration, setting
themselves outside the society of which they were still very much
apart, if they followed their literary dreams.

And though I had broken away—or imagined I had broken

away—from some of the ties that still bound them, I wanted this to be the one space where we could write (and speak) honestly.

The one kind of place that Mother had never had.

"Why did she write about all those *strange* people?" Mother had asked once of Flannery O'Connor, who, like her, had attended Georgia College for Women in Milledgeville, but who, unlike her, had been both less pretty and less a success as a belle, as well as a rebel of her times. Mother was referring to an O'Connor story in which the characters sounded to me remarkably like Mother and her garden club–attending friends. It was a question she would later ask of my own work, which she found even more shocking because of its sexuality. (Though I had fulfilled her ambition of becoming a writer, I had, through the virtue—or vice— of its content also become, as it's said down south in whispers, "ruined.") She also disapproved of Thomas Wolfe, and what she considered his betrayal of his Asheville family in *Look Homeward, Angel*, even while she avidly visited his "homeplace" as a tourist.

"What will *they* think?" had long been part of Mother's standard repertoire of reprimands to Anne and me. Part of her fear of being known as a writer undoubtedly had to do with her fear of being "peculiar" like O'Connor (who after all died early, an old maid and childless, possibly the worst of all fates for a traditional southern woman), or like Carson McCullers, who left Columbus, Georgia, with her soldier husband as a teenager to become a national success as a novelist at twenty-one. She had had to "go north," leaving her roots (and her sobriety) behind in order to do so. A University of Georgia dance program in which Mother is pictured as the sweetheart of Daddy's fraternity, Sigma Nu, included a photo of Miss Margaret Mitchell as beauty queen of another frat house. While Mother may have envied her peer, she may also have been vaguely aware of the misery that was heaped on Mitchell along with her success. The childless Mitchell and her ever-ailing husband lived in their self-described "dump" on Peachtree Street in Atlanta until her death when she was hit by a car. And then, like the joke about why the southern belle doesn't want to have group sex, there were all those thank-you notes. Thousands upon thousands of them, and Margaret Mitchell got up at five-thirty each morning to write them after the publication of *Gone with the Wind,* sometimes even writing a signed letter to explain why she couldn't send an autograph!

Despite Mitchell, O'Connor, and McCullers—and certainly despite Wolfe and Faulkner, with whom Mother, as a woman, couldn't possibly identify—Mother dreamed of a husband who would take care of her, and a pretty house, if not the columned mansion she had been led to expect as a girl. Suspecting an unbearable alienation from her roots had she done otherwise, she dreamed these ordinary southern dreams, rather than of the fulfillment of her considerable gift for writing—dreams that at one point, I, too, had dreamed, as had the women of Zona Rosa.

Unlike Mother, I was excited rather than frightened by books about people who were different. Nor was I deterred by difficult biographies. Stories of how others—especially female others—had surmounted obstacles inspired me to dreams of action, even anarchy. I would sit in my bed in Savannah, consuming, say, Robin Davidson's *Tracks,* her story of crossing 1,700 miles of Australian outback with the three wild camels she had trained; or Sarah Lloyd's *An Indian Attachment,* in which she lives in a remote village in India for two years with a handsome young Sikh she has met on a train; or even a Victoria Holt gothic featuring, inevitably, a feisty and courageous heroine as though these books were Godiva chocolates. After a while, I had written my own adventure story, *Sleeping with Soldiers,* an account of breaking class boundaries and gender imperatives by sleeping with many different kinds of men. More recently, reading Jill Ker Conway's *The Road to Coorain,* I thrilled to the story of her journey from a failing Australian sheep ranch to the post of president of Smith College, during which she had had the courage and the smarts to leave a male-dominated culture and a demanding alcoholic mother over 7,000 miles behind her .

But my literary and emotional loyalties were divided. Through the years, I also had become acutely aware of others, especially others like Mother, who passionately wished to write, but who felt burdened by the strikes against them. Long before Zona Rosa, I had always had, without really thinking about it, such women sitting around my living room—however small or shabby— talking about books, creative writing, and life. Just as I had always been drawn to stories of more adventurous women's struggles, I was drawn by these womens' stories and their desires to express themselves: though they were not necessarily intimidated by gothic masters or tyrannical husbands, and had not, like many women throughout the world, been victims of genital mutilation or a Muslim patriarchy, they felt equally barred from within, by the effects of a society that cared not at all whether they fulfilled themselves as individuals: just so long as they filled in the blocks, doing "the right thing," or what others expected of them, they were considered by their families (or school principals or ministers or garden clubs) a success. That they would veil their thoughts in feelings in a kind of emotional chador was expected of them, both by themselves and others. "Writing is an act of aggression," I would tell the women in my classes over and over. "Nobody cares whether you do it or not. And often as not, they would prefer not to hear what you have to say, what your real feelings are." The anger I felt on their behalf was like the anger I felt when I realized that the lone explorers of the Old West, charting out new territories, living off the land, adventurously going where no white person had been before, had all been men.

When La Donna Harris, Comanche Indian and Woodrow Wilson fellow, visited the college where I was teaching, I shared what

she had told us with the Zona Rosans. There was respect between tribesperson and tribesperson, she said, from the youngest
down to the oldest, among both male and female. No one ever
spoke with an impediment, such as a podium or a table, standing between themselves and their audience. When the pipe was
passed during tribal meetings, during which each member had
an equal voice, its purpose was to provide a pause for reflection.
Even within the small space of the teepee, respect was shown by
never walking directly in front of another. Also, anyone called
Mother or *Aunt* truly took on that relationship; Harris had had
many on whom to depend within the tribe. This was becoming
my vision for those of us in Zona Rosa.

I had always held the truth of individual experience as a value
in my writing, believing that whatever I had experienced, someone else had, too. The personal is the universal, I would say to
my students; if it's true to you, it's true. More and more in Zona
Rosa we experienced a marvelous, almost magical synchronicity.
If one month, one woman wrote about teenage foibles, or the
time she had felt close to a breakdown, it seemed that all of us
had; if she had used an image—say, dust motes—we would laugh
as we listened to yet another manuscript drawing on the same
imagery. As Melinda quipped, "Soon, even our menstrual periods will be synchronized!"

One day as I walked down the cobbled streets of Savannah,
deep in anxious thoughts about a book-in-progress, a car slowed
to a stop beside me, and a woman's voice asked directions to a
local inn. I looked up into the face of the older woman on the
passenger side, and clasped her hand. "Are you Louise Nevel-
son?" I asked. I had just been reading of how she had believed in
her work as a sculptor for a lifetime, finally to receive recognition
for it in her seventies. It was as though in the midst of my doubts
about my own work, I had suddenly been given a gift by the
universe.

Later, sharing the moment with the women of Zona Rosa,
I found myself experiencing it again—in the same way that I

was always moved by reading certain poems aloud, no matter how many times I had read them before. These were poems that related directly to my experiences as a woman: Anne Sexton's "Grief for a Daughter" or "The Red Night Gown," and almost anything by Sharon Olds or Erica Jong. Now, I discovered that the women in Zona Rosa responded to these poems in the same way.

And then there were the many women authors of the past, who unlike Virginia Woolf and Edith Wharton in their privilege, or even Anaïs Nin in her exotic travels and associations, had written out of ordinary, yet exceptionally difficult lives as women. From the Brontë sisters, dutifully attending their minister father, their drunken brother; to Louisa May Alcott, taking in washing and writing to support the family; to Harriet Beecher Stowe, with her many pregnancies and seven children, her moody and impecunious husband, kept out of the literary establishment through the concerted efforts of Nathaniel Hawthorne and Henry James.

We did not have to turn to patriarchal culture, academia, or even the *New York Times* for our credibility as writers; we could turn to ourselves, to women *like* ourselves. Unabashedly, we would (in Erica Jong's words) "wear our ovaries on our sleeves," for as long and as openly as we wished. On the other hand, we would openly discuss the feelings that went against the ideal of ourselves as long-suffering nurturers and, at last, even creatively transform them. We would give one another courage, I told them.

We may have been in a small, sleepy city, even a repressive one. "*Where?*" a former debutante and guest of Savannah's Oglethorpe Club, in which one's white, non-Jewish, non-Catholic ancestors must date back to Oglethorpe, asked incredulously when I questioned whether there was any place in America still as rigid as that portrayed in Wharton's *Age of Innocence*. "Why *Savannah*, of course!" she said, answering her own question. Or as

Helene, a poet visiting from Maine, said, "A woman could rot here!"

But in that room, the clannishness and class differences that are still a part of small-town southern life fell away, leaving in their wake support and connection. At the least, we were best friends, talking. At moments, we were a secret cell—some would even say, a subversive cell—made up of apparently conservative women telling, often for the first time, their truths.

After a while, we women, who ranged in age from sixteen to eighty-seven, knew one another so well that we were celebrating birthdays, weddings, births, and sometimes divorces, commiserating over illnesses, and later, mourning deaths. We talked and wrote of our darkest secrets and of our greatest joys. We congratulated one another on writing acceptances and consoled one another at rejections. No triumph, no disappointment, no problem was too small for our attention. We shared recipes, and the artists and craftswomen among us sold their products. Courtenay, also a visual artist, sketched and resketched us, noting the changes made by time.

And at times, for many of us, one might say that Zona Rosa even became an occasion for worship. "Not only in their songs, but in their whole lives, they seemed to do nothing but praise one another," the poet William Blake had written. That was what we shared in Zona Rosa.

Around the time I began writing seriously, *Mademoiselle* magazine ran a series called "Disturbers of the Peace," in which writers such as Jean Genet or Colin Wilson were interviewed. I avidly devoured these articles, as well as Wilson's book, *The Outsider*, yearning for nothing more than to become yet another literary anarchist, a bona fide "disturber of the peace." It was a goal that in some small degree I have achieved, given the degree of irony, even anarchy—the dedication to political incorrectness, or what a writer friend calls an "in your face" quality—of much of my writing.

"Multi-miracles, testimonials, exotic origins . . ." advised a TV ad warning against false claims for untested drugs used in the treatment of AIDS, and watching it, I thought of how some might also doubt the healing power of the creative arts. Yet I can honestly say that I, a dedicated skeptic—some would even say cynic—have seen miracles happen in Zona Rosa. As therapist and screenwriter Marcie Telander mused to me one day, "It's impossible to be a victim when you're creating." She was reflecting on a recent news account of trend-watcher Faith Popcorn's prediction that chautauquas and writing groups would take the place of twelve-step groups during the '90s, but I knew what she meant.

For one thing, I knew how healing writing had been in my own life. I had started *Fatal Flowers* during a period of great pain, just after Mother's suicide, Daddy's death from cancer, and after a third divorce that had left me feeling as though I had been cored by a serrated knife. In the worst of circumstances, writing had been my constant and loyal companion, the one medium on which I could concentrate, and through which I could express my grief. I had written books revealing my most shameful secrets and had dealt successfully, I thought, with my dysfunctional childhood.

In Home Ec at Tucker High School, I had learned how to turn a flat-fell seam in which no raw edges showed. In the same way, each time I wrote out my pain, I would feel the stitching and restitching inside my brain, as though festering tissue was actually being trimmed away and sealed over, to at last heal. The longer each book had taken to write, the longer had been the revision process, and the stronger the fabric of that healing.

I had been in the habit of asking myself, during times of minor physical illnesses, what my body was telling me. The answers had sometimes become published poems, such as one titled "Cystitis," and another, "The Loss of the Soul & Other

Sicknesses," based on a fever after a trip to Mexico and an en-
counter I'd had with an Indian woman. One only has to look
at the relationship between the body's erotic longings and feelings of spiritualized love and romance to know our mind-body
connection.

During the late '80s and early '90s, I, like many people in
America, had become interested in other forms of healing. And
like many of them, I had been motivated by events in my own
life, events that, despite my writing skills, I couldn't quite get a
handle on. When two of my adult children developed diseases of
the brain and spirit—one, an opiate addiction; another, a mental
illness—I was thrown in a way I had never been by anything in
my own life. The wisdom I had found within myself in regard to
other matters suddenly seemed to escape me. (In retrospect, I see
that it was the distraction from my writing created by these
events that kept the work from having its usual healing effect.
When I finally got around to focusing on and writing about
them—letting the pain flow through me without resistance, to
be shaped into words, phrases, and sentences—I found that the
process had worked its healing magic once again.)

I had already had years of therapy, but now I indulged in an
orgy of self-analysis and guilt, turning to a revolving array of
"experts," none of whom gave satisfactory answers. "Do you
hope to be with her in this life? Or the next?" a life-after-death
doctor asked me about my daughter, while the sweaty Mexican
shaman who had just sold me a book on the rattlesnake designs
in the structures of the Mayans said that Mother and Daddy had
obviously been reborn as these two children because of my unresolved issues with them.

Finally, I would come to Gertrude Stein's notion (as she is
said to have responded on her deathbed) that the answer is just
to ask the question. Or at least to accept that life is not a problem to be solved, but a mystery to be enjoyed.

In the meantime, moving from Jungian therapists to New
Age literature to 12-step groups (which turned out to be the

best—and they were also free), I found I had inadvertently become an expert myself. When I saw and read Bill Moyers's *Healing and the Mind*, and again when I read Peter Kramer's *Listening to Prozac*, especially his references to the theory that traumas are not only encoded in memory but actually cause changes in tissue, I began to think about the fact that the opposite might take place—that the healing I felt during my own writing and what I was seeing happen in Zona Rosa might cause positive changes within the brain tissue.

As Moyers commented in his TV series, *Healing and the Mind*, healing can occur even when no cure takes place. In *Pain and Possibility*, Gabrielle Rico describes her theory of naming and framing: the way writing distances the pain, permitting healing to take place. When I read of a new therapy called EMDR (Eye Movement Desensitization and Reprocessing), in which the therapist passes two fingers before a patient's eyes while she talks about a past trauma, with the effect of historically distancing the event, I realized that this, too, was similar to what happens while writing.

I was a door until my parents slammed me, a second-grader had written in one of my Poetry in the Schools classes. And almost all of us, it turned out, had been slammed—by siblings, peers, teachers, and ministers, or some other person or group on whom our self-esteem had once hinged. Nurse Pat had told us a story of how we are all born princes and princesses, until the way we were treated turned us into frogs. Shame, it seemed, lay at the core of most of us, keeping us from the full flow of the present moment, and of our creativity. It was obviously hard for us to believe, as writer-therapist Claudia Black recommends, that "You are not bad. You never were. And you're not today."

"Write about the thing you most don't want to write about," I advised the Zona Rosans, wanting them to experience the healing I had come to trust. I quickly found that those who successfully overcame their fears, honestly tackling my suggestion, experienced near-immediate breakthroughs in their writing and their lives. "Sex and death are the only two things worth writing about," I said, quoting Yeats. These two subjects did seem to touch on our greatest, most quivering taboos. The most common experience never before spoken of, but written of in Zona Rosa, was that of having been sexually or otherwise abused as a child. (According to statistics gathered at a University of Kentucky Women Writers Conference, such abuse is more than three times more likely to have occurred in the childhoods of female writers.) We read aloud pieces of writing in which members of the group described experiences that they had never confessed to anyone, therapist or priest. Freed by an atmosphere of acceptance, people confessed to emotions they considered their greatest shame. Time after time, I've seen the innocence of human beings—how the most victimized among us often feel the most guilt.

Yet why did writing not have this healing effect for such writers as Sylvia Plath, Anne Sexton, Ernest Hemingway, and John Berryman, all of whom killed themselves? Aside from the fact that mood disorders such as manic-depression are more prevalent in writers, one might add the one substance that, according to numerous author biographies apparently destroyed so many of them—booze. But some of us have had the good luck to realize before it was too late that alcohol only intensifies the pain. "Alcohol just throws me *into* that guilt," said Pat Conroy, explaining why he had quit drinking during a bout of depression. Also, despite my admiration for the works of the poets who killed themselves, I had made a decision early on to be as happy as I could, and to not harm myself. For me, for some other writers, and for ordinary people just coming to writing, like those in Zona Rosa, writing was definitely a positive force.

In her book, *Nisa: The Life and Words of a !Kung Woman*, anthropologist Marjorie Shostak quotes the Botswanian bush woman of the same name: "I'll break open the story, and tell you what is there. Then, like the others that have fallen out on the sand, I will finish with it, and the wind will take it away." But it would be years before Shoshak, long back in the States and faced with breast cancer, would recollect this wisdom in the play *My Heart Is Still Shaking* that she wrote with Brenda Bynum. In it, Nisa, now an old woman, continues to describe how naming the pain of an unresolved relationship heals her: "No. There's still something in my heart about this that isn't finished. . . . I'm going to talk about it more until it does. Then my heart will be fine." "Diagnosis can't be made until the story is told," said Carl Jung; "Telling the story *is* the treatment."

As any good salesperson knows, a way of opening instant dialogue is by telling something about oneself. I was willing to use any means I could to entice the Zona Rosans. Good teaching, like good writing, requires a *soupçon* of amorality, I was discovering—a willingness to find what works and use it. Since I had written and spoken often about the most personal aspects of my life, I was able to ask the Zona Rosans to do the same. I described the rush of liberation that for me had come along with finally telling the truth. The fact that I had done practically everything "wrong" and had survived gave them courage. "Think of it this way," I would say, referring to a perhaps more risky way of raising self-esteem, "it's a lot less dangerous than nude fire-walking!"

A primary fear among beginning writers is the loss of love they imagine will befall them if they are honest in their writing. The irony was that the relatives the Zona Rosans were determined to protect were often the very ones who had abused them—the Uncle So and So or Grandma Kinky who had wielded the strap or shut them in the closet, as well as the sharp-tongued ones about whom "I just can't write until they die."

The other fear had to do with the shame of exposure, of being viewed as human, and thus flawed. "Yes, your hubris, or fatal flaw, *may* be exposed as you write, revealing you to be human," I said to the group, "but so what?" And how could they expect to become published writers if they held themselves to such standards of perfection? But there *was* a way to elude that initial shame, I explained—by sticking to the truth of one's own experience. "My own truth is the only truth I *can* know," I said, reiterating my belief that the personal is the universal.

I could honestly say this to them because of my own experiences. I recalled the fears I had had the night I signed the contract to write *Fatal Flowers*. I was afraid I wouldn't be able to write the book, because I had never written anything longer than a book review or magazine article and the contract called for a manuscript of "200 double-spaced typed pages."

But worse, I feared what would happen if I did what I knew I intended to do; that is, break the two taboos with which I had been brought up as a southern woman, the taboos against speaking honestly of anger and sexuality. I wanted to write the first honest account of growing up southern and female, and I knew as I signed the contract and put it in an envelope that I was committing myself to that end. But that night I dreamed that I'd been shot for the sin of telling the truth.

Yet despite my fears, the final manuscript was 460 pages in typescript, and, while the book was controversial, the bad things I had expected hadn't materialized. I shared with the Zona Rosans my experience of having told all—only to have bad relationships never made worse, and good relationships often made better.

My cousin Jo Anne, the other "bad" one in my family, and a bit older than I, had inspired me in my future wildness by eloping from a fancy private girl's school at seventeen with a young soldier and, to the shock of the family, becoming pregnant soon after. Mostly, though, I remember her for providing the images for childhood nightmares by telling me that the Empire State building was hollow and that visitors crawled to the top via a spiral staircase without a rail.

I had lost track of Jo Anne during the years, but when my fifth book, a novel, *The Hurricane Season*, was published, she called from Texas to say that she loved it. "Florance"—Mother's sister—"said she threw it down after the first twenty pages, then took it back to the library," she went on, "but I don't care *what* the rest of the family thinks of you!"

As she spoke, I recalled how Aunt Florance had said accusingly during my feminist days that Gloria Steinem was too old to wear her hair that long—the same length as mine at the time—and that she only acted that way because she hadn't met the right man (like my buttoned-up Uncle Howard, I wondered!).

With relatives like that, I told them, there was nothing to fear. And besides, I had always known exactly what Aunt Florance thought of me, from the first time she sensed that I had little desire to grow up to be a permanent-waved, pocketbook-carrying, Jell-O-salad-making proper wife and mother like her.

< FOUR >

The Goddesses of Excess
& Other Tales of Southern Womanhood

"I like you because you are cute / I like you because you are different / I like you because you are like / a piece of Juicy Fruit," my daughter Darcy wrote when she was seven. When I read her verse aloud to a group of kindergartners, a small black boy with big eyes and a wide white smile said, "I've got a friend, too, but he's mo' like a un-yun. Or a *grape*fruit!"

And that's the way we were in Zona Rosa. Our first group of four had grown and mutated, a colorful and ever-changing kaleidoscope. We now included New Agers and 12-steppers; Freudians, rationalists, and born-again Christians; one woman made her living giving tarot readings over a 900 number. We could almost see the waves of irritation emanating from Susan, who had never had therapy, when Jana, who was a true believer, referred every literary problem back to the inner child. Melinda was a passionate Jew, ever in search of new scholarship about her roots; Gladys and her sister Latrelle were atheists; Nancy and Nell were cool Episcopalians; Courtenay a not-so-cool one who preferred the Roman Catholic mass; while Danielle was a far-from-stiff Presbyterian.

Gladys and Latrelle had been raised in rural Georgia, as were Onetha and Ruby, who turned us nostalgic with their stories of the "olden days." Joan had grown up on the campus of the college in Jackson, Mississippi, where her father had been a janitor.

Lila had come to Savannah from Rome, Georgia, apparently a town with a bumper crop of beauties. Melinda and Betty had grown up in Brooklyn, where Betty had been a bona fide beatnik ("a beatnik, *not* a hippie!"). Courtenay, Lois, and I had once been belles-in-training in Atlanta.

For refreshments, Melinda brought perfect meringues and fat strawberries or sleek green grapes, dipped first in a beaten egg white, then in sparkling sugar. Nurse Pat contributed big bowls of shrimp salad, pink chunks jutting from a pale sea of mayonnaise. ("The Goddesses of Excess," she enthused, referring to our mutual passion for eating and the inclination of several of us to douse ourselves with Joy perfume.) Jana made architectural marvels from flour tortillas, cream cheese, and stuffed olives, the center of the olive appearing as an exact bull's-eye within each piece. When I felt ambitious, and the weather was right (dry days), I made pecan pralines that seemed to dissolve magically, almost like breath, between the women's lipsticked smiles. On the day I served pâté, shining within its gelatin casing, Onetha objected. "What is this? Dog food?"

As for clothing, Gladys favored existential black turtlenecks; Jalaine and Mimi, floaty California-style draperies; Onetha, the de rigueur good ol' girl costume of pumps, pastel polyester pants suit, and freshly coiffed and teased curls. Nurse Pat said that her collection of eye shadows, often applied in stripes of luminous greens and golds to complement her red hair, was the one thing she couldn't live without. Laurel affected a Marilyn Monroe style that complemented her blond waves and lush figure. I was known for a near-sick shoe fetish—I had them in every height and color, and they covered every surface of my small bedroom.

(When, years into the group, Susan cut her waist-length white braid usually bound tight atop her head, into a soft bob around her face, I experienced a moment of shock that made me realize what the subtle feelings were playing just beneath my consciousness whenever she was in the room. Though they couldn't have been more different in every other way—Susan was nothing if not cool and collected—she looked exactly like Mother: the thick curls, the heart-shaped face, the piercing dark eyes; a resemblance confirmed as Susan sat in her usual chair just beneath a photo of Mother at eighteen.)

I read poetry and the *New York Times*; Onetha, Mary Higgins Clark and the *Glenville News*; Ruby, the self-help books recommended by her therapist; Lenore, the *Dialysis Newsletter*; Pat, nursing journals and Armistead Maupin; and Gladys, the *Partisan Review* and *New York Review of Books*. In addition, it was often urgently explained to newcomers that although some publications—Madonna's *Sex*, or *Thin Thighs in 30 Days*—might appear between two covers and even on the *New York Times* bestseller list, it didn't necessarily make them *books*.

We were just as different in our writing goals. Some, like Gladys, yearned after the creation of a literature that was nothing less than what Kafka described as "an ax to break through the frozen ice inside us." Others aspired to romance novels: underestimating themselves in the traditional feminine way, they assumed that children's books or romances would represent the height and depth of their talents. Many of these women, if they stayed, ended up writing something more ambitious, moving perhaps from predictable housewife-style prose to literary poetry, or, as Melinda did, from *Cosmo*-girl essays to the serious novel. (Amelia Earhart may have once been the aviation columnist for *Cosmopolitan*, but I told Melinda that I preferred her novel.) Almost all had deepened their work, whatever their subjects or genres.

Because of our shared experiences as women, homely metaphors for the writing process popped into my mind like the bubbles in Diet Coke: "When I was young housewife, I said to my mother that I just couldn't make piecrust. Then the very next time I tried—just playing around with the ingredients, but not really expecting anything—my piecrust was perfect!" As I spoke, I was remembering my friend, the novelist and journalist Joyce Maynard, her hands deep in floury dough, as she made apple pies from

scratch. While I meant the image as one for the playfulness involved in creativity, the try-and-try-again notions inherent in revision, I also wanted the group to realize that their natural earthiness
as women was not necessarily a deficit to them as writers—that the
lessons learned from trying a new recipe or changing diapers
might ultimately be of as much use as any learned, say, through
a study of French literature or postmodern Deconstruction. In
fact, women don't even have to keep up with the news or read the
newspapers. Because, given a receptive spirit, we are given exactly
what we need for our writing; usually it is already inside us.

There was another lesson, too, that I had learned from my efforts to make piecrust: sometimes an internal giving up leads to
more success than constant, goal-directed effort—the breath of
relaxation is what allows creativity to flow. Permission to fail is as
important as success, I told them, quoting a high school science
teacher I knew: "Scientifically speaking, one cannot fail—unless
one stops trying."

Buffie Johnson, a grand dame among New York painters,
once told me the theory that she believed led her to getting most
everything she had wanted in life: "I visualize what I want, then I
set it aside, confident that it will come to me without any further
effort on my part. And that setting aside is the important part—
there is external will and there is internal will. But only the latter
works—external will is ineffectual."

And what about those inevitable days when we feel our writing
is no good, that our efforts are wasted—aren't those just like "bad
hair" days? We don't go around shaving our heads just because
our hair sometimes sticks out from our heads in funny angles, do
we? (Unless, of course, we're Betty Dodson, who did do just that
for the cover of her book on female masturbation, illustrated with
drawings of a dozen different vaginas, back in the '70s.)

"Accent-chu-ate the pos-i-tive, e-lim-i-nate the neg-a-tive" go the
lyrics of the Johnny Mercer song I had often belted out as a kid,
before my musically gifted cousin Jack had told me that I couldn't

sing. "*Jeal*-o-*see*! Cousin's full of *jeal*-o-*see*!" he had crooned into a fake microphone, putting me off singing forever.

"I felt like I was being actively discouraged from becoming a writer," said Beth, a talented young woman who ended up winning a *Redbook* short story contest, of the prestigious American writing school where she had gone for an M.F.A.

As that was exactly what I *didn't* want to happen to the aspiring writers in Zona Rosa, the words to Johnny Mercer's song had become the core of my method. A spirit of support, an ambience of wanting every other member to win, had fast become an essential aspect of the group. In fact, the few lapses in support that had occurred in the group had only strengthened my belief in this kind of atmosphere: competition, comparisons, don't work for prospective writers; support and encouragement of strengths do.

As the years went on, this approach became a formalized, stated aspect of the group: newcomers, such as a divorcee fresh from Harvard creative writing classes, were told up front that this and this alone would inform our perspective—that we were not in the business of tearing down, but of building up. Before long, it was almost as if there was a sign over the door: NO NEGATIVE VIBRATIONS ALLOWED HERE.

FOP, FOF, FOC, and FOS: Fear of People, Fear of Failure, Fear of Chaos, Fear of Shame, and Fear of Success—were the acronyms I used to describe what I saw as the most common bogs into which we might stumble. Most of us consider our own experiences too mundane, too ordinary, to serve as material for literature. Over and over, I saw the spurts of self-realization and the common forms of self-sabotage of which fear was always the common denominater, including the fear of good things, such as intimacy or success. Together, they coagulated into a great blob of quicksand, just waiting to suck us in.

"The Lady Who Spilled Poetry All over Herself," a high school student, referring to my zaniness, had labeled me. "The teacher must always maintain an air of eccentricity out of control," Pat

Conroy wrote in *The Water Is Wide,* his account of teaching on the then remote Dafuskie Island, off the coast of South Carolina. I had taken his advice to heart; in fact, it became my credo. Indeed, while working in Poetry in the Schools, I had learned shamelessly to do almost anything to grab the students' attention, from sitting on the desk in blue jeans in a decidedly unteacherlike manner, to claiming skills at mind-reading and hypnosis, to going around the room and getting each to tell (a) what he or she had had for breakfast that morning, and (b) a secret no one else in the room knew, even if he had to make one up. As I had taught in schools that ranged from a Mormon community where I wore long skirts in order to fit in to an Appalachian school where many of the kids came barefoot, these means had had to be all-purpose, even crosscultural.

When Zona Rosa began, one of the skills I was already proud of was my ability to get anyone—no matter how unlikely—to come up with an original, even significant, piece of writing. I was learning from the kids while they were learning from me, and I would have been hard-pressed to say who had learned more. Out of desperation, and by trial and error, I had developed diagrams, devices, and exercises that I could quickly write or draw on the board, which proved to work quickly and effectively with students from a shy, retarded fourteen-year-old in the state mental hospital to a highly reluctant and hulking football star, who above all didn't want his image tarnished.

I had also learned from working with kids to keep things simple. Now, in Zona Rosa, I learned to hone my advice to an even greater simplicity. "There are no writing blocks, only feeling blocks," I asserted to the group. "Take the greatest possible unknown, and say it in the simplest possible way." In discussing our writing, I said, I would always refer to *content and form,* rather than *form and content,* as in the more conventional phrasing, because without content, we would have nothing to apply form *to.* We would help one another fight *entropy*—that all-too-human inclination to let ourselves slide in a downward direction, rather than to make the habitual efforts that lead to personal and creative growth. I described my trick for getting started on the days when it was hard: JUST, for Just You Start Typing, the acronym I had hung above my desk. I shared my own private tricks, such as *thumb-tacking*, a method of hanging images on the wall of my mind in order not to lose them before I could get to writing paper; or *coagulating*, a method of bringing all like material together in a manuscript in order to find its natural form. Even little structural tricks, such as leading with an image or a quote. And I described my own one-sentence goal for anything I write, from a poem to a nonfiction book, which is *to bridge the gap between immediacy and depth.*

As I experienced Zona Rosa as an ongoing part of my life, rather than a temporary amusement or, worse, a distraction from my own writing, I began to put the same energy into developing methods of working with its members. Given serendipity and a steady audience, I found myself coming up with ever-newer ideas, some of which succeeded beyond my expectations. Before long, I had developed a thick packet of "exorcises" (as Zona Rosan June suggested I call them) and devices that I had learned worked for anyone who would sit down and do them—an important qualifier, as these were adults and I couldn't *make* them do *any*thing.

I further encouraged them by saying that the writing that came out of the exorcises would not be judged as pieces of writing, but would merely serve as a means for breaking through blocks and into new material (though often the assignments did become the beginning of a finished piece of work).

On the other hand, our critiques of one another's works in progress would be impersonal, based on clearly stated objective criteria that would evolve within the group. But always the author's own intent would be the final authority in judging a piece as successful.

Losing myself, feeling my creativity clicking in a way I had previously associated only with my writing, I dug out the notebooks I had tediously made years earlier, delineating my early struggles to write, and shared them. I found that the same methods I had rigged—often, out of near hysteria, *jerry*rigged—to help me in my own writing and with that of my oft-reluctant students in the public schools worked with these women, too. In fact, those notes became the basis for what I came to view as one of my more effective assignments—that each of us create our own notebook, analyzing our own process, listing and defending our own criteria. Those who took this approach experienced greater and quicker strides in their work; a personal style evolved as we began taking our own work as a precedent. "'About style, the less said the better,'" I said, quoting John Gardner. "Ideally, we will develop a style that becomes so natural to us that it is virtually invisible."

Whenever apropos, which seemed to be at some point during every Zona Rosa meeting, we discussed not only the fine points, the minutiae, of each manuscript, but the whole lifestyle around its creation. The genius of teaching, I was learning, was often as not just learning to pose the right questions. Were we giving ourselves enough leisure, enough dreamtime, time for meandering, or as we say in the South, just for "milling" around? Were we feeding ourselves good books, and taking the time for the solitary pleasure of savoring them? (Erica Jong believes that we may be the last literate generation. Given our Western culture, and our focus on constant action, whether the action is just having a manicure or checking out the new mall, doing "nothing" is a subversive notion even in Savannah, where time can still appear to move at the speed of sorghum syrup.)

Were we making full use of such direct paths to the unconscious as keeping dream journals and writing to music? What part did the body play in our writing—were we making the best use of our time and our biological clocks? And what, given the imperatives of our lives—a full-time job, or a sick, live-in elderly aunt to care for—could we safely give up, making way for these things?

On the other hand, were we feeding ourselves enough positive stresses? One of the ironies is that people who come to writing at midlife finally may have the time they need, but no longer the abrasive stimuli. I had begun writing as a young mother with three children under five; the constraints on my time and energy had goaded me onward. This experience had led me to another of my teaching and writing beliefs—that there was more than simple selfishness and curiosity behind the artist's drive to new experiences, and that aspiring writers must deliberately feed themselves these positive stresses. Also, that these stresses must be alternated with the alpha, or right brain, state required for the creative act itself.

Were we dislocating our preconceived prejudices? Detaching from nonsupportive situations and people (even husbands!)? What were we doing to affirm ourselves as writers? How were we dealing with envy, despair, and the sense of time running out? Most important, what were our greatest passions, our deepest and most profound experiences, and were we being true to them in our writing?

And what about our habits? For some of us, if it didn't happen a second time over the telephone, when we told a friend about it, it hadn't really happened at all. Were we willing to question what seemed fixed, almost mandated—answering the phone when we were merely "thinking," or watching the eleven o'clock news every night just because our husbands did? I knew from experience that solitude and personal space was hard to come by. But I had also discovered that the first step toward achieving it was to look at the way we did things with detachment—almost as though we were from Mars—in order to see the possibilities that we may previously have overlooked. The result was the chance to focus on what was really important to us, to enjoy that delicious state the psychologist Mihaly Csikszentmihalyi calls "flow." Though often our resistance ran deeper than mere habit: "Whenever I feel an emotion I don't want to deal with, I immediately turn on the TV," Lila admitted.

And what of our social lives? "One of the things my writing has cost me is the time for friends," said Josephine Humphries, wife, mother, and author of the novel, *Rich in Love*. From a social Charleston background, Jo was a graduate of fashionable Ashley Hall, and I suspected that she meant obligations and friendships of a certain sort, a paring away of what was not close to the bone in the first place. Most of us were imprinted with the notion that we would always put immediate family, or even a large extended family, first. But for some of us, an early imprint in social noblesse oblige carried almost the weight of family in its imperatives, imperatives that included a lifelong attendance at a certain church or synagogue or membership in the local Junior League or country club. "I've spent the last eighteen New Year's Eves at the Oglethorpe Club!" half-moaned our Savannah native, as shockingly, she found herself in other company for the nineteenth.

Frequently, those around us, even those we think should know us best, don't want us to change. The feminine camaraderie of going out to lunch was one of the first things to go in my own life. "There *will* be things you have to give up in order to write," I told them. "Some of these may be things you enjoy. And some may be subtle, such as the approval of certain friends. But you may find those things weren't so important to you after all." Habits die hard, and change is hell, I said, citing addictionologist and author, Earnie Larson.

On the other hand, I noticed that those of us who resisted such analysis, clinging like Saran Wrap to the belief that creative expression is somehow magical—too mystical, too ethereal, to be tampered with—hung behind, remaining static in their skills and ideas. For though it is true that art is magic, the greatest magicians know how the tricks work, just as Michelangelo knew how to apply the paint that resulted in the Sistine Chapel.

I described three women who had inspired me by questioning the way things were: Jane Smiley, author of the Pulitzer prize–winning novel, *A Thousand Acres*, lives in a part of Iowa she describes as not merely boring, but "blank"; she also says that she can write anywhere, sometimes even while talking on the phone. "If you can only write in a certain way, that's ritualistic, and it's the rituals surrounding writing that we need to break down," she told an interviewer for *Mirabella*. After the success of *Women Who Love Too Much*, Robin Norwood gave up her therapy practice and began the seven-year hiatus, sans television, radio, and newspapers out of which evolved her next New Age work, *Why Me? Why Now? Why This?* In her second autobiography, *Stations of Solitude*, Alice Koller describes the process by which she came to the decision to spend much of her life independently, away from human habitation. And while few of us might make that choice, it's good to realize that relationships *are* a choice.

"To tell someone how to write is to tell them how to live," mused Carolyn, a high school English teacher and one of Zona Rosa's more sensitive poets. "Yeah, it's a lot easier to talk about how to write a query letter than how to find your voice," added Jana, a striking brunette who had left a job planning special events in Washington, D.C., to move south with her musician husband.

I told them of my belief that while the creative tide may go out, it *always* comes back in—provided we live in a way that encourages it. Almost all of us can live in a more continuous state of flow, a more intense state of creativity than we generally allow ourselves. Creativity has to do with what we feed ourselves, and the kinds of thoughts we choose to emphasize. "Seek out the shock of the new," I advised, "in ideas, art, and experiences; as well as positive stresses, if you find life becoming too predictable." Reframing our thinking, shifts in life orientation, changes of all kinds, whether pleasurable or painful—stimulate our creative juices. Important, too, is developing an overview of ourselves within the context of the totality of the human experience. All these, I asserted, could lead to a creative burst, a constant rainbow of creativity.

Then there was what I thought of as *writing in the gap*, getting into those mysterious interstices that, as flitting as dust motes or a hummingbird, are hard to capture, yet when we do, add true creativity and originality to our writing. The only method I knew to capture these fleeting thoughts was by paying *attention*—to passing feelings, thoughts, and the world around us, as well as, over a period of time, the provisions of the unconscious, generously made manifest by our dreams at night.

"I always remember what you say, 'Let the chaos flow,'" said Courtenay, who had written a finished yet unsatisfactory, stiff first novel as part of an M.F.A. program at Florida State and was now 500 pages into a different, much freer, manuscript. In order to free ourselves to write at the top of our abilities, the unconscious must be dealt with. The proper order was content and form, not form and content. Then, and only then, would we have something to work with, to revise. "Problems in revision are always a problems in clarity and vision," I told the group, "and finally, revision revises *us*."

Revision is also a necessary part of writing, along with the view that both our original ideas and language are malleable—that we can mess around with them and try them different ways. "Think of how a room always looks dirtier when you start to clean it up. Though a better analogy might be looking at a house in the process of renovation, and imagining it totally redone," I said, using a familiar image. We who lived in Savannah were surrounded by gorgeous Victorian houses in a constant state of transition, from derelict dump to showplace, and sidewalks and yards were often strewn with rotting boards and the dust from hacked walls. For those of us who've been writing long enough, that sort of chaos is often the fun part. The group was shocked when I told them that at this point in my life—after years and years of writing, and hours and hours spent at my desk—I feel just as at ease while writing as I do, say, reading a book. But most of us had initially shared Carolyn's feeling: "I always felt stupid when I didn't write it right the first time. I didn't know language was something you could just play around with."

The poems, essays, stories, and books we will write will *never* turn out quite the way we had envisioned them; in fact, that may be why we write them over and over. Also, if each of us is our own ideal reader, one of our motivations for writing is to write what has not yet been written—the one piece of writing *we* would want to read.

The trick was in thinking of oneself, one's thoughts and feelings, as special (remembering that the inner critic can be as merciless as any outside one), but at the same time remaining as humble, as simple, in one's work as a carpenter. This was the kind of healthy arrogance, combined with realistic patience, that I wanted to inspire in Zona Rosa—to teach these women that there were no limits on what they might aspire to in their writing, but that it was the process itself that was the thing.

Years before, while I was at work on *Fatal Flowers*, my editor, Jennifer Josephy, visited me in Savannah. As we discussed a certain portion of the manuscript, whether a particular character had been disguised enough, I said, "It doesn't matter—she's moved to Seattle anyway." Jennifer looked at me in surprise. "Don't you know this book will be published in Seattle?" I had become so immersed in the process—in my hundreds of revision notes, the strips of yellow second sheets thumb-tacked all over my rose-printed wallpaper—that I had forgotten the reason Jennifer was there was because I was writing the book under contract to Holt, Rinehart and Winston, and that it would be published all over the country.

Indeed, it was a period during which I reverted to doing what the architect and thinker Buckminster Fuller had recommended: "going back to what we were doing before somebody told us we had to make a living." The girl who had scribbled in her five-year diary with the pretty pen from Japan had taken over, for a time, the woman with a serious adult commitment, a book contract to fulfill.

This delicious unconsciousness—this ability to lose oneself completely in one's writing—was a state that would take more effort to achieve during the completion of each future book, conscious as I was by then of the reviewers lying in wait, not to speak of the sales reps and their inordinate power to dictate which books would be salable, which not. But it was a form of naïveté that I had learned to resuscitate through the act of writing itself, one that I wanted the members of Zona Rosa to enjoy for as long as possible, even for a lifetime.

"A frog can only see what it can eat," I had read. It was an idea that had thrilled me, coming to stand for the way an image is almost always more than just an image. If we resonate to an image, it probably has significance for us, serving as a metaphor for something deep within, perhaps something as yet undiscovered. Our task as writers is to uncover and clarify that meaning.

Some of us work outward from images, not knowing at first what they mean to us; others work from meaning and must uncover the images that match and express it. Whichever way I find myself working, *loaded imagery* is the way I describe such material to myself. Loaded imagery is the perfect word picture that, miraculously discovered out of the myriad available, feels like a ripe plum in the palm of the hand, heavy and fleshy and visceral in its rightness. Time after time, I've heard writers describe how, out of the blue, they came upon just the right image, the perfect material for a work in progress; it is as if their very concentration put them in touch with some universal law of supply and demand. And how satisfying it is when such an image appears on the page, fitting itself perfectly, becoming one with one's meaning. For wasn't it the cup of tea, steaming in a white bone china cup, that we remembered from a favorite novel? Who can think of John Donne's poem "A Valediction Forbidding Mourning" without thinking of the separation of the two lovers as "an expansion, / Like gold to airy thinness beat," or not hear the very buzz of the insect, reading Emily Dickinson's "I Heard a Fly Buzz When I Died"?

We don't have to read or be one of the great poets to be receptive to sensory language. Terry McMillan created her best-selling novel *Waiting to Exhale* out of the mundane world of shopping and everyday black life. "Don't worry so much about good writing—just tell the reader what they want to know about," she told her students at the University of Wyoming. I found that, using this approach, I could show almost all the women in Zona Rosa the effectiveness of concrete imagery (*almost*, because I could never quite explain to Joan, who, as one of the more intellectual, formally educated women in the group, seemed to think almost totally in abstract concepts).

Indeed, I hammered home my belief in concrete images so often that Melinda came up with this poem:

> *"Write of concrete things,"*
> *you say, "not abstract."*
> *So on my Beautyrest I lie*
> *having concrete thoughts.*
> *I see Egyptian pyramidal blocks*
> *shlepped by Hebrew slaves.*
> *And tabby-crusted granite walls,*
> *pockmarked by Union bullets,*
> *surrounding Fort Pulaski.*
> *Enormous terracotta planters*
> *mingle with angels' statues of cement*
> *in a yard beneath a skewed pink sign,*
> *POTTERYLAND.*
> *Above me on my ceiling*
> *jagged cracks are splayed like mini-creeks,*
> *black lightning traceries*
> *on roughly textured alabaster plaster.*
> *So tell me, R.D., is this poem*
> *concrete enough for you?*

"Would Emily Dickinson have worried about that?" Evelyn asked when someone brought up publishing. Her question echoed my own thoughts exactly. My belief that writing and publishing are two totally different processes—a source of confusion for many beginning writers—had to be reemphasized whenever newcomers appeared in the group. The simple notion that one must first do a good piece of writing before seeking to market it seems, in our desire for prestige and fame, to escape many of us. It was the '80s and New Age affirmations had become the order of the day, but too often they took a secular form—visions of ourselves on *Donahue*, "laughing all the way to the bank." This led to self-hatred when the desired reward didn't materialize, not to speak of lessened enthusiasm for one's work. Indeed, such narcissism is the enemy of art. "If you're good enough, you will be published," my editor had told me early on, giving me courage. Yet becoming that "good" requires total focus on the goal of excellence.

The writers I knew to whom those things had happened usually had experienced them as a side effect of their efforts, their passion to bring a vision into reality. "Everybody all over the house was looking for a check I was supposed to have received," Raymond Moody, the med student-to-millionaire author of *Life after Life* told me, "and all the time it was stuck in the book I was reading!" As he spoke, I recalled when I almost threw a check for $12,500 for a grant from the NEA into the trash while clearing my desk so that I could work. Pat Conroy had been so naive about the publishing process that when his agent called him to say that his first book, *The Water Is Wide*, had been accepted, citing a sum of $5,000, Pat exclaimed, "Is that all we have to pay them!" John Berendt had worked so long, seven years, on his best-selling *Midnight in the Garden of Good and Evil*, that some people in Savannah, the book's subject, wondered whether he was writing at all. During that time, he made his living writing dry annual reports for corporations. Louise Shivers, once a sales-clerk at Sears, also worked for seven years on her first book, *Here to Get My Baby Out of Jail.* While writing her New Age classic, *Beyond Codependency,* Melody Beattie subsisted on welfare, sometimes going to a public food bank for food to feed her children, and once, in a fit of discouragement, almost threw the manuscript that later made her a millionaire into the trash.

The list goes on and on, from Henry Miller, who even as an icon of American literature placed ads in *The New Republic* asking for donations of money and used clothes, to William Kennedy, who submitted his classic *Ironweed* to seventeen publishers before receiving acceptance, to John Kennedy Toole, who died a suicide after his comic masterpiece, *Confederacy of Dunces,* was turned down by Knopf, only to be published years later at his mother's and novelist Walker Percy's persistence.

"Better to kill a baby in its cradle than nurse an unacted desire," wrote William Blake. A Zona Rosa "exorcise" asked the newcomer to free associate on her wildest fantasy of what she wanted to achieve with her writing. It was designed to give full breath to usually half-formed thoughts, then to painlessly break through the bubble. A stockbroker who had never written a word, but who assumed that she could, wrote that she wanted to make so much money from her writing that she could retire to an island off the coast of Italy. I noticed that after giving voice to this fantasy, she never reappeared: apparently speaking it aloud had been enough to dissipate it.

Reading books about how to write has always seemed to me to be like reading books about how to have sex—vaguely titillating, but a poor substitute for the real thing. In addition to the exorcises and the usual readings from such books, I dug up material to stimulate the group from every possible source, from women's magazines to cartoons to meditation books to inspirational tapes to marriage manuals. We talked about the music of jazz musicians—about how artists like Miles Davis knew how to leave stuff out—and about how some performers created a deliberate cacophony. We discussed the relationships between musical composition, and composition in writing, especially poetry. We looked at works of visual art deliberately chosen for their disturbing qualities—a print of a Mapplethorpe photo or a dark drawing by Käthe Kollwitz, a poster I had brought back from Berlin, just after the fall of the Wall, delineating a bird with nails instead of wings.

Onetha hated snakes, but my living room was full of them—carved from sticks and brought back from Mexico, hinged ones from Guatemala, even rubber snakes from the five-and-ten. "Won't you please *move* that?" Courtenay pleaded, referring to a new painting I had hung behind my chair, depicting a dancing nude Pan in primary blues and oranges, complete with penis, balls, pubic hair, and painted toenails. I had always been inspired in my work by other art forms, and it turned out that the group was, too, even when art had never been a part of their lives before, and even when that "inspiration" took the form of a shudder. "I *still* remember that day you held up that poster from Berlin, and the way I felt!" Tyler, a former Zona Rosan, called to say three years after the fact.

"It's like you're tickling us, or *goosing* us," said our Jungian therapist, Barbara, amused. Already well into the unconscious, she understood exactly what I was doing. A reader of William Burroughs, D. H. Lawrence, and Camille Paglia, her own low-ceilinged cottage was like the dark underside of the brain, with scarves veiling low lamps and mysterious photos on the walls.

For one thing, I wanted the women to realize that they could become mental anarchists, destroying in the way necessary to create the new without necessarily becoming anarchists (à la Jean Genet or Jane Bowles) in their lives. After all, they didn't want to become leather queens, heroin addicts, or run away with the circus (though any of the above, had they lived through it, might have facilitated their creativity), they just wanted to write. And the abrasion of new ideas, the shock of the new, I had found, was an invaluable resource.

"Creativity is like a shark or a jungle cat. Basically amoral, it has perfect form and aim," I said. "It doesn't ask, it doesn't judge, it just *does*." Some of the women in the group thought that the British poet Ted Hughes had driven his wife, Sylvia Plath, over the edge with his looming presence, his adulteries. Nevertheless, I read to them from his poem, "Thrushes," in which he asked what gives the birds such single-minded purpose: "Mozart's brain had it, and the shark's mouth. . . ." To further emphasize this point, I quoted Thomas Hardy: "Literature is the written expression of revolt against accepted things."

I felt that Deconstruction, in which works of art are considered as ideological rather than aesthetic artifacts, would only further inhibit us. As women, imprinted early with the notion that we were the vessels of a culture's morality, this idea of giving ourselves over to a nonjudgmental creativity was a difficult one. (A survey conducted during the 1970s reported that women feared feminism because they feared a life without limits, which they saw as the decline of the family.) From my own and from Mother's life, I knew only too well how our minds had been split off, divided, on others' behalves—how they still were, day after day, so many times a day, in fact, that we may not even realize it. (My life, without a nine-to-five job or children still at home, was simpler than that of many of the Zona Rosans, but I quickly realized whenever I went off to a writers' retreat just how complicated daily life, with its phones, television sets, chores, and demands, is for *any*one.) Yet hadn't we all, at some point in our lives—especially the mothers among us, bent with a tigress's fury on our infants' survival—been as intent? Couldn't we once again reclaim that intensity, this time for ourselves, for our own writing and purposes?

"Weren't there many loops and nooses, seemingly imperative, that we could simply step out of," I asked, introducing a poem they had inspired me to write, "The Cowgirl Speaks to Her Daughter of Life":

The ropes   they're like men—
some're lassoes some're nooses.
Most can be   stepped out of—
others lie on the ground as
simple & flat as rattlesnakes—
but watch out for the rope
tightening tightening—
tripping you by an ankle.
Instead step out smartly
raise it above your head—
& throw with all your might—
toward the wildest mustang
toward the highest mountain
toward the distant stars—
rope what you will girl: you have
nothing to lose but yourself.

A subversive's guide to literature

I read to them from essayist Vicki Lindner's "I Was a Comman-
dante in the Sexual Revolution." Lindner first describes her own
pre-AIDS period of sexual freedom then makes the connection
between such risk-taking and later achievement, as evidenced by
her women friends, who had been as experimental as she had
then gone on to fulfill themselves creatively and professionally.

I told them about Carol Schneeman, the New York performance artist who performed nude, pulling her poems from her
vagina before she read them. I spoke of Beatrice Wood, the ce-
ramics artist whose autobiography, *I Shock Myself,* was published
in 1985 when she was 95. She describes her bohemian life in
Paris and New York, and her ménage à trois back in the '30s with
the Dadaist artist Marcel Duchamp and with Henri Pierre
Roche, the author of *Jules et Jim.* It was not until age forty that
Wood discovered the passion that would change her life: pottery.

I described a friend's interview with Elisabeth Kübler-Ross, the expert on death and dying who had brought the hospice movement to this country. "Did she seem depressed after dealing with the dying for so many years?" I had asked. "No, she seemed deliriously happy, and her clothes looked as though she had rolled around on the bed, and whatever old rags had been lying there had simply stuck to her body," he recalled, laughing. For Women Who Still Wore Slips, as I sometimes thought of some of the Zona Rosans, the idea of not being properly dressed alone was a shocking one.

I mentioned the philosopher-author Thomas Moore and his empathic views even of the Marquis de Sade, who he says was driven by his daemon to write of the dark side, yet never recanted his works despite being imprisoned for them for twenty years. I talked about an NPR interview with the filmmaker John Waters in which he began by saying, "I require the company of murderers at least once a week," then went on to describe the reaction of the hardest-core criminals in the prison where he was teaching to his film *Pink Flamingos*, starring the corpulent drag queen Divine. "They were as shocked as my parents would have been," he said, "but I wanted them to see that there were other ways to act out against society—that one doesn't have to do it through violence . . . that one can write a poem, paint a painting, make a film." (Was *Serial Mom* simply his expression of the traditional feminine role gone berserk?) "So shock yourselves!" I told the group.

Often the Zona Rosans themselves provided the shock waves. When I read a poem on tongue-piercing by one of our younger members, Lisa, a conversation ensued regarding the different body parts we had known to be mutilated in the name of sex, beauty, or identity. We talked about some art students around town: "She looked as though if someone grabbed that chain that ran from her eyebrow to her nose, her whole face could have been ripped off." Lisa mentioned a young man who pierced foreskins for a living; I told about the acquaintance who'd had a small pearl stud inserted in her labia as a gift to her bridegroom.

"It took me sixty years to decide to pierce my ears!" exclaimed Virginia, a conventional, sixtyish lady, who wore a short white bob, small gold earrings. "And even then, I didn't want to. But my earlobes are so small, and my face needed something beside it," she went on, using an expression common in the South. As she spoke, her rosy countenance was radiant, awash with thrilled and horrified delight. Indeed, where else could she safely sit in a room discussing body piercing, fire walking, trances, and self-mutilation—and also hear the word *fuck*? (Though not everyone thrilled to this approach: "It was the worst experience of my life!" gasped a tightly coiffed, fiftyish woman who had sat primly, stockinged legs tightly crossed, as I read from Anne Sexton's poem, "The Ballad of the Lonely Masturbator.")

I described women I knew who had taken other risks, such as my friend Diana who, after years of working three jobs as a single mother while earning her Ph.D. in political science, had given up the possibility of tenure. Taking her student loans and ten boxes of worldly goods, she moved to a sixth-floor walkup in Prague, in order to follow through on her research on the people of the Czech Republic. Diana was a living example of the book title, *Do What You Love and the Money Will Follow*. After making her decision and resigning her college teaching job, she was offered a position opening a Yale Law School branch three days a week in Slovakia, six hours away from Prague by train. But Diana had the first prerequisite for taking the kind of risk that was inherent in her choice: unlike many who follow the rules, she knew what she wanted, just what that voice inside was telling her.

I related what had happened to Judith, another friend who had given up preconceived ideas only to experience the synchronicity of the universe. A midfortyish psychotherapist, she had been deep in grief at the failure of her marriage and her lifelong inability to have a child when we met at a bioenergetics workshop in Atlanta. When I ran into Judith again, at the Jung Institute in Houston, she told me what had happened to her in the interim: she had remarried an engineer and, setting aside her own career, had gone with him to Moscow, where he worked. While taking her teenage stepson by train to a camp in a remote area, she had begun bleeding from her vagina; when she consulted doctors in a nearby rural town, they made her understand—despite her inability to speak Russian, theirs to speak English—that she was pregnant, and that they must perform an abortion; amazed and saddened, she consented. Yet back in Moscow, the bleeding continued, and she decided to fly to New York to see experts. During the journey, the hemorrhaging became so bad that the airline put her off the plane in London, where she spent two weeks in a clinic. Finally in Manhattan, she received a diagnosis—she was still pregnant, with a healthy female fetus! Apparently the Russian doctors had done an incomplete abortion on twins. As she told me this story, her face glowed: her beautiful daughter was now two years old, and she was back in the States, a single mother working as a therapist again.

When women first came into Zona Rosa, many of them, like the prisoners John Waters referred to, were prisoners of the belief that you were allied either with the light or the dark, that if you gave in to your creativity, your wild side, you would inevitably end up destroying families and yourself. "Is this anxiety, or unsupported excitement?" I asked them, repeating the question a Zona Rosan had been asked by her therapist. Some of us, if we have habituated ourselves to the mundane, the world-as-it-is, find creative excitement uncomfortable, just as preorgasmic women find sexual excitement uncomfortable.

Early in my writing life, the excitement of a new inspiration, a new idea for a poem—of sitting down to write—was so overwhelming that I required small physical rituals—the fresh cup of coffee, the wooden pencils on which to chew, the books by poets I liked stacked nearby in case I needed a jolt of their words—in order to calm myself. But as time passed, and my skills grew, I realized that one can learn to live comfortably inside this level of excitement, that we can tolerate more novelty, more mental pleasure than we believe. For beginners, floundering with technique and feelings of inadequacy, writing is *work*; for longtime writers, it can be work, too. But it is also life, the light: Van Gogh in his blazing cornfield, Emily Dickinson with her secret life. Indeed, just before writing this paragraph, I felt compelled to jot the first draft of a poem that had been growing inside me during the night, and afterward I felt as I usually do at such moments: shaken, a bit amazed at my own sudden explosion. But it is a shakiness and an amazement I've grown used to. "What seems unusual to other people is just everyday to us," a drag queen pal said to me back during my wilder days. And I had to admit, even the novelties of free sex could become mundane. But this—this is an excitement that never fails.

As Erica Jong states in *Devil at Large*, "Women must claim their sexuality (and their wild woman) in order to write." But we also saw how such honesty affects us as readers. When *The Bridges of Madison County* was published, it was the subject of controversy within the Zona Rosa groups, some Zona Rosans defending it despite its literary flaws, others affecting nausea at the very sound of the title. "I enjoyed it," Latrelle admitted. "I was turning the pages as fast as I could." But then she added reflectively, "But I know *why*. It was because the woman character was so passive, so *repressed*—just as I have been for so much of *my* life." "Yes, she took off her clothes in front of that man, and for a lot of women, that would be a *big* thing," said Nurse Pat. I agreed that for a woman reader who was more sexually experienced, the protagonist's one-night stand with the roving photographer might not feel quite so charged, and the book might not be such a page-turner.

"You always say exactly the *right* thing—the thing that person needs to hear," said Carolyn, making me aware for the first time that this might actually be a gift, one developed albeit through concentration. All I was doing, really, was talking to myself, saying the things *I* sometimes needed to hear. But now I recognized in myself an ability to focus, to truly listen. At the end of a Saturday afternoon workshop, after talking and reading aloud from manuscripts for as long as six hours, I was still exhilarated by the intensity of our time together. Many of the others, too, said that they were so excited when they went home that they immediately went to their desks to write.

Support, Stimulation, and Standards—these were the three S's, I was realizing, that made Zona Rosa work. "You give people hope," Mary, a department head at a nearby junior college, told me. Despite her degrees and achievements, when Mary had come into the group she still imagined herself to be the fat awkward teenager who populated her touching stories. Yet the secret of the group's success is not only in its support and stimulation, but in the fact that these are provided simultaneously with the highest standards for the writing itself: never once in Zona Rosa—despite our good times and camaraderie—has the hard work of writing well been underestimated. We agreed that what counts is what appears on the page. In fact, if there was one common thread we had developed through the years, it was this: *No sentimentality allowed.*

Writing in the Pink Zone was the way I thought of it, a circular, nonlinear approach, using the power of the feminine, the intuitive: in the zone of joy in writing for its own sake, taking all the time in the world. We, within our mortality, became like the woman who was diagnosed with a fatal illness, took her life savings to cruise around the world, and came back healed, if broke. Best of all, our approach *worked*, taking into account our realities as women (and later, for the men who came into the groups, the too-oft unacknowledged feminine parts of themselves).

There were still those who considered the feminine to be pejorative, and this was merely a further challenge. When a soon-to-be-famous male writer from the Northeast visited the group to sign books, a *Washington Post* reporter in tow, the resulting piece called me a woman "who writes about the labia-pink South," and termed Zona Rosa "a group for aspiring women novelists." Jana responded in a letter to the editor: "Given the company he was keeping, your reporter might be forgiven his glib oversight. But as a former member of Zona Rosa, I would like to correct your writer's description. . . . Zona Rosa is more accurately part literary salon and in part incubator for talented women writers, both published and unpublished." I had devised and handed out a list of precepts to the group.

PINK POWER, OR THE BASIC TENETS OF ZONA ROSA

That writing in the Pink Zone gets us there deeper, and sometimes even faster.

That the ordinary experiences of our lives are sufficient thereof.

That making love, cooking a good meal, or changing a baby's diapers, and being mindful of the above, can be as conducive to good writing as reading the New York Times Book Review.

That age is riches and wisdom—the older we are, the more we have of them.

That we can bless our own writing hands.

That there are few limits on what we can achieve, other than those we allow set upon us.

That a little anger, and a lot of self-respect and keeping the focus on ourselves, is healthy.

And finally, that menstrual blood is as powerful as, and more vivid than, semen!

< FIVE >

How to Be a Belle without Crossing the Mason-Dixon Line

"What *is* this thing about southern women?" Susan would demand rhetorically, in what was becoming a recurrent theme in the group.

"I'm Sunshine Harmonious Appleby," a graying, unmade-up woman said to me at an oyster roast on a Savannah bluff. She went on to explain that she had been born and raised in Savannah, but had moved "to northern California where I changed my name and lived on a women's commune." Looking wistfully at my red chiffon blouse, my dangling red enameled heart earrings, she went on, "I used to be able to dress like that, too. But now, I'm in a therapy group to deal with the 'shame of being a southern woman.'"

I knew what she meant. A lot of people still agree with the character August Evans, as quoted in Elizabeth Moss's *Domestic Novels of the Old South*: "'We have thousands [of ladies] who are graceful, pretty, witty and pleasant, but their information is . . . scanty, their judgment defective, their reasoning faculties dwarfed, their aspirations weak and frivolous. . . .'"

It was true that we southern women didn't seem to mind appearing girlish, or even diminished: "My name is Sybille Summers, but most people just call me Silly," a middle-age neighbor said to me, introducing herself. In the South, monickers abound, leading Carolyn, who had grown up on a South Georgia horse farm, and who had no truck with such leanings, to exclaim, "I can't stand *any* woman whose name is Sissy or Missy!"

Then there was the joke about the three southern belles, sitting on a verandah in Mississippi: "I'm jus' the luckies' guhl in the worl'," drawled the first. "For our twenty-fifth weddin' annivers'ry, mah husban' gave me a three-karat diamon' ring." "Oh, you *are,* you *are* the luckies' guhl in the worl'," said the second. "Oh, thet's nice, thet's *so* nice," murmured the third. "But ah jes' might be the luckies' guhl in the worl'," the second went on. "For our twenty-fifth weddin' annivers'ry, mah husban' rented a yacht, 'n took me on a cruise aroun' the worl'." "Oh, you *are,* you *are* the luckies' guhl in the worl'," agreed the first. "Oh, thet's *nice*, thet's *so* nice!" echoed the third. "'N what did *yore* husban' give *you* for yore twenty-fifth weddin' annivers'ry?" the first and the second asked the third. "He sent me to finishin' school," said the third. "But *why*?" chorused the other two. "Yuh have such nice manners now—you surely didn't need to go to finishin' school!" "Well, before, I used to say, 'Fuck you, 'n fuck you, too!' But now, I jes' say, 'Oh, thet's *nice*, thet's so *nice*!'"

It was clear that we southern women had a reputation for hypocrisy. But there was a chauvinism among us, too; a prejudice some considered well-earned (the brunt of one too many jokes). Even the more educated sometimes let drip the pejorative *Yankee,* the battery acid of her anger. Jalaine had just been awarded the prestigious Robert Frost poetry award at Agnes Scott, the college where she had started as a freshman at age fifty. But still, that didn't stop her from murmuring when piqued, her red curls dripping around her heart-shaped face, "She just thinks that way because she's a *Yankee.*"

The whole thing had come to a head when Lois wrote a piece on the Coca-Cola parties she had attended as a girl in Atlanta. These innocent spend-the-nights had been the occasions for instruction by the mother-hostesses on how one should behave as a proper young lady. "I'm so glad now that I had those experiences!" Lois enthused after we read her story. "We learned how to get along, what to say to boys when they got too forward, when we should wear white shoes or white gloves."

"Oh, thet's nice, thet's so nice," agreed Joan. As she spoke, one could almost see the white gloves *she* had worn, sitting for examinations forty years before in Jackson, Mississippi.

I nodded, too. Though I had attended E. Rivers grammar school and Lois had gone to the prestigious Washington Seminary—or "Washwoman's Cemetery," as it was dubbed at my school—we had already shared fond memories of being on the teen board at Davison's Department Store, with luncheons afterward at the Frances Virginia Tea Room.

But Nancy, a retired businesswoman from Minneapolis, was having none of it: "*That's* what I *hate* about southern women— they always think there's a certain way to act, rather than just saying what they mean!"

"Yeah. They're manipulative—hell, dishonest!" tossed in Jana, who had grown up in New Jersey. "You think they're being friendly, all this 'y'all come' stuff; then you never hear from 'em again!"

As the others joined in the fray, Lois sat silent and ladylike, rising above it all just as she had been taught to do at those spend-the-night parties. To smooth things over, I told about an evening when my literary agent and I had dined in a Greenwich Village trattoria. "I hate to go out to eat with southern women—they always flirt with the waiter," she complained to my surprise, after I had smiled at the boy pouring the wine.

But the worst came when Betty Blank visited from New York to promote her new novel, a steamy tale of upheaval and black-white sex in Haiti. During what was supposed to be a question-and-answer period, Betty talked nonstop, drinking straight vodka from a jelly glass while the rest of us sipped white wine or Coke. Once she got up to go into the bathroom, which was just off the living room, and left the door open while urinating loudly and continuing her monologue. The Zona Rosans looked politely off into the distance—hadn't anybody ever told that poor girl *how* to act?

Afterward Lila, who was to write a piece for her paper on our visiting writer, went with Betty and me to a nearby bistro where Betty immediately ordered a triple Stoli straight up. The meal went swimmingly enough, until Lila's current beau, a handsome attorney in an expensive suit, came over to our table to say hello. "Who's *that*?" Betty asked when he left, a rude edge to her voice. "Why, he's my boyfriend," Lila answered sweetly. "If *he's* your boyfriend, you've got *problems*!" Betty snorted. "What do you mean by *that*?" Lila said, the color rising in her face. "Well, if you don't know, honey, I can't tell you. You crackers just don't know anything anyway—" At that, Lila stood to leave the table, at her full five foot ten, a rose on a prickly stem. But she already had enough notes for the article that would appear the next morning in the *Savannah News-Press*: "Yesterday at Zona Rosa, a Savannah writing group for women, Betty Blank was holding forth. And holding forth appears to be what Ms. Blank does best . . ." her piece began, beneath a full-color photo of Betty, her gray-blond bun askew, her mouth twisted in a sneer.

At the next meeting, all the Zona Rosans, even the Yankees, complimented Lila on her fine coverage of the author's visit. But not before Betty, truly puzzled and for once sober, had called to ask, "Why did that pretty little reporter write such mean stuff about me?"

On an afternoon when Pat Conroy visited—at 4:30, as specified for male guests—we were still reading manuscripts, and Pat sat at the top of the stairs to listen. We were reading Helen's story of a woman in a relationship in which she was being battered, a natural for Helen, as director of the city's Victim's Witness program; then we went on to Joan's newest poems, which were as usual tender and lyrical and addressed the issue of grief and her own impending death (she was eighty-nine). But despite her subject matter, Joan was far from joyless. In fact, I had told Pat and others that simply being in Joan's spa-like presence felt like having a soothing salve spread over one's entire body.

The Zona Rosans were excited: most had read Pat's novel, *The Prince of Tides*, which was set in nearby Beaufort, South Carolina, and had heard him read from his forthcoming *Beach Music*, his massive manuscript in progress. Indeed, he was their favorite male guest. I felt good about his coming, too, because I knew that, despite his aging football player's build, the biceps bulging beneath his short-sleeved knit shirt, we were in little danger of testosterone poisoning. Indeed, he was among the least sexist of southern male authors, regaling us with his love of the works of one woman poet or another, and appearing to appreciate the Zona Rosans' stories as much as I did.

A favorite story was of the time Adrienne Rich had thrown him out of a poetry workshop at an Atlanta arts center back in the '70s. I was responsible for this, he claimed, first because I had invited Rich to teach at the conference but had not specified the workshop would be for women only; then because I had sent Pat out for coffee for the gang of us, and when he came back, balancing a cardboard tray containing steaming styrofoam cups, he was severely set upon by the aggressive Ms. Rich, who chased him from the room, despite her limp, her cane.

Now, as we finished reading Joan's poems, I wanted Pat to know more about her, about how special she was. Recapitulating a number of the stories she had finally put into prose at our gentle nudging, I told how she had come straight after college from Jackson, Mississippi, by train in 1925 to live in the dormitory at Savannah State College, where she would teach sociology for the next forty years. I talked about how she had met her husband, history professor Asa Gordon, and had finally been persuaded to marry him, then left for her honeymoon trip sans a nightgown—though she had cunningly left the wedding night out of her story, leaving what happened to our imaginations. I repeated her account of the times she and her new husband had visited Tybee

Beach at midnight, where no "Negroes" were allowed, to watch the moon rise above the tides.

There were other poignant aspects to their story: Asa, an early desegregationist, had written articles for the *Savannah News-Press* calling for an end to Jim Crow as early as the '40s. His activism had cost him his job at Savannah State, forcing him to leave the fieldstone house he had built for himself and his bride—to take whatever teaching jobs he could find and join his growing family in Savannah only during the summers. Joan had now lived in that big cool house for fifty years, the last thirty of them, since her husband's death, alone.

"I was bad 'bout writing," Joan interjected, warming to her own story. "So bad that once I sent him a telegram saying that I was writing him a letter. 'Gentlemen,' he announced to his colleagues at a faculty meeting, 'My wife just sent me a telegram saying that she's about to write me a letter. Now I *know* it will be a long time before I receive one!' "

At my prompting, she added that as a bride she had called him Mr. Gordon and he called her Mrs. Gordon; that when she became pregnant with their first son, she had not known what was "wrong" with her until he had told her.

"And what did you call him after that?" Pat asked.

"Oh, then I called him 'Daddy.' "

"You know who you sound just like?" Pat teased. "Rosemary Daniell, in her book *Sleeping with Soldiers*!" A running joke between the two of us was that I was able to write about sex, while he could not—or at least, not until all his aunts had died. He had always avoided having an affair with me, he told the group, because he was afraid I would write about him in one of my books. I ribbed him about what he didn't know about women: when he described a beautiful, yet passive Zona Rosan as being enigmatic, I countered by saying that we women considered her nice-girl reticence to be frustrating, if not downright boring.

I also knew Pat had the southern male's ma'am-calling respect for "ladies," especially elderly ladies, and I wanted to tease him a bit, too. Also, I knew something he didn't: that despite her lady-like demeanor, Joan had sat patiently and nonjudgmentally through the years, during discussions of everything from incest to oral sex. When he began a funny story I had heard before, about taking his ten-year-old daughter to a march against the gulf war in San Francisco, I realized he was omitting a certain part—probably because Joan was in the room. "Pat," I insisted, "Tell us again what the gay contingent were chanting—"

"I can't say that in front of Joan!" he protested.

"Oh, she can handle it," I insisted. Pat looked embarrassed, but finally mouthed the words: "Gays suck dick / Lesbians suck labia / U.S. get out of / Saudi Arabia!" As a blush suffused Pat's broad Irish face, the women laughed.

Yet Joan merely sat as she always did during times when the talk turned raunchy or argumentative—elegant hands folded in her lap, a faint, pleasant smile on her still-pretty face. It was much the same expression my Grandmother Carroll had worn whenever someone had tried to tell her what the *real* subject matter of my writing was; instead, she merely collected my reviews and any media coverage of my career without reading them, leaving the packet to me when she died. (When I said in a '70s interview in the *Atlanta Journal-Constitution* that I no longer believed in marriage and was in fact living with my current lover, my sister Anne said that the article quickly disappeared before Grandmother could see it, and was mentioned by my aunts only in whispers.)

"Joan's such a lady I'll bet she called her husband's dick 'Mr. Gordon,' too," Pat said to me later, still marveling that he'd been able to say such words before the woman I called the Last of the Black Southern Belles.

I chuckled. Joan had heard a lot worse through the years, and never for a moment had she lost her perfect composure. I suspected she even enjoyed it.

Zona Rosa and the Birth of the Book

"I was told to change into a hospital gown. Then I lay on a bed and a dark-skinned nurse lifted up my gown—what was she, a lesbian?! I wanted to kick her hand out of the way, but she was coming at me with a razor. She proceeded to give me a shave where I had never expected to have one. Next, she wiped my mount, and stuck something up my rear end . . ." Melinda was near-singing in her Brooklyn accent.

Over the years, three contenders had emerged among the Zona Rosans to be the first published novelist out of the group— Susan, Courtenay, or Melinda. Susan had finished two books, and, in her usual businesslike way, was looking for an agent. Courtenay had gotten off to a good start, then had gotten mired for a time in divorce, family illness, and what I was learning was her characteristic procrastination. Today, Melinda was reading the last chapter of the book she had been methodically writing for four and a half years. Now she was down to the last few pages, reading faster and faster through a scene in which her protagonist, a delirious Evelyn, is giving birth on a rural kibbutz sans anesthesia:

"Think about something, anything, old records from my childhood, an Alice in Wonderland record where the Mock Turtle sings, 'Beautiful soup so rich and green, waiting in a hot tureen,' and a Purim song in Yiddish about the hamantaschen, the poppyseed-filled tricorner pastries, 'Hop, meine hamantaschen, hop, meine hamantaschen . . .'"

Just a few minutes before, we had raised our glasses in a toast as Melinda stood glowing pinkly in the archway between the living room and dining area of the tiny apartment that June, a single mother, shared with her small son. We were meeting there that Saturday because of the boxes filling my new-old house. On the way I had stopped to buy two bottles of champagne. Melinda, ever practical, and afraid that no one else would think of it, had brought two bottles herself, along with a platter of the special little noshes—tiny spinach balls or mock kishkas—for which she had become known in the group. The only ones not drinking were Kathleen, who was about nine and a half months pregnant with her first baby, and looked as though she had swallowed a basketball; Joan, who rarely imbibed; and the two recovering alcoholics in the group.

"It's like a torture machine, the medieval Iron Lady—woo woo woo woo woo, wif, wuf, wuf, I won't think about it I'll put my mind onto something else, somewhere else, north south east west, West Side Story my favorite movie as a kid the Sharks and the Jets and the crush I had on one of the Jets what was his name?—wuf, wuf—something cold Cool Ice or Snow Man he took over the gang after Biff was killed and he sang, Boy, boy crazy boy, stay coolie-cool boy, got a rocket in your pocket woo woo woo . . ."

As Melinda read, her voice quivering with the excitement of her achievement, I thought back to the beginnings of a manuscript that was now nearly 600 pages long. When she had first come to Zona Rosa, she had written that her wildest fantasy, the height of her ambition, was to learn to write humorous pieces to submit to *Cosmo*. She was a plump, rosy Jewish housewife who made her own challah bread (her detailed love of food would turn out to play a large—and delicious—part in her prose) and kept her house, within walking distance of a synagogue, immaculate for her stockbroker husband, her teenage daughter, and her preteen son. She didn't know how to drive, but liked to walk, despite the fact that she lived in a heavily trafficked suburb near one of Savannah's more popular malls. As I drove by on errands, I would often see her walking past the 7-Eleven or up the exhaust-filled main street.

At first Melinda's ambition seemed a fit to her quick, irreverent humor. But then one Saturday she brought in a story about Evelyn, an eleven-year-old girl whose mother had died of cancer not long before. When she goes into her thirteen-year-old brother Eric's room to watch Pee Wee Herman on TV with him after school, she's feeling especially pretty, despite the perpetual bane of her plumpness. She's proud of her new gold shag sweater, and asks Eric whether he likes it. Instead of answering, Eric wordlessly puts his hand on her breast. Back in her own room, she takes off the sweater, wads it in the wastebasket, never to wear it again. But she knows she won't tell her father because he is still reeling from the loss of his wife, and besides, Evelyn is the little mother now: it is her duty to hold the family together.

As I read Melinda's first serious piece aloud, I felt the tears spring into my eyes; we all drew in our breaths as the story concluded. That Melinda was Evelyn was clear, but we went on to discuss her as though she were a fictional creation, in order to protect the delicate fabric that had allowed Melinda to expose her feelings in this way.

Melinda told us something else that day—both her parents had been in the death camps during World War II; her mother had been a Polish journalist before the war, and she and Melinda's father had married in a Displaced Persons camp after they were liberated. They settled in Brooklyn, where Melinda would grow up, and, like Evelyn, her mother died when Melinda was eleven.

The next month, Melinda brought in a story based on an experience she and her husband, Steve, had early in their married life. During the early '70s, they had lived on an Israeli kibbutz, and Steve had gone off to fight in the Yom Kippur War, leaving behind Melinda, hugely pregnant and anxious, to tend the cows. I was stunned: wasn't the other story the beginning of a book, and this its possible end? The outline was already there, I suggested—all she had to do was fill in the dots.

For the next four years, we Zona Rosans waited—except in the months when Melinda was involved in one of her many family or religious activities—for her next installment. Her character Evelyn was a little girl growing up in Brooklyn who embodied Melinda's wit and cleverness; in fact, I told Melinda hers was the first *funny* book I knew of about the Holocaust. Year after year we followed Evelyn from early childhood in Brooklyn, where her life, because of her precocity, was filled with hilarious malapropisms. We lived with her first awarenesses of sex; through her learning to masturbate to her brother Eric's copy of *The Pearl* to her first menstrual period. We learned how Evelyn finds her mother's journals, in which her parents' hidden past with all its horrors is revealed, explaining her father's nightmares, the scars ridging her mother's back. In one of the more touching scenes, Evelyn dances with her mother, who is teaching her to foxtrot in preparation for her brother Eric's Bar Mitzvah, and feels the scars created when her mother was beaten by the Nazis. She and her sister were discovered sabotaging the bullets they were making in the camp by putting in only a half-portion of gunpowder. When younger, the precocious Evelyn had read the word *Braille* in a child's biography of Helen Keller, and misinterpreted it. For years she thought of the marks on her mother's back as *Brazil.*

As time went on, Melinda's voice grew in certainty. We also learned that she was not as traditional as she had first appeared. For one thing, she had less trouble writing about sex than almost anyone in the group. Indeed, she was an example of the power of passion and persistence. During those years she lost forty pounds, became a spokeswoman for her synagogue, and went to her son's private school in protest when she heard that a teacher had put Hitler on mock trial, saying perhaps he wasn't guilty after all. Because of her part-time job with a local abortion agency, she had also gone on national TV at two hours' notice to speak as an expert on teenage pregnancy. Now the daughter who had been born on the kibbutz had flown off to Columbia University, and Melinda had finished her first book.

"Oh Daddy, Mommy somebody woowoowoowufwufwuf I'm gonna push *right now* you fuckers and if you don't like it you kiss my wet and drippy ass unhh, uhnn . . . and I'm puuushing and uhnnn and uhhhnnn and UHHHNNN!" Now Melinda was reading even faster, deep breathing as though she were actually in labor herself. The Zona Rosans sat in a thrall, breathless with admiration and horror, until she ripped out her last line:

"'It's a girl!'"

"It's a book!" I said into the stunned silence, using the phrase my first editor had written in congratulation of my first published work. Then came our wild applause, followed by another sudden silence. "Has everybody forgotten about *Kathleen*?" June asked. Our heads all turned toward the couch, where Kathleen perched at the edge, her hands gripping her huge belly, her normally fair face blanched even paler by what she had just heard.

"Just say yes to drugs!" I said lamely, blurting the best advice with which I could come up, then went around the room, pouring more champagne as the other Zona Rosans, rising to the occasion, cosseted Kathleen with stories of drugged sleeps and easy births.

PowerBook Cooking & Other Signs of Commitmentphobia

Zona Rosa had now lasted longer than any of my marriages. But there were still times when I acutely felt the differences between us. It was not only that some of them still wore slips. For one thing, I feared losing myself in domesticity more than the Zona Rosans did, a fact that came to light when, thirteen years into the group, Zane and I became locked in a conflict over whether to buy a house with a yard and a garage. I had lived in my tiny Victorian flat, crammed with art, books, and manuscripts for fifteen years, and while I acknowledged that it held little room for a live-in spouse, it represented freedom to me: a beautiful place to alight, but a rental from which I could fly at the drop of a chance for risk or adventure. Never mind the gunshots that punctuated the downtown Savannah nights, or the fact that I had been mugged outside my door not once but twice. Also, I hadn't had a washer and dryer—something every other woman in the room considered an *a priori* condition—for over two decades. But I considered that a small trade-off for the sense of psychic liquidity I had come to see as essential.

I had gone through the same anxiety making the decision to marry, putting Zane off and then taking him back on again. Then too I had shared with the Zona Rosans the images that arose from my distress; then too, despite having been privy to the chaos of Zane's and my early relationship, they had looked at me, puzzled. When an acrylic fingernail—carefully applied, painfully buffed with a little circular electric machine, then dried under a heat lamp at a local beauty salon—became infected on my ring finger, causing the entire nail to at first mercilessly throb, then fall off, I took it as a sign. (Hadn't I also had my nails done that way in the first place—another disgusting sign of my willingness to please—because Zane liked them?) Finally, Zane had given me an ultimatum, and I had succumbed. But not before I had shared with the group the poem that surfaced to contain my fears:

> *I am a chicken*
> *about to have surgery—*
> *torturous distorting*
> *turning my wings rigid.*
>
> *In the yard*
> *I see the other chickens—*
> *already operated on*
> *unable to fly.*
>
> *Yet the scars make*
> *my wings stronger:*
> *I soar high higher*
> *dropping bright*
> *streamers & glitter.*

I knew there were internal reasons why I felt as I did, early imprints that had given me messages about what happened to women who followed a male lead. With Daddy, Mother had

spent more than half her life trying to reform an unwilling—
some would say no-good—man. When she married her second
husband, Wayne, her hopes of leading a "normal" life had re-
vived: they had moved to a rented house in Atlanta and, at her
new love's insistence, Mother had resigned her federal secretarial
job without notice, even before they left for the honeymoon. He
would take care of her for the rest of her life, Wayne said; it
didn't matter that she would lose the seniority and benefits she
had accrued through the years, that she would likely never be
able to get such a job again.

For a time things had gone smoothly, but when Wayne retired from his position as a federal forest service engineer,
Mother cried, protesting that she would be miserable cut off
from the pleasures of movies, shopping, and restaurants, not to
speak of the therapy she needed, if they moved back to his farm
in rural North Carolina. But her best southern-belle manipula-
tiveness was ineffective against his sense of male prerogative; job-
less and penniless, she had no leverage.

True to her fears, social life in North Carolina tended to dete-
riorate into conversations with Wayne's relatives that went something like this: "Planted me some tulips last week." "Oh, planted
yuh some tulips?" "Yep, planted me some tulips last week."—
each comment punctuated by five minutes of silence. After ten
years of watching her husband shoot squirrels and other "var-
mints" from the back porch, reluctantly canning an endless
stream of pole beans and summer squash, and making hundreds
of the homemade biscuits that the closemouthed Wayne required for his breakfasts, Mother's depression deepened. Her
sense of isolation and hopelessness led to her suicide.

Indeed, my own feelings had deepened as I approached the
age Mother had been when she died. Instead of mellowing out, I
valued my fluid, risk-taking side more than ever. More than ever,
I feared being tied down.

But many of the women in Zona Rosa still wanted—or
claimed that they wanted, despite their frequent asides to the

contrary—husbands to make dinner for (and organize their lives around); washers and dryers, and built-in gas grills; even positions of esteem within the community (Courtenay, for example, still taught Sunday School). They looked at me, puzzled, as I expressed my disdain for such luxuries, or more accurately, my fears of what would happen to me if I imbued them with too much importance. I thought that they, on the other hand, had bought into a set of beliefs, one that stretched thin their sympathies and their self-focus, immobilizing them as surely as though their feet were embedded in concrete.

In the case of the house, they were proven right. "Oh, you'll like it when you're moved in," Helen assured me. "I felt the same way when we moved recently. I cried and cried, and then wondered why I had hesitated." And as I looked out at the oaks dripping Spanish moss, the palmetto dancing at my bedroom window, the play of light on pale walls dancing through that new space—not to speak of the purr of the washer and dryer from the distant laundry room and the knowledge that a red-lit security system protected me from rape and, more important, my manuscripts from fire—I felt an archaic satisfaction, almost like a memory from a past life.

But the matter was not truly resolved for me, I told them, until I dreamed this: I was cooking a pot roast inside my Powerbook, and I was terrified that it would ruin the computer forever. Instead, I took out the perfect roast, and the machine ran just as well as before: despite my commitment to teaching, my new domesticity, my creativity was still intact.

"Artists and children disobey," Jean Cocteau, the poet and artist, had written in an epigraph to the French cookbook for children he had whimsically illustrated, which I had bought for my daughters. Whenever I felt rebellious—as I still did about once a week—I remembered not only my wild sexual past, but how we poets—traveling and living together or near one another in temporary or communal arrangements, working in schools away from our home towns—were childlike in our good times. Like the members of a traveling circus or theater, we had sometimes shocked the local populace.

At the school on Lookout Mountain, Tennessee, on a Monday when I had risen at 4 A.M. to make the four-hour drive from Atlanta, I lost it as an afternoon class of fifth-graders, many of them hulking boys—barefoot, in overalls, and taller than I was— repeatedly disrupted our discussion. "Dammit! That bores the hell out of me!" I yelled. A hush fell over the room. I had forgotten for a moment how deep into the Bible Belt I was, and as I walked out to my Fiat that afternoon, the boys called out to me from a safe distance, "Why doncha cuss for us agin, teach?"

The next morning, after a night spent dreaming of lynch mobs in my room at the Fairyland Courts Motel, wondering if I would be hung from the nearest tree, I was called into the principal's tiny office. "It's been said that you used *language*," he began, looking embarrassed, as though he couldn't quite bring himself to repeat the offending phrases, especially to quote them as having fallen from a *woman's* lips. Hastily, I assured him it would never happen again. This was a school where the teachers often took a full-grown girl, complete with breasts and a woman's body, into the hallway to "paddle" her in full view of passersby. I knew they certainly wouldn't put up with any uppityness from a female from "Etlana."

It was also the same school district in which I had been taken to meet the superintendent by one of the school principals: "See? I told you she was qualified!" the principal exclaimed when the superintendent asked where I had done my "work," and I confessed to being a high school dropout.

A widow in whose home I stayed in a town in South Georgia had hung velvet pictures of Jesus thoughout her house, and perhaps suspecting my true nature (she had already declined my invitation to a reading of my poetry, as though she feared what she might hear), offered me a tattered paperback of Eugenia Price's account of how she had been "saved." I read the book avidly as I lay in the widow's back bedroom while drinking Jack Daniels in bed at night (familiar with the mores of Bible Belt towns, I had known to keep the bottle hidden in my luggage). But the only "sins" Price appeared guilty of were drinking and smoking, and her salvation seemed to have appeared simultaneously with her relationship with the woman "friend" with whom she had lived ever since, a coincidence that I imagined had escaped the notice of the widow woman.

In fact, Jesus and sex, or at least mixing the two, as I had done in much of my writing and life, was a major taboo. Just before a reading at a small Methodist college in southwest Georgia, I was served dinner, sans cocktails, at 5:30 P.M., and nibbled at my dry roast beef, canned English peas, and mashed potatoes beside the college president, who was also a Methodist minister. "Just don't mention Jesus or sex," the school librarian whispered in my ear as he guided me toward a podium on a stage before which sat 200 teenagers, plus an array of faculty. "We'll lose our jobs!" Having destroyed my whole plan for the reading, he led me into a spotlight so bright that I could see nothing but a sea of bobbling blackness. At that moment, the wide belt to my new Norma Kamali dress, held in place in back by a strip of Velcro, leapt from my waist as though alive, and with my suddenly released breath, I felt as though I had been given permission. I concluded my performance with "Over Chattanooga," a poem in which a southern teenage girl commits suicide during a ride at a county fair, driven mad by sexual guilt. It was then that the bobbling black balls before me came alive, shaking the space with their applause, and I stepped down, beltless—still hoping that the librarian and his colleagues wouldn't be fired *right* away.

One morning, a male poet and I sat in the first-period class that we were team-teaching. We were hung over from the Black Jack we had consumed the night before while listening to a blues guitarist play over and over on his steel guitar a composition that had only one line: "I used my last nickel to call her on the phone and her goddamn husband was home." We had asked our ninth-grade Macon classroom to come up with the characteristics of a religion they have invented for themselves. As we chalked their answers on the board, we became nearly hysterical with laughter. "Do you realize we could have been run out of town on a rail for that?" he said later, referring to the fundamentalist nature of the community.

But at the moment, it had made us feel as though we fit right in with the kids. "THE VACANT LOT AT THE GEORGIA POWER COMPANY IS OFF LIMITS, REPEAT, OFF LIMITS," the principal had boomed over the loudspeaker during homeroom that morning, adding, "The person whose blanket was found on the vacant lot should report to the office immediately!"

Indeed, our antics seemed to endear us to the kids. "Miz Daniell, how did you get that hickey?" a tenth-grade girl shouted from the back of the room one Monday, after I had spent a passionate weekend at home. As the whole room rocked with laughter, I looked up to see that several of the girls wore the same faint blue bruises on the sides of their necks.

Needless to say, the teachers, representatives of authority and order, didn't always appreciate this fun-loving, anything-goes approach to teaching poetry. At one school in a small town near Atlanta, the governor's riot squad had been called out because of racial problems within the school. "Someone has been setting fires in the wastebaskets," the principal declared over the intercom; "If that person is your friend, he is sick and needs help. Please turn your friend in, and we will see that he gets help. We will prosecute him to the fullest extent of the law."

Applying, as I often did, what was situational to the day's curriculum, I told an anxious-looking young white teacher that I had a brilliant idea: I planned to ask the black students in his classroom to write about how it might feel to be white, the white students to write about how it might feel to be black. "Pul-LEE-ease!" said Mr. Smith, swishing a huge handkerchief across his forehead. "I think I might be getting a mi-grah-eene!"

"How can you read poems like that, and wear a dress like that?" a university professor's wife asked me disapprovingly at a party after a reading. She was referring to my favorite flowered crepe dress, cut in front to show the tops of my breasts. She was also, without knowing it, commenting on a certain blind naïveté. When I wore a form-fitting cherry crepe dress, along with pink fuck-me pumps—without my usual pink felt cowboy hat—to speak at the prestigious Atlanta Historical Society, I was surprised to hear later that someone had commented on the inappropriateness of my costume.

"You really know how to play a crowd!" another woman said somewhat bitterly, after I told the sedate audience that I was cutting a four-letter word from a poem during my reading of it. "After all, this *is* the Atlanta Historical Society," I explained. But rather than being disingenuous, my cut and my comment had simply been in response to my notice of an elderly woman on the front row, a woman who reminded me of my grandmother, whom I knew would be offended by such language.

I had become used to being called to task for my writing. At a writers' conference on Saint Simon's Island the Poet Laureate of Georgia, a plastic surgeon who looked as if he had been the beneficiary of his own art, challenged the use of "bad" language in poetry. "I think any language that accurately expresses the human condition and mirrors speech is appropriate for poetry," I told the audience, knowing it was really the content of the poems, a woman's honest expression of cultural anger, to which he objected. "Certain words are commonly used to express anger in our culture—thus, such a word may be the right word, the mot juste, in a poem expressing that emotion."

"The great thing about you is that you never get mad," a woman professor said, observing our debate. But the truth was, I was just weary of it. I had long been irritated by the fact that male writers seemed free to blithely embrace, even flaunt, their sins in print—to go down the garden path recklessly, certain that their risks might even be applauded, while we women were still held to the role of moral role models. It was even worse when women held us to those standards.

(On the other hand, given my faithfulness to my own vision, I had had problems with feminists, too; "not politically correct," they would say of my work, or "too macho." Once I sent some poems to *Ms.*, only to receive a note saying that the editors concurred that they "had too much blood in them." I wrote back, saying, "When I have some bloodless poems, I'll send them.")

Indeed, some people didn't even think I should read my own writing. As the years went by, after my first poetry collection, *A Sexual Tour of the Deep South* (1975), went out of print, I took to searching out copies in used bookstores. "Yes, I have a copy," said a young man in a bookstore in Atlanta. "I got one just last week—I sat down and read it straight through." Not knowing that I was the author, he looked me over, taking in my conservative dress, my heels and hose. "I don't think you would want to read it, though!"

"Somebody should write about the connection between sexuality and writing," said Bruce Feiler, who at twenty-nine had published two books and was at work on his third. Bruce *was* one of those privileged ones—the right schools (Yale and Cambridge, England), a supportive family. He seemed, in my mind, to fly through the air unencumbered, like one of the trapeze artists at the Clyde Beatty Circus, where he had worked for a year as a clown in preparation for writing his current book. But despite our differences in age and background, we had become fast friends because of our mutual love for one thing: good writing.

We were talking about how we had both had our first inklings about sex through the movies, and how that factor had affected our creativity. We had both been about nine, but because of our age difference, Bruce's had come, he said, when he saw *Saturday*

Night Fever, featuring an object he didn't understand, and mine through *The Outlaw,* starring a voluptuous Jane Russell. He had been puzzled by a jar of Vaseline beside a bed; I hadn't understood what it meant when Jane, in her low-necked blouse, leaned over the wounded outlaw hidden in the barn.

"But it's not that you have to have an unusual or exotic sex life in order to write," Bruce went on. "It's just the awareness of the *connection.*" He cited a night when, traveling and broke, he had crashed at the home of an aging and famous screenwriter in a small town in southern Mexico. "If it"—your manuscript in progress—"doesn't turn you on while you're writing it, it's probably no good," the great man had advised.

I knew what he meant. Whenever the writing was going well, there did seem to be some direct flow between Eros and typewriter or ballpoint. But I also knew from my experiences as a person who had written openly about sexuality that it was hard for some aspiring writers to embrace that part of themselves, much less accept it as a part of their creativity. Because of the degrading of sex in our culture—and the resultant demands that we women look/be/act sexy, however serious our other roles—it was hard for some of us in Zona Rosa to view our sexuality as a positive force.

And then there were the women who had been wounded by either their sexuality or someone else's, such as a husband who had strayed. "This book has upset me more than my divorce after thirty years of marriage!" Courtenay called to exclaim after reading my novel *The Hurricane Season.* "It's the *sex* in it I can't deal with!" On another occasion, she asked a question of a new piece of writing I had shown her. "I hope you will take out that part about fellagio!" she exclaimed. I looked at her, puzzled—was she suddenly speaking Italian? "You know, *oral sex,*" she explained indignantly. ("Yeah, it's that place in Italy that men love to visit!" Pat Conroy said, amused, when I told him of her comment.) As she spoke, I thought of the photo of her, made at Wesleyan College for Women, where she had been a beauty queen;

in her white strapless gown, her long blond hair in a smooth pageboy, she had been as lovely as a young Marilyn Monroe. But since she had started writing seriously—before and after her divorce—she had started masking her natural beauty with dowdy clothes, a layer of fat, as though seeking to establish her identity along more serious lines by keeping her sensuality at bay.

Courtenay wasn't alone in her reaction, and there seemed to be a common denominator among the woman who felt that way: they were women who early in their lives had achieved identity through following the rules, even if later they had been betrayed by those same rules. Elsa, the conservative Catholic who had found herself pregnant and betrayed by an American GI during World War II, was shocked by the sexual "looseness" of even the primmest among us, and driven to near breakdown by the more liberal. She stood up, shouting, "I don't have to listen to this!" after a chapter from a novel in progress describing a married woman's affair with her gynecologist.

Yet after my midlife abortion, it was Elsa, her devout Catholicism countering my skepticism, who had comforted me. Some, like the then age eighty Joan, managed to bypass the whole controversy: "You had some beautiful images and some very good insights in that book!" she had called to tell me after reading *Sleeping with Soldiers*, despite its oft-graphic frankness.

I knew that there were great artists at either end of the erotic spectrum. Courtenay, Emily Brontë, Emily Dickinson, and E. M. Forster (who, it was said, was a virgin at the time he wrote *Room with a View*) sublimated their desires into great literature. Courtenay, for example, may have objected to the sexuality in my work, but she had another vision in her own that was equally deep for her—a genuine religious thrust, an obedience to theological imperatives, which deepened and informed her work. She shared her credo with me, quoting the mystery writer, Dorothy Sayers: "'God is the idea you seek, Christ is the action of writing about it, and the meaning you see as you read. What you write is the Holy Spirit.'"

On the other hand, there were the Erica Jongs, Henry Millers, and Norman Mailers of the literary world. Freud had told us how our sexuality, even unconsciously, compels us. *The Intimate Sex Lives of Famous People*, collected and edited by Irving Wallace and family, reveals the difference from the Western monogamous heterosexual ideal in the lives of high achievers, a large number of them artists and writers. As W. B. Yeats wrote in his poem "Crazy Jane Talks with the Bishop": "A woman can be proud and stiff / When on love intent; / But Love has pitched his mansion in / The place of excrement." In her memoir, *Virgin Time*, Patricia Hampl decries her inability to present herself as anything other than a good Catholic girl. And some of us, identified with fiction writer Grace Paley's comment in regard to whether the writer Kay Boyle, who had been married three times, had many affairs, as well as six children, had suffered regrets. "I don't think anyone who has had a sex life *has* regrets," Paley is said to have remarked.

Nor was it only the literate in literature who believed in sex as a good. Nisa, the Botswanian bushwoman in the book of the same name, says, "If a woman doesn't have sex, her thoughts get ruined and she is always angry." She also believed that "a woman can bring a man to life, even if he is almost dead. She can give him sex and make him alive again. If there were no women around, their semen would kill (them)."

Whether we sublimated our sexuality or openly embraced it in our work, our common denominator as writers seemed to be a passionate nature. However cool we may strive to appear, most share this larger-than-life investment in our passions, whether they be romantic relationships, involvements with family, or certain ideals. Throughout history creative people have lived at extremes—from Emily Dickinson remaining true to her private fantasies to Emily Brontë's imagining of a story of passion and obsession as she sat, virginal, before the fire in her minister father's house. We are nothing if not *obsessive*. And obsessiveness seems to be the one characteristic a middle-class, mainstream experience, filled as it is with daily duties and responsibilities and passive entertainments that further tamp the psyche, seems designed to stamp out. I wondered if our fear of our sexuality might be caused in part by the fear we feel of becoming one of those at the far end of the spectrum—after all, criminals, addicts, and the mentally ill are obsessive, too. (In fact, there is a relationship: research shows that if one has a manic-depressive sibling, one has a higher than ordinary chance of being creative.) As the Spanish philosopher Santayana wrote, "What is happiness to the artist is too rarefied for the average man."

Indeed, the great psychologists have long puzzled over the riddle of creativity: "In his capacity of artist [the poet] is neither auto-erotic, nor hetero-erotic, nor erotic in any sense. In his work, he is objective and impersonal—even inhuman—for as an artist, he is his work, and not a human being," wrote Carl Jung. In Erich Fromm's view, our greatest problem as human beings— our sense of isolation in the universe—is best overcome in two ways: through personal relationships and through artistic creation.

But as every artist knows, artistic creation is not just from the head: it pulses from every cell in the body, even those of the reptilian brain and our basest desires. Writing may *seem* like a head trip, but what is the brain, after all, but a part of the body? As Swinburne wrote, "Body and spirit are twins: God only knows which is which." During ecstatic sex, or the peak of joy following the agony of childbirth, or even the peaceful pleasure of looking down at a small head nursing at our breast, we all know without question that this is true.

I didn't want the women in Zona Rosa to fear this part of themselves, this source of potential energy. To totally renounce one aspect of ourselves rarely worked to our advantage as writers. What was writing about but the human experience, in all its nuances? Sometimes our self-rejection could turn us away from our best and most honest material. Danielle was my daughters' age, and, unknown to the others in the group, had had a wild rock and roll history, replete with the a priori drug-and-sexual experimentation on New York's Lower East Side in the late '70s. By the time she came into Zona Rosa, she had long since renounced her "sins," and had already made plans to go to graduate school to study religion and literature.

But Danielle was blocked in her writing, she earnestly told me over sushi one night, and it was not until she had told me her full story that I understood why. She had cast out as unacceptable certain of her experiences, experiences so deeply rooted in her consciousness that it was making it impossible for her to write about anything else. Her psyche, her daemon, obviously had its own imperatives, I told her.

True, the other Zona Rosans were momentarily shocked when, at my behest, we read from her honest account of the months she had worked in a foundry by day, done drugs by night, and shared a flat with an ever-changing array of street people. Prior to that moment, they had thought of her as the serious even devout young woman about to go away to theology school at the University of Chicago. But as we listened to her first-person story of an experience very different from our own, we felt our own inner spaces expanding. At the same time, Danielle found that what had been blocking her creativity through the years, this material that she had so long denied, was suddenly rolling away, like a stone.

"To be *any* gender is a drag," said the rock poet Patti Smith, and we southern women sometimes seemed more afflicted by the limitations of gender than most. A southern woman, it seemed, was always in drag. Some, like Courtenay, had come from families rife with a kind of craziness that may have been a form of distorted creativity and had spent a lifetime trying to fulfill middle-class expectations. As Courtenay talked about her young mother and father and the chaos in their home, I thought of Mother, her desire to shake off the discomforts of creativity, of intellect—wearing a new hat, to fit in, to laugh and smoke at the bridge or garden club. "I just want to be *normal!*" she would cry over the phone to Anne or me, her melancholia deepening in the years just before her death.

For this was the idea to which Mother and many of us had subscribed, and that the church, the media, the women's magazines, and talk shows presented as a possibility: if we obeyed certain rules, we would somehow, someday, achieve a balance, a stasis.

Among us in Zona Rosa were women who had been living in the purdah of propriety and those who had not totally obeyed convention, but had disobeyed in conventional ways, perhaps through caches of mad money, or even secret affairs à la Anaïs Nin. (Erica Jong and I had once discussed with chagrin the fact that while we had written openly about our "sins," and had been castigated for it, we were shocked to learn that many women, seemingly far more conventional, had secretly been leading more flamboyant lives.)

In an essay on Nin, Erica Jong explains how Nin had made the choice, from the choices available to her as a woman and a writer, to deceive her husband, Hugh, rather than live a life she felt would be untrue to herself. Jong describes Nin's courage in writing honestly about her experience of girlhood incest and of her recreation (and resolution) of that incest through her seduction as an adult of her own father. Nin wrote of these matters in *Incest*, one of the unexpurgated journals she left for publication after her death ("Perhaps the only married woman to write honestly of her life," Jong states in her essay).

Like Jong, I, too, had once disliked Nin for her duplicity—in the same way some of us sought to tamp the creativity, the energy of women whose choices we didn't approve. While deception of any sort punched my particular buttons, other women didn't like those who didn't fulfill their social roles (the very roles they themselves might be agitating against) or who had adventures they considered outrageous; that is, beyond what they might allow themselves. ("She's *ruined* in this town!" announced a Savannah blue blood of a New York author who had danced topless on the bar of a local pub a couple of years after her move there.) When I took the manuscript for *Sleeping with Soldiers* to a local computer center for transcription, it was returned to me, undone, the next day. "It upset the women so much, they refused to type it," explained the young man who delivered it.

I admitted to the group that I sometimes had to tell myself, as Flaubert had advised, "Be bourgeois in your life so you can be flamboyant in your art." One could argue that the risks I had taken in answer to my daemon had, often as not, led me *away* from my creativity. I had always had that little voice deep inside me—the daemon that always told me what to do—and I obeyed it, even when doing so looked unwise.

I also believed in the Taoist circle in which one can travel toward enlightenment either through asceticism or hedonism. It was because of this belief that I could agree when my friend Helene from Maine, a late-blooming poet who had been with only one man in her life and led an otherwise sheltered existence, said, "I feel like we're just alike—that I've known you all my life." I knew what she meant, for beyond our different choices, we had come full circle to the same place. In fact, during recent years, more and more involved in my teaching and writing, I had almost become the Nun of the Pink Zone.

But I hadn't always been that willing to sit still. "Freedom's just another word for nothing left to lose," Janis Joplin belted time after time on the tape player in my car, making famous the song by Kris Kristofferson. The line had given me courage as I wrote *Fatal Flowers.* Getting into my little red Fiat with my bags packed, driving off into the distance, or boarding a plane (even in bad weather) had always excited me, however nervous I might be about the responsibilities—a speaking engagement, a week of teaching fourth-graders—awaiting me at journey's end. The sense of dislocation provided by new faces, a different place, jarred my creativity in a way I found pleasant. Rather than the desire for stasis, I had a hunger for the shock of the new, a hunger that other writers have evidenced through the many books on their travels.

When my first therapist asked me to draw a man and a woman, I sketched an effeminate-looking man, suitcase in hand; "Off to New York to see friends and lovers" and a woman seated beside a pond much like the one in my backyard, looking reflective, "pregnant with thought." Though I had been writing seriously only a short time, I knew that creativity required self-discipline. But I already knew that for me it was associated with freedom and adventure, and that that sense of freedom was, in turn, tightly wound to my sexuality: when I felt creative, I felt sexual, and vice versa.

The important thing for us as writers was the sense of permission, the free flow of feelings, and the acknowledgment of those feelings. It was imperative that we respect *whatever* choices a woman felt she had to make on her own behalf, whether on behalf of her survival or her integrity of vision.

I thought of my visit to Sarah, a painter whose "outsider art" had been featured on the cover of the literary magazine that sponsored my reading in her area. Sarah, her husband, and three children lived on the edge of a national forest in North Georgia, and even as a friend and I arrived, I was enchanted: the children, like small wild deer, greeted us shyly at the edge of a creek, then skittered around us, showing us a half-finished house, surrounded by chickens, goats, and wildflowers. Inside, as our plump hostess greeted us in an unfashionable flower-printed cotton dress, I was even more thrilled: the house was in utter chaos, of the kind I like best. The living room was obviously Sarah's studio, with paintings in progress including small works being done by the children. Finished and half-finished paintings, books, foreign magazines, and odd artifacts were everywhere. From the corner of my eye, I saw a shirtless boy of about eight tacking a piece of cloth up over the door to his bedroom with a power tool. As we sat on a cluttered couch drinking beer, my eyes drank in our surroundings—the gigantic deep forest through the plate-glass wall, the profusion of art and ideas all around us.

My friend and I bought two of the more affordable paintings. But as we drove away I was amazed when she commented (as though Sarah's outsider art could have existed anywhere, could have been created in the most pristine or conventional rooms), "Can't she keep her house any neater? And what *is* it going to do to those children, growing up like that?"

As she spoke, I thought of Sarah's wild vibrancy hanging on my friend's neat wall—how it would look like a burst of flame in a nunnery, a red embroidery on a plain gray dress. I wondered if she realized what she had asked, and how impossible it was: that Sarah should create her glorious art, and at the same time be just like the rest of us.

< SIX >

Self-Sabotage
Or the Anna Quindlen Syndrome

"We don't see the light by only looking at images of light," I said, nervily paraphrasing Carl Jung. "We see it by looking at the dark." What the great psychologist had actually written was, "One does not become enlightened by imagining figures of light, but by making the darkness conscious." But given my bent for simplifying, I was merely saying it a little differently: "Queens of Denial need not apply."

Since the advent of humanistic psychology, I had been a true believer. I believed in the power of denial and in the spiritual benefits of getting at the truth about oneself. Over the years, I had sought out these truths through forms of psychotherapy ranging from Bioenergetics to Jungian to Gestalt. I had also read widely in the field, especially enjoying the authors who gave their readers a positive view of the possibilities inherent in such truths—Abraham Maslow, Fritz Perls, and more recently, Mihaly Csikszentmihalyi. I found little more exciting than such explorations, and I don't know whether it was a genetically induced optimism that inclined me to such views—as Katharine Hepburn said of herself in a television interview, I have been blessed with a fortunately happy nature—or if it was a desire to find a satisfactory replacement for the negativism of the fundamentalism and dysfunction with which I grew up. But needless to say, this intense interest had informed much of my writing.

As I began to take my teaching more seriously, I found that this psychological approach, this ferreting out of blocks, blank spots, and denials, worked for the Zona Rosans as well, and was in no way contradictory to my view of the group as a support system. Instead, a gentle self-scouring of the psyche by those who were willing left strengths as writers standing out in strong relief; many of my assignments were designed toward this end, resulting in some of the most courageous and profound pieces of writing we shared in the group. Though this approach occasioned remarks—"What *is* this, a writing group or a therapy group?"—most seemed to welcome a method that took them to account as whole human beings, rather than just clichéd seekers after "plot ideas" or "dramatic structure." In Zona Rosa, we were not just "writing hands," once more advised to set ourselves before a typewriter for a certain number of minutes or hours per day, though that works, too. (Flannery O'Connor said she didn't sit down at her desk *because* she had ideas, but in *case* she did.) We were people struggling with problems with our writing—problems that were often highly individual and different from one another's.

Virginia Satir was one of the psychologists who had long interested me. A pioneer in family therapy, she had not maintained a home of her own toward the end of her life, but instead lived out of a suitcase, staying in the homes of clients to whom she administered hands-on family therapy. As I became more involved with the members of Zona Rosa, I found her example an inspiration. To make the caring phone call, to be concerned about what was happening in a student's life, was often just as important if not more so than advice in syntax or editorial marks on a manuscript.

My daughters and I were in the habit of sending one another clippings that we thought might be of interest. This had started when Mother, perhaps too overwhelmed by her depression to speak more seriously of herself, had sent me her latest recipes and the news of her garden in North Carolina. I, in turn, had sent my two daughters, on their own for the first time, my recipes for fried chicken or a thrifty casserole and had been impressed when Laura, then a student at New York University, held a party at her tiny Greenwich Village apartment, serving up her own version of Mother's and my southern fried chicken. (Later, as she surpassed me as a cook, I became the recipient of *her* recipes.)

My study was cluttered with clippings saved for various students, as well as the notes and clippings for my own work, and for family members. The Zona Rosans populated my consciousness; it bubbled at all hours with what seemed to be the key to one's problems with content, another's difficulties with syntax. I loved watching a talented poet or prose writer struggle with her material, finally to win. On the other hand, I hated seeing them go through the discouragement of rejection letters. There seemed to be no limit on the number of psyches my own psyche could entertain. I was like a mother with forty children—forty children who I wanted to see do well.

The ideas came in the same way the ideas for my own poems or prose came. And though I worried at times about them filling my mind too much, they seemed not to conflict with my own work at all; instead, they were just another sprouting of my creativity, confirming my belief that most of us only use a minute part of what we have been given. I would wake in the night with solutions to the Zona Rosans' writing/work problems, just as I woke with ideas for my own writing and life.

One woman, for example, might need to look at the whole, the structure; while another might need attention to significant detail; and yet another to character development and subtext. Always, we dealt with Resistance to Revision. But these were the kinds of problems that were easy to point out. More often, the blocks had to do with life habits and perspective. Early imprints, character, and personality traits inevitably influenced writing habits, giving flesh to my belief that there are no writing blocks, only feeling blocks. The more right-brained, the more clever one was, the more inventive were her means of self-defeat.

As the years went by, I saw over and over the same forms of self-sabotage: Courtenay's Web of Procrastination, Lila's Lack of Affect, Elsa's Denial of Differences, Carolyn's Carelessness, Rebecca's Fear of Living Relatives, Abbie's Excess Activism, Anne's Other Directedness, and Susan's Enslavement to Her Inner Critic. Many blocks appeared to be entrenched, such as Joan's Resistance to Imagery, and Mimi's Need for Recognition (Mimi, near seventy, felt time was running out—would she ever get her due in this world? Yet Joan, in her late eighties, felt she had all she could need, and more). There was Laurel's Lack of Focus (she could have written *three* books as she flitted from one project to another), and the refusal of Cynical Sisters—as I dubbed Gladys and Latrelle—to believe that their subtle, well-wrought prose *mattered.*

(To say that Gladys and Latrelle were sisters was an understatement; rather, they were soulmates, each vibrating to the other's feelings more acutely than one would to a spouse's. During the years they had been in Zona Rosa, they had both lost husbands of many years to cancer—husbands they had both been able to convince to sleep in other rooms. "He was happy about it once I got him a little radio," laughed Gladys. Obviously, no one mattered to them like each other, and their relationship was often the subject of their exquisitely ironic pieces in which, like aging Bobbsey Twins, they quit smoking together, canoed down a water moccasin–infested rural creek, or packed the kids in two cars to drive cross-country— "the southern route, the Mojave Desert in August!" quipped Latrelle—and otherwise explored the mysteries of the universe.)

Whatever was our weakness, it became apparent over time. (Was my own form of self-sabotage fast becoming A Passion for Zona Rosa, or Not Putting My Own Writing First? One of my own flaws was a vulnerability to flattery, and what could be more flattering than feeling I was needed?)

A common mechanism was the Drive to Create the Perfect Workspace. This was an activity one could always veer off into, given moments of discouragement or reluctance, and because we did, many of my students wrote in environments that were far more posh than any I had ever known. In New Orleans, publicist and television personality Rosemary James had shown me around her Bourbon Street offices, complete with ruffled curtains in the elevators, French chaise lounges in the waiting room, and tromp l'oeil flowers and vines hand-painted on the file cabinets. Some of the Zona Rosans worked in spaces that near-rivaled hers.

When some students began doing public readings, there was Appreciation of Applause, or Two Hands Clapping Together Are Enough, after which, failing to notice that they were simply applauding one another, several no longer considered necessary the long hours spent on the minutiae of good writing, let alone the ego blows of sending manuscripts off to strangers (even though I explained time after time that if they wanted to enter the true marketplace, competition with strangers was inevitable: but again, *only after the work was done, and done well*). "Nine times out of ten, I may not hit it. But then, that one time I do," said Marna, a beautiful blond helicopter pilot. It was hard to see her settling for doing less than she could. "You can strike ten out of ten if you're willing to analyze your process, and learn how to do so," I told her, to no avail, a mother talking futilely to her adolescent daughter.

Some veered off into Literary Good Works, substituting planning readings and editing literary magazines for writing themselves. Then there was the long wait for Economic Elysium, that heaven in which one would be freed, either by a long-awaited retirement, winning the lottery and moving to the South of France, or the death of a spouse who had left insurance and a silence in which one could, at last, write. Perhaps most bitter was Paralysis-by-Envy, which, like a spear tipped with curare, shot directly into the heart could—if one did not have the antidote—

bring one's creativity to a rigid halt. A recent offshoot of this was the Anna Quindlen Syndrome, during which one reasoned that if one couldn't be Anna Quindlen, with the perfect career, perfect family, and perfect success, one might as well not write at all. For some, Quindlen had become the kind of Impossible Dream that Martha Stewart had become for homemakers.

Perhaps the most insidious was the Pursuit of the Perfect Lifestyle and its offshoot Perfect Mental Health, as defined by New Age criteria. Unfortunately, many books the Zona Rosans read and raved about—Barbara Sher's *Wishcraft*; Shakti Gawain's *Creative Visualization*; Gabrielle Ricco's *Writing the Natural Way*; Clara Pinkola Estes's *Women Who Run with the Wolves*—contributed, in their own way, to this notion. In *Writing Down the Bones*, Natalie Goldberg suggests that writing has as much to do with attitude as with action, and that all we need do is sit in a cafe or Burger King and write a first draft. According to these works, affirmations are everything. Though fun to read, and initially encouraging, such ideas can be ultimately deceptive, implying that writing is far easier than it is. (In a later book, *The Long Silent Road*, Goldberg emphasizes the mindfulness necessary for good writing.) Martha Sinetar, author of *Do What You Love and the Money Will Follow*, was finally driven to protest that readers often misinterpreted her message: "Do what you *love*—not what you *feel* like!" she declared.

"Would Van Gogh have painted more or better if he had lived in California and belonged to the right support group?" I asked. "After all, he was poor, and his lifestyle wasn't much to speak of. In fact, he probably couldn't have afforded a therapist if he had wanted one. But he got the work done!"

We didn't have to be perfect people, or even healthy people, to write, I told them. All one had to do was look at the drunken and otherwise defective *men* who had written books that were called great! Most of those who have created the great art through the ages have done so under the worst of circumstances, and few had instructional manuals on how to do it.

"Look at it this way—you might eat a Hershey bar the size of a license plate, or even have one too many glasses of wine at night," I said, "but you wouldn't live off them, however soothing."

Many of us had grown up with *Good Housekeeping*, the *Ladies' Home Journal* and "Can This Marriage Be Saved," not to speak of historical and genre romances. It was important to balance such feminine pornography—as I had come to think of the masses of print that tells women what's wrong with us—with works by the great poets, novelists, and essayists, and by looking at and listening to the great works of art, however much we addictively enjoyed the other stuff—and however much unacknowledged nostalgia we might hold within our bodies for contexts in which our roles might seem simpler. (To give perspective, I cited a *Ladies' Home Journal* column from the '50s in which a battered woman was encouraged to have her husband's dinner ready on time and to avoid needless chatter that might irritate him.) "Women Who Don't Read Well Enough" might be another title for them, I suggested. Our brains usually need exercise more than they need salve; the trick was in knowing what was called for at the moment. (The most effective antidote for Paralysis-by-Envy—aside from the humility provided by writing regularly—is exposure to great writing: if envy is merely inverted desire, reading what is good will inspire us, lifting us out of despair.)

I knew that we women, given the earthy realities of our lives, tend to be more practical; at a certain point in our lives, every woman but the most deluded knows (in a way that men rarely know) that the fantasies of romantic love and patriarchy just aren't that realistic. I asked the Zona Rosans to look, for example, at the use of irony in good women's writing, serious fiction and nonfiction (*not* romance or genre novels), as opposed to that in men's.

As Mihaly Csikszentmihalyi says in *The Evolving Self*, flow doesn't come from avoiding complexity, but through integrating it. Or, as Robert Fritz put it in his nuts-and-bolts book, *Creating*, involvement is what people want, not satisfaction, as they imagine. At moments, caught in that divine involvement, I have totally forgotten everything, from a no longer steaming cup of coffee at my elbow to, I'm ashamed to say, my daughter's birthday. Once, forgetting the time of month, I bled all over a very nice chair. On another occasion, absorbed in a manuscript near completion, I went out for a much-needed air-conditioning filter, a 99-cent item, and came back with a $100 collection of pots and pans I didn't need, sold to me by a man in the back of a pickup truck. But the distracted involvement I was experiencing in my writing was worth far more to me than the price of that shoddy aluminum ware.

"Sometimes I feel a big block of resistance as I listen to what you're saying," said Mimi. "I ask myself, 'Do I want to hear this? Can I absorb it?' But the main question is, 'Will I be *able* to do it?'" As far as I was concerned, there were only three positions: entitlement (we shouldn't have to do it); victimization (we can't do it); and empowerment (we can and will do it). Marshall McLuhan, in *The Medium Is the Massage*, spoke of convergers and divergers: convergers zero in on the obstacles; divergers veer around them. Through perseverance, we could leap over impossibilities, going straight to empowerment, or we could get stuck in the mire. So it's true, for example, that women haven't been given their due as artists through the centuries: should we wallow in that fact, or should we go forward, leaping over the odds? (Not that we shouldn't be angry; anger can be a creative energizer, especially for women, who have been taught to keep it tamped.) The great British mystery writer P. D. James worked for years in a bureaucratic office, supporting herself, her children, and her husband, who had been left emotionally disabled by World War I, before she could even begin writing.

Like many complex things, writing, when broken down to its elements, is simple. For every act of self-sabotage, there is a possible counteraction, and I tried to share the ways. For Laurel, I recommended a book on Morita, a Japanese form of therapy in which one plans out one's day and follows that plan, whatever distractions or emotions might arise (given our New Age thrust toward following feelings, this old-fashioned idea, ironically, is radical for some). I suggested to Anne that she not answer the many telephone calls she receives each day from family and friends quite so readily; to let her answering machine accept most of them, and set aside a time each day for returning them. While Anne might not actually be writing, she might be thinking, and that was excuse enough. I asked Courtenay to stop reorganizing her study and sitting up late with her adult son watching old movies; to give up some of the volunteer activities that were a hangover from her garden club days; and to make chapter-by-chapter deadlines for revising and completing a manuscript with pages now numbering over a thousand.

In addition, I gave out a simple list, headed by a quote from Michelangelo: "Lord, grant that I may always desire more than I can accomplish":

SELF-SABOTAGE, OR HOW GOOD WRITERS SHOOT THEMSELVES IN THE FOOT

- *lack of self-discipline*
- *failing to use biological time positively*
- *creating distractions/giving in to them*
- *fragmentation: failing to finish individual pieces of work*
- *failing to set goals that are high enough*
- *not reading well in terms of goals*
- *failing to analyze one's own process and strengths*
- *failing to develop a personal criteria*
- *not honoring one's own unique material*
- *failing to acknowledge the duality within the creative process*

One of the "exorcizes" was to write about the thing you most don't want to write about (or, short of that, to write about *why* you don't want to write about it): we would go into the dark place where the writing comes from. The concept of voluntarily entering into their pain was naturally the one the women were most likely to resist. But I knew that those grains of sand, those irritants, often became a motivating force in my own writing; also that my own intellectual development had been primarily emotional, induced, as likely as not, by an unwelcome discomfort. A week of excruciation often became a week of blessing and epiphany, filling me with the blinding light of new insight. As the novelist Reynolds Price says in his book about his battle with spinal cancer, *A Whole New Life,* he finally came to the place of saying to God of his pain, "Bring it on!" Since the discovery of his illness twelve years before, Price had written more books than in his whole other life. Poet and essayist Nancy Mairs had learned to integrate her crippling multiple sclerosis and her husband George's battle with melanoma into her creativity, writing book after book in which she referred honestly to her struggles. Years before his fame as the protagonist of *My Left Foot,* Christy Brown, one of twenty children in a poor Dublin family, taught himself to type with his toes, and wrote his autobiography, *Down All the Days.* Flannery O'Connor wrote some of her great oft-comic Southern Gothic fiction while lying in a Milledgeville hospital bed dying of lupus. Apparently, virtually no external situation need interfere with the ground from which art springs. As Jungian scholar Marion Woodman writes in *The Eternal Feminine,* even incest, if resolved within the psyche, can result in creative energy. When *Fatal Flowers* was published, one reviewer wrote, "It's hard to see how anyone could have lived through this." Instead, my experiences had become a work through which healing had taken place.

Some forms of self-sabotage were more complex and subtle, with an almost irresistible imperative of their own. This was especially true if they represented something we felt we had to do in order to live with ourselves and our idea of ourselves. Not amenable to mere changes in habit or attitude, they had a visceral reality. ("But that's your *material!*" a friend said once when I complained of what had seemed a dozen years of relentless family crisis.) "Always live with death at your left shoulder," Carlos Castenada wrote in a credo I took as my own. For me, that meant doing in life that which I could look back on from my deathbed without regret. And when such choices come up, the best we can do is integrate them, making them part of our creativity.

Indeed, the most unavoidable of these have to with family ties and responsibilities. Paul Bowles, author of the rediscovered *The Sheltering Sky*, spent years and sold valuables caring for his wife, the writer Jane Bowles, after she suffered multiple strokes. Tennessee Williams provided for his fragile sister Rose even after he was in none-too-good shape himself. The list of writers who have made such familial sacrifices is endless.

In my own life, these were the kinds I had come to know best: when a conflict arose between my desire to work and to please my husband and children (or worse, *save* a child), the division could feel as though I was literally being torn apart. But family almost always won—no contest. When my daughter needed me in Savannah, my husband, Zane, wanted me in Germany (where he was stationed in the army), and my editor was awaiting the final draft of a manuscript in New York, I tended my daughter as best I could, revising the manuscript between visits to doctors or in their waiting rooms; then made reservations on a flight to Hamburg. The last days before the trip were spent racing back and forth between the treatment center into which I'd finally gotten her and my desk; I shipped off the novel the very morning of my departure. Yet afterward, I was shaking: I had typed the final paragraphs with my daughter lying on my bed six feet away, writhing in opiate withdrawal. When I arrived on European soil, I immediately fell apart in Zane's arms, disappointing his hope that I had come to comfort *him* after his experiences in the gulf war.

One evening after our Zona Rosa meeting, Courtenay and I were on our way to our favorite Cantonese restaurant when she told me that she was taking a full-time job, teaching eighth grade at a rural school fifty miles from her home. Like a mother whose child has just said she's dropping out of college, I screamed in protest. I thought of Courtenay as my southern Virginia Woolf: she was four-fifths through the novel she had been working on for five years, and I could see the whole thing going up in smoke.

But as Courtenay explained further, I realized why, being the person she was, she had to do this thing. She had a chronically ill adult child, medical bills had been heavy, and she wanted to show her husband her goodwill in sharing the burden. Though the job later went against her in her divorce proceedings, her lawyer spouse attempting to prove thereby that she could make her own living and that he needn't pay so much alimony (this, despite the fact that the sick child would remain with her), Courtenay transformed this situation into one in which she demonstrated a great creativity, as she did with all the challenges with which she had been met in life. First, she related to the deprived children she taught in an innovative way, adding a great deal of culture and warmth to their lives; then she ended up integrating this new material into the conclusion of her novel, giving it a dimension and sense of closure it would not otherwise have had.

Yes, however we did it, and with whatever pleasure, it was going to be *hard*, I admitted to the Zona Rosans. To become good writers, we would need every ounce of insight and stamina we had.

Or, as Gail Godwin said when asked why her female protagonists in her novels of southern family life were so forbearing and long-suffering, "That's what we call *character*, honey!"

Obsessive Love, or How I Do It

When I was five, a black snake wound around Mother's ankle as she stood talking to neighbors on the grassy strip beside the sidewalk outside our little house in Atlanta. She screamed and Daddy came out and killed it. The picture of this scene is still vivid in my mind, despite the fact that it didn't happen: there were no snakes on that fairly busy suburban street, and no one else remembers such a thing.

While that picture is not a literal one, it expresses a larger truth. For Mother, still girlish and trusting, was indeed about to be done in by sinuous and insidious powers against which she would be helpless, and Daddy, rapidly sinking in his own quicksand, would be unable to save himself, much less her. The scene, for me, is symbolic of what writing can be: an expression of an unconscious truth, a dream from deep within the layers of consciousnessness. Ferreting out those hidden crevices, those mysterious interstices—those only half-true but oh-so-true images—was part of the excitement. "Beauty is truth, truth beauty—that's all we know on earth, and all we need to know," wrote John Keats. Carl Jung put it more succinctly: "Sanity is facing reality." The truth—not the literal, but the emotional truth—had come to mean everything to me.

"Set the goal, and the means will come," a therapist friend said to me. And once I had committed myself to searching out that truth through the medium of writing, I began, floundering at first, to find a way.

One of the first questions aspiring writers ask is how and when do you write? Where do you sit, what kind of pencils do you use, do you write by hand or on a computer? And so on, as though the mechanics might give a hint of the magic of the real process. "No, do tell us about those things—it helps to know how others do it," Mimi said when I protested that such matters are mundane, boring. There may be merit in her request, because the rhythms of the process are often a part of setting it in motion.

E. M. Forster's imperative, "Only connect," may be the most profound advice ever given to writers. I have long held to the old-fashioned notion, unpopular among some experimentalists, of writing as primarily a form of communication. ("Tell the reader everything they need to know. But never tell them more than they need to know," I would say to the Zona Rosans in an effort to get them to keep their readers in mind.)

But for me "only connect" also means writing in the gap, filling in between the dots, as I did in the drawing books I had as a child. What could be called the tedium of composition—dealing with problems of syntax and structure; searching out the perfect image, the right word; devising rhythms, or working out meter and form—becomes purposeful, a mission. Poetry, especially, is a kind of stitching and restitching of the truth, a form of needlepoint that soothes me, the shame of dysfunction or some other pain disappearing into the white spaces between those small black squiggles we call language.

It is as though there is a jumble of words, images, ideas rattling like dice in my brain, and if I throw them down on the page often enough, their meaning finally comes clear—as charged, neat, and linear as a pair of sixes. Working with rough phrases and ideas, feeling the unshapely become shapely (the raw edges turn inward, a perfect Home Ec seam) is a visceral pleasure, as satisfying as a cup of hot cocoa on a winter day. As the tumble of words align themselves to form meaning, I feel the healing begin.

Indeed, in my alter ego, I have sometimes imagined myself as a maiden lady, living off tinned sardines in the attic bower I share with my cats; rather than the woman with a lifestyle complicated by children, husbands, friends, responsibilities. It was inside the maiden lady that I went when I wrote, retreating into a welcome clarity, simplicity, and control.

Once, as an artist friend and I sat looking at a photograph of a painting by the Swiss-American painter Mark Tobey, I commented that Tobey's uniform drops of white paint on white canvas were less interesting than my friend's more varied drops of black, white, and sienna on a white background. "No," my friend protested, "his is by far the greater painting—he has achieved perfect simplicity!" Out of his words developed an image that I use as a guide for the finished work: that is, of a cellophane or transparency; something that was once murky, unfocused, becomes crystal clear.

These are processes I have learned through the years to trust. Too often, the Zona Rosans were turned off when their first, inevitably rough drafts didn't match the smooth stanzas or paragraphs from their favorite works, or even those resonating in their heads. To encourage them, I sometimes would drag down from my attic some of the fumbling drafts from which virtually everything I've ever published has emerged. I consider the right to fumble—to make mistakes, to write awkwardly—an inalienable one as a writer. For it is only out of this kind of permission that the finished work can finally flow, at last falling into place as effortlessly as those dice.

"You have a language for it, know how to talk about it," a college student in Massachusetts said, amazed as I discussed with her the more subtle problems of her story in progress. She didn't know how long it had taken me to develop that language, and through what trial and error. How through the years I had exhorted and instructed myself in the same way I now exhorted her and her classmates, and, back in Savannah, the Zona Rosans. The little tricks I shared with them were merely the tricks I had come up with to help myself along the way.

For every writer's craft is a homely one, devised by trial and error to suit one's inclinations, limitations, and strengths. M.F.A.s in creative writing aside, we all struggle with writing in our own way. I remember James Dickey's comment that he had to balance out the mental with the physical as he worked, whether by chewing a pencil or drinking a cup of coffee. I think of John Irving writing at his dining room table amid kids and family, Pat Conroy's 1,400 pages of manuscript written by hand, and John Berendt's meticulously kept loose-leaf notebooks, paragraphs written and rewritten. For me, it has often been a simple curiosity—a drive to observe, to listen, and above all, *record.*

I recall the notebooks I've kept over the years: first in my efforts to teach myself how to write, then as repositories and greenhouses for ideas. These hundreds of composition book-journals are where the germ of an idea first appears and then develops amid the chaos of other materials—recorded dreams, bits of overheard dialogue, images that resonated for me, whether I knew why or not; jottings on movies, books, and television programs; struggles (many struggles!) with personal problems (and *drawings* of personal problems, because I had learned that making pictures of my conflicts, however rudimentary, was an aid toward resolving them); even my efforts to budget my money. Fortunately, my Savannah flat had an attic, which had long been filled with the notebooks, as was Zane's gift to me of a fireproof file cabinet so heavy it couldn't be brought up the stairs.

("Listen to this!" Leila, my twenty-one-year-old assistant, exclaimed when I sent her up into the attic and she came down, carrying one of my journals from 1971. "After Ben and I made love, I was no longer interested in going to the Women's Liberation meeting. . . ." Little did I realize when I wrote those words that my experiences two decades before would have meaning to a young woman of the '90s, in the throes of her own conflicts.)

Today, after thirty years of writing, the notebooks have evolved into a system in which one notebook is reserved for the personal stuff; the front page also lists my current writing projects, however far into the future they advance, usually at least five years, plus my personal goals and desires, such as "learn French," "live six months in another country," "pay off Master-Card," or "resolve issues with the kids." These goals, too, may extend long into the future, but I include them because I have found that those I put into writing have more likelihood of materializing: I write in this notebook at any time, but habitually write in it upon waking, before dreams with their delicious images and wild but meaningful stories dissolve like cotton candy. I will suspend this rule if I wake with something else on my mind, something that belongs directly in a manuscript.

Three other ongoing notebooks are respectively for spontaneous notes on writing ideas in general, first drafts of poems or poems in progress, and notes for my current prose project. The two with various notes are titled at the top of each page to show the poem or potential writing project to which the page belongs; I later tear these pages out and place them in the proper file folders, until the folders have fattened enough to form a substantial basis for a piece of writing.

(Not all notes become part of a finished work: the choice of ideas from among the many is another of my challenges as a writer. But this note-keeping system reveals to me how ideas I may previously have considered unrelated may indeed be part of the same project. Unity is everything in art, and the greatest challenge may be bringing together previously unrelated ideas— "making order out of chaos," in Wallace Stevens's words—then contriving that they live peaceably, wild animals within one fenced garden, or at the very least like the ingredients in one of those *New York Times Magazine* recipes that contain such disparate ingredients as apricot jam and jalapeno peppers.)

It is through my journals that I have kept in touch with and developed the images of my life—images that evolve out of my personal myths. For a long time when I was younger, the image of Jesus, lifting me in his arms on a white cloud, was one I used to relieve my pain. A bit later, the image of a round-faced china doll, fat tears rolling down her cheeks, was one I hung on my bulletin board over my desk, along with my eight-year-old daughter Darcy's drawing of me sitting hunched over my manual Royal, hair and eyes wild. More recently, Danielle, a student of world religions, described to me the origins of the Sacred Heart of Mary, how the chakra that parallels the genitals moves up into Her heart as the source of empathy, and I knew that this, too, was a picture that resonated for me. The journals give me a way to track such images.

Later, the images changed, coming to me more and more often through the medium of dreams. I began to dream of rooms—

rooms of unusual shapes, often empty of furnishings or with floors that sloped, but always high-ceilinged and spacious. As I gained control over my dreams by recording them, I found I could even, at times, go back to these same rooms: one was an apartment in a cave carved into the side of a mountain; another was a second-floor flat that went on and on, room after endless room, more space than I have ever had in my life. But there was one common denominator: in all these rooms, I was both free and safe (and, except for my daughters as children, often alone in them): the rooms were my creativity, the very feeling my creativity gave me.

Recently I recorded another room-related image: on a drive through Milledgeville not long after a tornado, Zane and I saw two houses on a slope off the road, their roofs neatly blown off, leaving the interior rooms, complete with furnishings, as perfectly revealed as dollhouses. At the moment, I didn't know what the image meant to me, only that it meant *something*, something that, if I preserved it, I would discover at a later date. The clue was the heightened feeling I experienced around the image, even if I did not yet know what it was a metaphor *for*. Gradually, true to my trust in them, the images began to take shape as a series of poems, *Rooms, or the Comfort of Enclosed Spaces*.

Food Dreams is another set of recurrent images in which I dream whole meals, often ones that Mother, now dead almost twenty years, prepared for Anne and me as children. Recipes I had forgotten—Spanish pork chops simmered with onions and green peppers in red rice, sour cherries caught in red Jell-O along with stuffed olives and pecan halves—emerge in these dreams as though dictated. Recently, I dreamed a meal of stuffed pork chops (for which Mother had the butcher cut little pockets in the sides of the chops), apple fritters, and black-eyed pea croquettes. I had never heard of the last dish, but at the supermarket the next day, thumbing through a woman's magazine in the checkout line, I came across the near-exact recipe I had dreamed, contributed by an acquaintance, Elizabeth Terry, the cook and owner at Elizabeth's on 37th, a renowned restaurant a mile from my apartment. The experience confirmed to me the magic of the unconscious.

I always prepare these dream meals as soon as possible. Over the years I have learned that acting out, whether through writing, painting a picture, or cooking, gives me a visceral satisfaction, a certain creative jolt. When the dreams are made up of recipes handed down to me by Mother, I also feel that by honoring her memory, she is again with me, puttering in the kitchen. Despite our family's miseries, those had been happy moments— Mother, Anne, and I in the kitchen, laughing and talking as we prepared the evening meal, a ritual that Mother, no matter how out of sync with our lives, always managed to keep intact.

I find that recording my dreams continues to result in miracles of enhanced synchronicity. I had long believed that time is multilinear—it is only the limitations of our awareness that keep us from realizing that everything is really happening at once. As a writer, I had always found that synchronicity—the phenomenon in which the universe seems magically to supply whatever imagery one needs, especially as a work hurtles toward completion—was an important part of the process. But now I find synchroncity bombarding me from every angle. While teaching among the mesas and buttes of Wyoming, I suddenly awoke to images of the swamps of southern Florida where I had not been in fifteen years, and a poem seemed almost to flow from my ballpoint. "This guy called you three times this week, asking if you've fallen out of any canoes lately," Zane said on the phone, and suddenly I remembered my oil-rigger boyfriend Bobby, with whom I had once canoed those swamps. At other times, an uncanny premonition was as scary as it was amazing: when my younger daughter called to tell me of the sudden death of her infant son, I realized I had bought the black shoes she would wear at the funeral the day before in her size instead of my own.

On the morning when I told Zane of my dream of a tidal wave, whirling away one of my daughters, as well as my niece and nephew, he came into the bedroom carrying coffee to say, "I hate to tell you this, but on the weather channel this morning, it looks like Laura"—my older daughter who was teaching at medical college in the Caribbean—"is in the center of Hurricane Luis."

Despite such messages, the journals also serve as a safety valve for my sanity. For my whole life, I have dealt with a recurrent inner pain, a sensitivity to experience that often kept me awake at night, burning in the hellfires of my own emotions (doubtless a remnant passed down to me from Mother's more severe depression—a sensitivity I undoubtedly have passed on to my own young). It was not a condition I would wish on anyone, but I sensed that it was also a part of my strength, my creativity: to this day, I can't say which is the chicken or the egg. In such moments of desperation or despair, I still prayed to the God and Jesus of my childhood. I also had a bit of the dazzling if uncomfortable craziness that I suspect is part of the makeup of many creative people. Listening to a lecture by Dr. Fred Frese describing the moments leading up to his first psychotic breakdown, I recognized my own thought processes—my obsession with making connections, with finding patterns in what others might find meaningless. I had merely stopped short of the kind of moment Dr. Frese experienced when, obsessed with the number three and the Holy Trinity, he found himself kneeling at an altar before a packed church while barking like a dog. Over the years I had had the good fortune never to go quite over that edge. Also, I had found one sure cure for the circular thoughts that kept me from sleep: simply get up and write the thoughts in my journals, thus naming and placing them outside myself.

All four notebooks sit in a briefcase beside my bed, ready to be written in at any moment or be carried away immediately on any trip. (Like many writers, my yearning for travel, dislocation, is near-constant. Is it the act of sitting down to write that makes me want to be elsewhere, or is it the act of writing that excites me, the internal journey reminding me of the thrill of external ones?)

Like everyone, I lose confidence at times, so I keep two other flower-fabric-covered notebooks on my bed table—one of quotes from every possible source that never fail to refresh and inspire me, and another for "strokes," those compliments and bits of positive reinforcement that we forget all too easily, especially when we need most to remember them, that we *have* been a success, sometime, someplace, at some moment in our lives.

Another little mental trick I use to keep going when discouraged is telling myself that if this is not working out any better in a year, I'll give it up and go on to a new life, a different field altogether. Yet at the same time that I'm employing this trick, I know that the whole notion is a fantasy, and that by the time the year is up, I'll be totally involved in my writing again, my period of discouragement forgotten.

While writing *Fatal Flowers*, I was living in a furnished railroad flat in Savannah, without a telephone or a television set (admittedly, I did have what meant more to me—a raspberry carpet, a four-poster bed, a mirrored French armoir). I had sold my house in Atlanta and didn't have savings, depending on occasional stints in Poetry in the Schools to provide a minimal income. Yet most of the time, with my upright Royal perched on a wooden table in the living room, my hundreds of notes on yellow second sheets tacked to the rose-printed wallpaper, I was exquisitely happy.

But one day midway through the manuscript, I had an anxiety attack: What did I think I was doing? Who did I think I was to believe I could finish this book? Why didn't I just get a nine-to-five job, like everyone else? Awash in a feeling of nausea, I walked down the oak-lined street, looking down between the cracks in the bricked sidewalk at the moss, which seemed to be growing far more effortlessly than my manuscript was. Suddenly, a new thought came to me: "Oh, *no!*" I said aloud to myself. "Then I would have to work on it at *night!*" In that moment, I realized how committed I was—because of that commitment, I would finish the book *no matter what.* It was also my first inkling of how little control I had over my daemon.

I'm not the kind of woman who dreams of diamonds and furs (although I do require more affordable luxuries, such as pretty sheets and fresh flowers). Instead, I long for mauve file cabinets, big work tables, and walls and walls of bookshelves and the high-ceilinged spaces to hold them. My idea of ecstasy is a true library, with all my books indexed and alphabetized, and one of those little rolling wooden ladders. (When it comes to the actual choice of how to use my time, I always choose to write, rather than to arrange the books, or to look for a space big enough to hold them; in a bookstore, I'm as likely to buy something to write *with*—new felt tip pens, or a reference text—as something already written.)

My wish for a notebook computer, a dream ever since I first saw a PowerBook in a shop window in Amsterdam, was one of the desires written in journal number one. In my fantasy, I saw myself with it perched on my lap on a jet plane, or better yet, as I lounged in bed or on the couch—*languid* (one of my favorite words)—as lazy and relaxed as a cat. (Visualizing myself sitting before my word processor, completely relaxed as I write, is another of my little preparatory tricks.) And here, several years after adding it to my list of "desires," the PowerBook sits atop my thighs, amid the flowered bedsheets, just as wonderful as I imagined it.

But during those years before such a thing existed, before I had ever dreamed of such luxury, the old upright Royal, then two manual Hermes typewriters, which literally fell apart just as a book was completed (one with the carriage held in place by a rubber band, as I hacked out the final pages); then a huge and bulky but at the time magical Kaypro computer, all served me like a trusty old Ford. Yellow second sheets, carbon paper, Wite-out, glue-on correction strips, cut-and-paste—I've used quantities of these throughout the years (here again, that obsessiveness, the willingness to do whatever it takes). But all a writer really needs, once his or her vision is established, is any writing tool, as was proved by Jean Genet, writing on toilet tissue or brown paper in prison, or throughout the centuries, by those who dipped nubbed pens into messy bottles of ink.

I've found that what I do the night before, just before sleep, effects my writing in the morning. A depressing made-for-television movie or an interpretive news show, or even just the stridency of voices from the television set, will spoil the whole, affecting the next day. It's the time for a good movie on video, for reading a poem or two, for devouring a good novel *slowly*, like the last pieces in a box of Godiva chocolates, or even for perusing a passage from a meditation book. I may also look over my list of long and short writing intentions, or ask a question of my unconscious, hoping to be answered during the magic of sleep. I reserve fast-forwarding through book reviews and magazines for mealtimes; gauging my mood, I save the kind of reading that requires the least attention for a time of day when I'm open to distraction. (Indeed, I find such materials especially amenable on tape, for listening while one is already doing something physical, like walking or driving.) An interviewer described James Dickey's house as being practically unmaneuverable due to the stacks of books that filled every room, and he is not alone. Writers, strangely, never seem to tire of print; for most, reading is a favorite activity, no matter how long they've been at it during the day.

I save the best times of day, morning, for the serious work on a manuscript in progress. "What fresh hell is this?" Dorothy Parker responded each time she answered her phone. Like her, I hate the thing. Since I have to use one, I set hours when I will answer and hours when I will not, voice mail taking care of the rest. During certain hours, I also write letters, read manuscripts, plan my teaching, and even pay bills.

About once a week, I cop out of the whole thing. Secreting french fries, a McDonald's Quarter Pounder with Cheese in my purse, I sit in the back of darkened movie theaters once or twice a week at the luxurious hour of one in the afternoon (researching screenplays I might write, I tell myself).

I am also a true believer in a few glasses of wine and the suspension of disbelief that follows. Since writing is such a head trip, the sensual pleasures are mini-vacations. Sometimes I like to go to places where live music or a jukebox is playing, and gangs of people who may never have read the *New York Times Book Review* appear to be thinking of nothing more than whether they should have another scotch. More often, I cook in the evening, go out to dinner, or call or see friends. (Even ironing, which I hated as a young housewife, is relaxing to me as a writer. And driving the car from Savannah to Atlanta, a five-hour trip, is the perfect time for the mind to drift.)

And there were those more dissipated years, spent going out with men I barely recall; after those evenings, I mostly remember hangovers from which I had to recover for a half a day before doing any work at all. (The most vivid in my memory is one in which I hung over the toilet bowl, imagining myself spewing forth a hundred tiny men, symbols of all those with whom I had slept.) And since it is impossible to think of much of anything while one feels that bad physically, perhaps those hangovers did constitute a kind of release.

Fortunately, after a while, I found better ways to distance myself from my obsession. I've finally learned what I *don't* like to do, and I try to avoid doing those things at all.

I do like to walk or otherwise get out of doors, even if it's just a brief trek to the grocery store, where I chat with the clerks from over the years. I don't mind painting a table, or some other homely chore, but always these little vacations exist, however pleasurably, to prepare me for the main thing in my life.

The truth is that there have been many, *many* periods during my life when these conditions have not been, or could not have been met—when I've been teaching full-time, leaving my children at home with notes and menus tacked on the side of the refrigerator; when I was exhausted at night, or was sitting, hour after hour, in hospital waiting rooms. Indeed, there have been huge *chunks* of life taken out, times when I had to write in any way or any moments in which I could. Times when only books could get me through—I found that no matter how bad things were, a good book, a chocolate bar, a shot of Black Jack before bed, could help me survive. As Oscar Wilde wrote, "It is only through the senses that the soul can be cured," and at such times, the pleasures of the flesh have been my salvation.

All these other matters are just habits of being, like the fact that I wash my lingerie out every night before I go to bed, and sometimes carry a gun. The life of the artist *is* as wonderful as I imagined it to be as a child, but not exactly in the way that I thought: it is *often* externally boring, but is *always* internally exciting (in fact, I now recognize the boredom as an integral part of the rhythm of creativity: the tide going out in order to crash back in). Indeed, for most artists, a stable inner peace is a barely possible dream, given our varying degrees of mania. However relaxed I may feel, however successful I've been in simplifying my life, there is always that underlying tension; I know the night will soon come when I will lie awake, my mind churning with ideas insisting that I turn on the light, write them down. And out of this many ideas, one will grow like a pregnancy, agitating its way through my psyche in its demand to be born.

Indeed, there is only one certainty for me (sometimes to the chagrin of family and friends): my life revolves around writing. I'm either thinking about writing, yearning to write, preparing to write, resting from writing, or actually writing. (And though my current writing project always informs my reality, a finished piece quickly becomes as foreign, as separate to me, as a seashell washed up on the beach. "'Watching ducks on deep water, seeing them upright in white casings, I think them balancing on magic balls,'" my husband Paul quoted one evening as we walked with the children beside a lake studded with the white birds. "That's beautiful—who wrote it?" I asked. "*You* did," he laughed, incredulous.) I've heard many writers moan over the time *not* spent on their writing; I've never heard one complain that she or he had written too much. When writers talk about writing, it's not mere shoptalk—it's *life*; everything else is just polite conversation.

These are merely the means, however makeshift, I have evolved for myself, I told Mimi and the others in Zona Rosa, and though we can learn from one another, each of us as writers can and will come up with our own ways. I have learned as much from failure as from success. If anyone needs further proof that I wasn't a natural, she need only flip through the pages of my five-year diary, peruse the stacks and stacks of notebooks and first drafts filling my rooms and my file cabinets, or plunge her hand into that fat box of rejection slips kept as a reminder of my efforts in my attic.

"Thinking is better than knowing," said Goethe, "but looking is better than either." Over the years, I had come to appreciate this truth. Otherwise, if I could synthesize what I have learned, it would simply be titled *The Mystery:*

1. Of the gift of the five senses (and the food, air, and water that nurture them); of all things sensual, from food to flowers to sex.
2. Especially of COLORS.
3. Of DREAMS, and other mysteries: the upward spiral of the human spirit; of the number 3 and the number 5.
4. And of the greatest mystery of all, other people: of loving, rather than being loved; of appreciating, of caring.

5. Of always, in so far as it's possible, being simple and centered.
6. And of staying, at the same time, dislocated enough to see with fresh eyes.
7. Of FOCUSING, of allowing myself total obsession with PROCESS, which for me is creative writing.
8. And of being ever mindful of, and grateful for, the above.

< SEVEN >

I Was a Doorway,
Filled with Azaleas & Oleander

Sam had given me a Tibetan fungus, brought over from monks, he told me, to make a special daily yogurt drink that purportedly had healing powers. Soaked in milk, the fungus doubled until I too was giving it away. Over the past fifteen years, Zona Rosa, like that fungus, had thrived and expanded, becoming almost as organic to my life as breathing.

When the first group outgrew my living room, a second was started, then a third in Atlanta, five hours away by car. When men persistently asked to join the groups, a mixed-sex group was added, giving me the chance, through teaching men, to deal with some deep-seated lifelong problems with them—to learn to relate to them at times authoritatively, to tenderly receive their dreams, and, perhaps for the first time, to do these things without relating to them as sex objects, breadwinners, or political enemies. The younger among them wanted to avoid becoming their fathers. The majority were those for whom being macho, breadwinners, or conservative hadn't been enough—like the women, they had come to a point when they wanted more from life.

There was one other common denominator among the men who came to Zona Rosa and stayed: they were men who, no matter how masculine they might appear to be, found it acceptable to be part of a group led by a woman. They were also men

173

who found acceptable our nonlinear, non-goal-oriented approach, who could write in the Pink Zone and still feel comfortable.

(Indeed, simply knowing these men existed did much to en-hance my own feelings about the other gender. Through the years I had been exposed to so many "great writers" who felt they had to compensate for their creativity with macho, and often drunken, behavior that I had developed a theory: men, espe-cially southern men, subconsciously perceive the truth—that artistic creation is essentially a feminine activity—and bend over backward in their machoism, even obnoxiousness, in order to compensate.)

Lou had raced stock cars, and at fifty, built racing car engines out of a shop in his house. As a young, blue-collar James Dean type, he had sped about on his motorcycle, dreaming of moving to Portugal, but after Vietnam, he had settled down in the sub-urbs with a pretty nurse. Sig had been interned in Switzerland after his plane was shot down near the German-Swiss border during World War II; during his years as a husband, father, and businessman, he had put his yearnings to tell the story of his ad-ventures on the back burner. Walt, a youthful forty, had been married four times, had wrestled with drug and alcohol prob-lems, and had long experienced the conflict between his impera-tive creative drive and the goals set for him by his affluent New England family; as a plump boy, he had been sent repeatedly to sports camps in an attempt to help him conquer a world in which he had little interest, and for which he felt little aptitude. Sam, five times wed, had lived in the Caribbean for thirty years, during which he made and lost several fortunes; at sixty, he moved to the South Carolina coast, broke but determined to spend the rest of his life writing. He had been raised in a heady New York environment by a psychiatrist-aunt who was an asso-ciate of Karen Horney, one of the pioneers of psychoanalysis, but still, for a lifetime he had lacked the confidence he would be able to fulfill his goal.

This was only some of the variety among the groups. We have

had among us two women helicopter pilots, a special events planner for the Kennedy Center, a stockbroker, a retired army colonel, a city budget director, the owner of a fabric shop, a supermarket shelver, several sales clerks and visual artists, as well as students, college professors, and journalists (who, it turned out, had the hardest time with creative writing of anyone in the groups, accustomed as they were to work fenced off by journalistic requirements and then immediate publication). Yet all were bound by the desire to be known, to express themselves in language.

While there were rough spots along the way—hurt feelings, personalities that didn't jibe, and people who cared more about getting published or having their egos stroked than about actually writing well—I found I didn't have to worry about who I let into the group. Those who thrived on negativity, believing that anything that didn't feel bad couldn't be good, soon left (were they secretly looking for excuses *not* to write, I wondered?), as did the ones who were disappointed that it couldn't be done overnight. There were those who were put off by my very ordinariness—how could they have anything to learn from anyone who didn't fulfill their notion of the Great Writer? Sometimes, newcomers were intimidated by the quality of the work of the other members, until I explained that everyone there had once been a novice, too. Then there were those who, still clinging to an ethereal notion of art and artists, were shocked by the frankness in the group.

But after many fumbling missteps, I began to notice that something about Zona Rosa was working—the members were resolving problems in writing (and in life), having breakthroughs in content and form, finding their own voices and métiers, often exceeding their own hopes as writers, and ending up with publishable (and increasingly often, published) works.

Everywhere I went, I met writers and potential guests. I met Marcie Telander, a visiting screenwriter from Crested Butte, as she sat beside me in a shampoo chair in the beauty salon. Hearing me mention my stay at the tiny Virginian Hotel in Medicine

Bow, Wyoming (population 450), back during my poet-in-the-school days, she exclaimed, "You stayed there, *too!*" John Berendt and I chatted about Hitler's flatware at a dinner party given by Jim Williams, the subject of Berendt's not-yet-started *Midnight in the Garden of Good and Evil*. Pat Conroy was so beloved as a guest that we named him our first honorary male member. And long before she wrote *Rich in Love*, Josephine Humphries came to read to us from her first novel, *Dreams of Sleep*. Indeed, the serendipity that seemed as though by magic to bless Zona Rosa was as lush as the azalea and wisteria that blazed outside my window in Savannah each spring. Through the years, well-known and soon-to-be well-known authors visited Zona Rosa to read from their books, letting us see that they were just people like us. And even better, perhaps, was when a Zona Rosan from one group shared his or her work with another group.

Now more than fifteen years have gone by, and literally hundreds of people have passed through Zona Rosa. Some members have considered the healing they found through their writing to be reason enough. For most, the goal was not to change their lives, but to become writers. Yet lives were sometimes changed incidentally in the process. We had watched the more personal changes take place—romances begun and ended, smoking or drinking stopped or taken up, not to speak of the family deaths and illnesses. We listened as Courtenay, former garden club member and college beauty queen, struggled through an initial stiffness in her writing to get to the authentic rage that lay beneath it; we sat at sober attention, some of us understanding alcoholism for the first time, while Delta read a brutal scene in which she crawled naked across her kitchen floor, looking for any kind of booze during the last of her drinking days. A number of us were in 12-step programs or in long-term therapy. When Prozac came on the scene, its merits and drawbacks were debated; about a quarter of the group, it turned out one day, were on it.

Zona Rosans also affected the community: Rebecca, Lou,

and Robert started the *Savannah Literary Journal* and a reading series; local alternative papers were filled with works by people in the groups. (Frederick Beil, of Beil Publishing, a small elite house that had moved to Savannah from New York, commented to me that the best pieces always turned out to be by people from Zona Rosa.) Will and his wife, Ruth, began a small press (I felt doubly honored when, as their first publication, they reprinted my first collection of poems, *A Sexual Tour of the Deep South*).

Despite her pacemaker and bad health, Jane Ann, perched on a stool because of her height, became a favorite poet at the open mike readings. Evelyn's review in the *Savannah News-Press* of James Dickey's novel, *Anilam*, was so esoteric that few could understand it. Onetha, still the city clerk of Hinesville, had become a regional Erma Bombeck with a large following, her humorous, down-to-earth columns appearing in three local newspapers. Mimi appeared on *Donahue* on the subject of older women, younger men, looking glamorous while satisfying her bent for the limelight. Melinda also appeared on national television, and was interviewed by the *Savannah News-Press* regarding her views on the Holocaust.

Laurel and Jana published essays in a national anthology on sexual harassment, and Laurel took the train to Washington, her toddler daughter in tow, to read with a group of contributors. Jana had hated Savannah's racism and the good ol' boy mentality, but when she moved back to Washington she missed the group so much that she flew back every other month "for my Zona Rosa fix." Danielle decided to put off graduate school for another year to stay in Savannah, attend the group, and get a headstart on her novel.

Over the years, the women helped me select titles for my books and decide which producer to go with for a movie option. ("This one has the more trustworthy handwriting," said Pat, the nurse-therapist. "The other one looks like a sociopath.") We visited Ruby in the hospital; after her death, it was hard for a while for anyone to sit in the wicker chair that had been hers. We heard the poems and memoirs Joan had written in the group read at an event honoring her as Professor Emeritus at Savannah State College. Aside from her image as a fashion plate, Joan's one weakness was sweets: a few years later, we celebrated her ninetieth birthday with a cake Onetha had heavily iced with sugar flowers, each reading aloud a tribute to her. A year after that, near tears, I spoke at her funeral. The day before she died at a Savannah hospice, her friend Thelma reported, Joan had demanded a lipstick and Lancôme face cream in order to ready herself to receive a last visit from the aging beau who had traveled from Charleston to see her.

Susan got a New York agent for her second novel, and we all breathed a sigh of relief at the deserved success that was surely now in sight. Latrelle broke down and published her exquisite piece on quitting smoking, and we toasted her breakthrough. In fact, we were having so many successes that champagne bottles being uncorked was becoming the sound of our soirees. Gladys's play was given a professional reading by the Southeastern Playwrights Project in Savannah, and again in Atlanta; we were impressed by the ease with which she parried questions during the question-and-answer period.

We listened to Lenore talk about her pleasure at sitting in the shopping center, watching the people, or playing her guitar and singing her song lyrics in her small, uneven voice. We voted Abbie down when she didn't want Lenore to sing at a planned reading, saying her voice wasn't good enough, and that her performance would be a disservice to blacks.

We went to a party for Lenore, celebrating her graduation from technical school (institutional cooking), at her apartment in a ghetto area, where she lived on disability. Lenore died, too, but her face, between a royal blue mortarboard and gown, still shines from the side of my refrigerator, which has become a virtual gallery of photos from Zona Rosa, held in place by magnets shaped like chocolates or shoes.

Stories from Zona Rosa

"Pictures are better with people in them," said the friend with whom I was traveling through rural Costa Rica, taking the camera from me, insisting that I pose before a hedge carved into an airplane in a topiary garden in a town square.

It's no accident that most journalists and writers are liberals: they've heard too many stories not to be. When I was single and meeting men in bars, I felt burdened after a while by hearing their griefs, sliding out in a rush of alcohol, about the women who had left them, the children they had lost, their regrets about careers or about Vietnam. I felt that way because these stories were unprocessed. But I felt differently about the stories I heard in Zona Rosa. Indeed, I experienced them as blessings, indicating as they did the healing powers of the group and of art.

"I knew I was truly accepted when you read aloud my poem about wanting to take my false teeth out and give my young doctor a blow job," laughed Jane Ann, a short, feisty, white-haired woman. She had come to the group in her early sixties, on the advice of Nurse Pat, after many hospitalizations that had led to having to resign as anthropology professor at Armstrong State College. "Before that, I was so inhibited that I had completely bypassed a section on masturbation in a sociology course that I taught. But in Zona Rosa, I found the first real acceptance I had ever known, and the friends who have kept me going." Jane Ann had such severe asthma that climbing the stairs to my apartment was painful to her; often, she had to go into the bathroom to use an inhaler. At seventy, she had an operation to place a pacemaker, then another to correct problems with it, and five operations since. "If it wasn't for Zona Rosa, I'm sure I wouldn't be alive today," she said. Carolyn, Latrelle, and Gladys had become intimately involved in her life, cutting her grass, driving her where she needed to go, or, above her protests, taking her pots of her favorite split-pea soup.

"Writing *totally* changed my life," said Laurel, a thirty-year-old single mother. For most of her life, Laurel had lived with a secret: the man who had been the first of her mother's four husbands was not her father, as she had been told. Her real father lived in Savannah where Laurel grew up, and though *he* knew and *she* knew, his paternity had never been acknowledged by Laurel's mother or anyone in her family. For years, trying not to repeat her mother's pattern, Laurel had gone in and out of a depression that drained her of her naturally bubbly, effusive creativity, but after she wrote of her secret and confronted her mother (who, in the southern way, went to bed with a migraine), Laurel had become more focused and began writing the powerful poetry that was to become her forte. "I go to bed now, and I fall right asleep," she said, despite having to deal with the money and baby-sitting problems of a single mother who also worked full-time. "Whereas before I tossed and turned all night, angry about everything."

Sam's poetry had been rigid and pretentious at first. But then he wrote about a "forgotten" experience with an older male cousin in a bathtub as a small boy and the hurt he felt when his aunt—his foster mother, a well-known psychoanalyst—came into the room but overlooked the incident. The very next month, there was a new flow in his ideas, a relaxation to his language.

Indeed, the level of trust in the group helped many Zona Rosans shed the burden of secrets that they may have carried with them for a lifetime—secrets that, like dead weights, had held their creativity in thrall. Rebecca, in her fifties, described what her male cousin had done, a story she had never told because he had threatened to kill her mother, a thrall that, when broken, immediately led to a rush of energy in her poetry. Jana's account of being raped at knifepoint in a garage near Berkeley as a student was so well written—the image of the strawberry ice-cream cone she dropped when accosted, walking down the street, provided a poignant counterpoint for her soon-to-be lost innocence—that it appeared in a national anthology. And Leila, a gorgeous young blond video artist whose aversion to the boys her own age had puzzled me, finally told about the rape in the woods by a teenage neighbor when she was five: in that case, too, the worst part had been that her mother insisted they not tell her professor father—"It might upset him." Within months, Leila had a boyfriend and had begun her first screenplay.

Charlene, a housewife with teenage children and a husband whose heart surgery had left him impotent, was one of the several who had joined Zona Rosa on the recommendation of a therapist. Her dark brown hair was cut in a neat cap, and she always wore slacks and a sport shirt. She had already written a piece on how she hated to wear jewelry, makeup, or other "feminine" forms of dress. For the assignment, she confessed that for all her life in her blue-collar family, people had wondered whether she was a lesbian, until—examining her close friendships with women, despite her frustrated passion for her husband—she had begun to wonder, too. Beneath that doubt lay the memory of the rape she had experienced as a child, plus the physical and sexual violence she had seen her mother endure. Whether or not Charlene would go on with her writing was beside the point; the level of acceptance she experienced as we read her piece in Zona Rosa had, at the very least, freed her from a lifetime of self-doubt.

Edna, near fifty, worked in a supermarket deli and was married for the fourth time to a man on disability (for brain damage). As a teenager, she had had two babies out of wedlock; one of the pregnancies was caused by a rape. Awaiting the births, she was kept locked in her room by her father and stepmother; then the babies were taken from her and given up for adoption. As she worked on her story, often actually sobbing as she wrote, she began to recall the sexual abuse that had occurred even earlier. Edna was an inexperienced writer—not a natural, but a woman with a story to tell. After I gave her some simple advice on editing out abstract modifiers and nouns, and sticking to the concrete details of what happened, we read a first draft within the group—to tears rolling down almost every cheek.

I once attended an Adult Children of Alcoholics meeting in Santa Monica; instead of hesitating shyly at telling their stories, as members of such groups often do, wannabe and working actors vied for a chance at the microphone, eager to tell the huge crowd the most intimate details of their lives. Because of the variety of our stories, the openness of the telling, attending Zona Rosa was often better than a bunch of actors, or going to the movies. Kay's tale of trying to sleep in a bomb shelter in war-torn London, her bunk in standing water from a nearby creek that had flooded the refuge, was as vivid as *Mrs. Miniver*. As she described her mother, who had to go to work the next day to support Kay and her sister, and who had already lost one husband to the war and would soon lose another, sitting in the dark, smoking a cigarette, we sat stunned by the image of such ordinary heroism.

Often, such accounts provided us with much-needed courage. Just before Jalaine's long overdue divorce, and the completion of her first collection of poems at age fifty-two, she visited her aging parents' home, next door to her own, to find, like a tableau deliberately laid out for her, that her father had shot her mother through the heart and then had shot himself. The night of the double funeral, she called to tearfully tell us why she had missed the meeting. Through the coming months, we cosseted her, watching her pretty face gradually relax. Two members wrote poems for her, and I shared with her (my own heart of the heart of darkness) the story of how Mother had killed herself just after the publication of my first book, *A Sexual Tour of the Deep South*, and how I had come to realize that the anger in those first poems had been Mother's rage speaking through me, that I had been a surrogate voice for all Mother had been unable to say.

We learned lessons in listening and truly hearing from Paddy, a grandmother and Franciscan nun, who had long been putting her faith to work. As the founder of a controversial inner-city shelter for the homeless, she was often an item on the front pages of the *Savannah News-Press* representing a position unpopular among the city's blue bloods and property owners. On the night we read her piece on the spiritual benefits she received by serving meals at the shelter, we also had as a guest a young black poet who embarked on an angry monologue about whites who condescend to those they "help." But Paddy was an expert in empathy. As he talked, she sat quietly listening, and at the end of his diatribe, said nothing. At our next session, we heard her revised story: she had integrated her critic's perspective, making her essay even more moving.

One man had killed, and seen people killed and worse, in Vietnam. Another, a Green Beret during the same era, had hijacked a United Airlines jet to Cuba, planning to assassinate Fidel Castro. A woman had been shot in the head by her own adult daughter, who had then turned the gun on herself. Others had had bouts with mental illness or addiction; some had spent time in mental hospitals; one had been taken there in handcuffs. An elegant woman who had been hospitalized for depression after her husband died was now dealing with an unexplained alienation from an adult son. Some wrote of more subtle but equally forbidden experiences of envy, rage, or shame. Ronald, a four-times-wed sailboat captain, still bore the guilt of having sought out another woman during his first wife's long, fatal bout with breast cancer. Then there were the socially unacceptable feelings of being unattractive, the fears of poverty or becoming homeless; of failure, and of being out of control of one's life. We all had our myths and our failures. But whatever the "secret," the sharing of it in writing and the reading of it aloud within the group presaged a rush of energy and clarity. When the Zona Rosans realized that they *could* write honestly and still be accepted, shame evaporated like the morning dew.

A Thicket of Roses

Most of us stretched our boundaries in Zona Rosa. I could feel my own capacity for empathy expanding viscerally, a rubber band that continued to stretch as my own growth deepened. (That "Only connect" again!) In what felt like a miracle of suspended judgment, I loved even those who in ordinary life had traits that might have punched my buttons—laziness, narrowness, unkindness, emotional dishonesty, or a need for self-aggrandizement. It was as though, once they were in Zona Rosa, they were each *mine*: I could no more feel permanently cross with them than with one of my children. Their flaws had only become flaws as they related to their writing.

In addition to the members who were just ordinary folks with ordinary dilemmas and neuroses (though they, too, as various as the designs in a kaleidoscope, constantly amazed me), there have also been those with real and special problems, conditions or situations that made them behave in strange ways, ways that they were "not s'posed to," which maybe because of our fear of the dark, the unknown, are painful even to see: the kinds of diseases of the mind and spirit that challenge our ability to love.

I have long received messages from unlikely sources in the universe. Because of Zona Rosa, I have become close to people who could easily have been considered hopelessly mad, addicted, or otherwise crazed. People who are mad or addicted are not *just* mad, addicted, or otherwise disabled, they are *also* accomplished, intelligent, or whatever else they may be. As Jean Kennedy Smith and George Plimpton point out in *Chronicles of Courage*, their book on disabled artists, such people are not just their problems, but the sum of many parts and possibilities.

"Marvella was so refined as a young woman—she was traveled, elegant, slender, with her dark hair in a chignon. She spoke several languages and played the piano. I was in total awe of her," a visiting poet who had grown up in Atlanta around the same time said of a member of our group, a woman in her mid-fifties who was from an artistic and aristocratic Atlanta background.

But while the Marvella I knew was a poet with the passion, rage, and talent of a southern Anne Sexton, she was also a graying woman, a ponytail often sprouting directly from the top of her head, who emitted the acrid odor of the mad. She dressed in a way that made one wonder if she had closed her eyes while choosing her attire and I twice had to put her out of the group because of the disruptive outbursts brought on by her manic-depression.

More than once, I had coaxed her to sit quietly, writing down her random thoughts as she listened, to share with me later. But when she began to interrupt my reading of the others' work with such comments as "There's nothing I like better than a good two-or-three day session of sex!" (this in the mixed group) and asking the others if they'd like to go with her to a nudist camp, I knew things were going downhill again. "I thought of a good bumper sticker," she said when she called to ask for another member's number. "It came to me when I saw one that said 'Have you hugged your child today?' Have you fucked your mother today?—don't you think that would be a good one?"

When I saw her in public in Savannah's small downtown, Marvella would complain loudly about my having put her out of the group. Pushing a shopping cart, she went into a store where another Zona Rosan worked, asking his help in "raising money for Rosemary." She called others, requesting help in getting donations, even offering to send little boxes with my picture on the side, like the ones in supermarkets requesting change for people in need of organ transplants. She gave my home address as her return address, and made such strange calls ("It is not safe for you to work with me. I have blood on my hands.") that I put a phone block on her number. She left raw steaks, clothing, bank statements, legal correspondence, her house keys (with the offer to buy her house), and what could only be called love or hate letters on my porch. My poems drove her crazy, she said, invading her mind, and keeping her from concentrating. Envisioning her pulling a gun from her purse, I took to carrying my own to places where I might run into her. When she left a painting by her deceased husband (which she insisted was of me) outside my doorway in the rain, I decided contact had to end.

Yet ten minutes later, when I saw her standing motionless in the rain outside the supermarket, gazing forward almost catatonically, something lurched inside me. I remembered the brilliant lines from her poetry, the way we had talked about Bartok, Thomas à Kempis, and Emily Dickinson; even how something she had once said had given me spiritual guidance in a personal matter. I knew that there was something deep and refined inside Marvella, the thing to which I, and the visiting poet who had been awed by her, had initially responded. Knowing that, and seeing her standing there, knowing that nothing I could do would help her, caused a great gap to open, that feeling of being cut off from one of one's kind, someone you would like to love and appreciate, but who, because of her illness, could not allow that to happen. All I could do with our frustrated connection was to begin a poem that night, titled "One Woman, Insane," putting Marvella in that place where I placed all the unresolvable mysteries of life: my writing.

Bearing out my belief that, given certain atmospheres, people *do* change, some called or wrote years after the fact to say how Zona Rosa had changed their lives. Often these were the very ones whose needs I thought I had failed to meet. There must be something about our situation, the level of honesty, combined with the acceptance, perhaps, that gives people the strength to do what they needed to do, even if they needed time for the experience to sink in.

Mike was an offbeat guy near forty, and it was easy to see why some people would find him strange. "But hey, people probably thought Leonardo da Vinci's ideas were strange, too!" I told him, encouraging him to express himself. He first wrote of a tower he wanted to see built 200 miles into the atmosphere, providing living space to deal with the overpopulation problem. He told us how he had gone to a cabin in the woods to fast for forty days during Lent and had followed a forest prayer path each day in the pattern of the Stations of the Cross. He had hitchhiked all over the world, he told us, starting out with $17 in his pocket and the belief that God would take care of him. When he worked at a Catholic shelter for the homeless in Washington, D.C., he sent a romantic valentine to a young Irish girl whom he thought fancied him in return; the nuns promptly fired him for sexual harassment. He was painfully shy—too shy to call a woman on the telephone; as he began to trust the group, he read a hilarious piece in which he told of how he had waited ten years to call the girl he was attracted to in high school. When I last heard from him, he still had some of the same ideas, but he was dating, and was running for the U.S. Senate.

Sometimes, half a decade would pass before I would learn that Zona Rosa had worked for someone. When Tyler came into the group, she had just survived a midlife divorce and a manic-depressive breakdown. She had saved $20,000 as a successful real estate agent in Atlanta, and had fled to Savannah, where she found herself driving around in a fugue state. For a time, she worked on a moving story of her hospitalization, then suddenly dropped out. Late one night, five years later, I answered the phone sleepily to hear Tyler's thick Buckhead accent; she reported that she had moved to Mississippi, where her sister lived, and where she was continuing her writing and going to college as an undergraduate. "Ah remembered ev'rythang you said, 'n it's kept me goin' through the yee-ars," she went on to my amazement. I remembered distinctly how disappointed I had been when she dropped out of the group, and how I felt I must have failed her somehow.

I was puzzled when Teresa suddenly dropped out of Zona Rosa when she had only been a part of it for a few months. Attractive and mysterious, she was one of our more brilliant newcomers. When she called again, using a different name, she explained her secret: she was being treated for multiple personality disorder and had found it hard to sit still, staying within one personality, for the entire afternoon. One of the ways she was dealing with her disease, aside from intensive therapy, was taking karate. I suggested that she try the second group, a mixed-sex group that met at night, using her alternative name if she wished. She did, coming into that group each month in her white cotton uniform, fresh from her karate lesson. As time went on and she felt more accepted, she began writing freely and with great subtlety of the strange states of being she had experienced, and was continuing to experience.

Bobbie, an alcoholic from a blue-collar background, was painting houses for a living, and at forty struggling to get a college degree. She came to her first Zona Rosa meeting drunk and obviously nervous; throughout the evening, ignoring my offerings of coffee and Coke, she gulped tall nameless drinks from an opaque plastic cup. On the way home that night, she had an auto accident that brought to light nineteen previous D.U.I.s. "You know that country song, 'I've got friends in low places?'" she wrote me from jail. "Well, think of me when you hear it." She said that the one thing that was keeping her going was her commitment to her recovery from alcoholism, her writing, and her dream of coming back to Zona Rosa when she got out.

Not all my efforts turned out so well; early on, especially, there had been the failures: when Emily, whose son had been shot by his lover, a wealthy antique dealer (a story that later became the subject of John Berendt's *Midnight in the Garden of Good and Evil*), came into the group to begin a touching memoir of her son, I happened to be writing an article on the case for a national magazine. When I was asked by the defendant to bring Emily an offer of a financial settlement in her civil suit against him, I did so, thinking how much the money might mean to her. But Emily decided I must be collaborating with the man, and nothing—not my article, or anything I could say— would convince her otherwise. Years later, she was still writing me letters, threatening suits if I wrote anything about her and her son.

Yet whatever its outcome, every story from Zona Rosa bore

out my belief that such sharing—the sense of being a part of one another—is an imperative part of our drive to literature. According to astrology, we are nearing the end of the Age of Aquarius when it was predicted that there would be excesses of compassion. But because of it, Zona Rosa had come to feel, over the years, like the theologian Martin Buber's imperative to relate as *I/thou,* made flesh.

"Art makes that pleasurable, even beautiful, which in life would be painful to observe," wrote the critic Lionel Trilling. And Zona Rosa had become my art.

As Nurse Pat said about her work with the dying, "Being with them at that time is a privilege." But it took me a long time to realize that I was also the one being healed.

"I used to be a frog. Then I became a teacher. I wish I was a frog again!" a second-grader had written in one of my classes.

For a long time, this was the way I felt about teaching—that my creative self still resided solely in my writing, and that teaching was merely a related way of earning the money I needed to indulge that self.

There were those who wrote, and those who taught, I thought. I kept time management notebooks to make sure I spent more time on my own writing than on preparing for classes; just as I had, in my wilder days, once kept notes on the number of men I slept with. I wanted to make sure I slept with "enough," thus saving myself from turning into a mere intellectual (even then, I knew that experiences were sometimes as important to the writing as the writing itself).

For one thing, I had hated school. During my brief sojourn there, I had been a rebel and a troublemaker. My seventh-grade teacher, Mrs. Brown, had me sand my desk a half-hour each afternoon until I had removed my boyfriend Troy's name from it, which I had carved deeply into the wood. When I was talkative, she made me leave the classroom to go outside and write poems about nature and spring, which she would then read to the class. When she took me aside to tell me that I shouldn't get married young like the others, but should go on to college because I was bright, I scoffed—to do what? Become an old fogey like her? And besides, my first goal was that baby blue satin wedding, complete with six bridesmaids in blue net, married as soon as possible to Troy, along with the vague fulfillment of the hidden fantasies that I had begun to have at night. Later, I would learn why Mrs. Brown looked so worn: she and her husband had moved to the South to escape the McCarthy hearings, in which he had been questioned, and after which he had suffered a heart attack.

In high school, often as not, I copied my algebra homework just outside my white-haired math teacher's door. I did listen avidly as Mrs. Conley read from *Ivanhoe*, but I didn't want to be like her, married to the school counselor, her hair tied back like George Washington. Lying to Mother that I was cheering at an out-of-town game, I cut school and got money from my boyfriend T.J. to buy the pink suit for $17.95, the transparent pink lingerie embroidered with tiny blue flowers, in which I planned to elope with him. That same day, we had blood tests and applied for a marriage license. When Mr. Conley asked if I wanted to order my senior ring, I told him mysteriously that I wouldn't be needing one. Mother had discovered my subterfuge, and grounded me, but T.J. and I had just gone ahead with our plans, changing the date on the license with ink irradicator.

The closest I ever came to fantasizing myself as a teacher was in eighth grade at the huge West Fulton High School, which I attended for a semester after grammar school, before our family moved to Tucker. There, I was surrounded in the halls by rougher, more pimply faced boys than I had ever seen, and in the restrooms by tough girls who wore heavy black Maybelline, and even heavier class rings taped to fit their fingers. My seventh-grade sweetheart, Troy, had gone on to West Fulton before me, and we were doing things that caused me pangs of guilt. Sitting every afternoon in a white metal love seat, dazed by the scent of the white autumn roses still ablaze in my Grandmother Annie's side yard, Troy and I had moved from my mashing the blackheads on his face to kissing over and over, the worm of loss of innocence wiggling into our relationship. I could tell that even he, a worldly ninth-grader, was disturbed by these developments. Feeling soiled—after all, I was a girl, and chastity was my responsibility, wasn't it?—I must have felt the need to purify myself. When my homeroom teacher asked each of us to write our fantasy of our future, I wrote, springing out of who knows where, "I want to be a dancer. Or a missionary," the latter a word that to my Methodist-Sunday-School-trained mind, meant giving up the pleasures of the flesh and teaching the heathen for the rest of my life (along with this might come the added chance to mortify the body by being tortured if asked to deny Christ).

True, since I had first Begun to Write—a demarcation defining Before and After, as boldfaced an event in my life as being Born Again—I had been inspired by several teachers: Herb Francis, of the modern poetry class; Van Brock, the earnest young graduate student who had led my first poetry workshop; and James Dickey, who, if at moments abrasively, had taught me much about modern poetry. At a summer workshop at the University of Colorado in Boulder (where I met my third husband, Ben), I had been encouraged by the poets Alan Dugan and Richard Eberhardt.

But it was only when thrown into the frying pan of Poetry in the Schools; then later, when I began Zona Rosa, that I recalled a thirteen-year-old's goal of becoming a missionary. As the years went on, I became more and more a crusader for creative writing—my missionary zeal had lain in wait all those years spent as housewife-poet, then as sexual and emotional adventuress.

I was a person who had long prided myself, like many artists (especially youthful ones, not yet sure of themselves) on my uniqueness. As Mother had always said to me as a child, and later when she saw I wasn't going to follow the rules, becoming a good wife to a good man, "Nobody could ever tell you anything!" That I would willingly give up the cache of safety my prettiness could have provided for me was something she, and my other female relatives, found hard to believe.

From the beginning, I had been as committed to writing as to my children (and *more*, some of my husbands would have said, than to my marriages). But I had never had a flash of evangelical zeal, a moment in which I knew I wanted to teach. I would have felt threatened had anyone assumed this to be true. My teaching was an incidental activity—something I wanted to put on the back burner. I was still merely a writer who shared my passion for writing, I told myself. Praised for my skills as a teacher, I protested, afraid of being diminished as a writer if I gave into my increasingly strong feelings about teaching. When Zane, thinking to compliment me, mentioned the guitarist Leo Kottke, saying he was more famous as a teacher than as a performer, I was cross, asking him to please not say that again.

Then there was the matter of my charisma, on which I felt that much of my teaching was based. "Calling this woman charming is like calling water wet," an editor for one of my books had written of me for an in-house memo advising that I be given the opportunity to promote the book on radio and TV. At the time, I was vaguely flattered (most southern women expect charm of themselves), but I barely recognized myself in what she had written. It was just something I had, like having brown eyes—and it was something that had the feel of snake oil to me. Modesty and a stiff upper lip were high virtues in my Scotch-English-Irish family. Writing itself felt natural to me, but to talk about, to glorify, what I did felt weird. I'd never known a female relative to effect others through the power of her tongue (except maybe my cousin Jo Anne, who had put the fear of God in me with her tale of the hollow Statue of Liberty). "Pretty is as pretty does," I had been told over and over as a child by my female relatives, despite that they themselves judged one another on the basis of appearance and charm, rather than achievement. Since teaching, and the students flocking to me, came so naturally, I felt uneasy about it, as though it were unearned, undeserved.

Too, there was the question of the morality of the teaching itself: was it right to encourage people in such a demanding and all-consuming discipline, to support them in feeling that this *was* something they could do? A common belief among my peers was that writing can't be taught, but I felt differently: sheer talent, commitment, perseverance—indeed, *character*—can't be, but writing can, at least to those who wished to hear. I had seen the evidence too many times. I had set myself a difficult task of retaining high standards in my own work, while facilitating those at the bare beginnings of the same goals. I couldn't make it any easier, and I might not be able to help the Zona Rosans get big advances, or on the Phil Donahue show, but I could support them in their desire to create. When Melinda, at the behest of her stockbroker husband, asked me how much of an advance she might expect for her near-completed novel, I laughed. "Well, if you're lucky enough to find a publisher, you might get $5,000, or $50,000—or $500,000!"

"Why does everybody in America want to be a writer? It's the worst paying job in the world!" authors sometimes gripe among themselves. Yet however much we writers might complain about the stresses that often go along with our commitment (statistics show that the average income among working writers is $5,000 a year; not to speak of our higher rate of alcoholism and mental illness), we secretly—in our best and most honest moments— feel lucky. We understand very well why others—whatever the loss in cut flowers, peace of mind, and other luxuries—might want to sacrifice to do what we do. Indeed, why else would so many of us have made so many sacrifices to that end? As Sam, a man who had made and lost millions several times over and moved at age sixty from St. Thomas to an island near Savannah to live simply and write seriously, for the first time, said to me, "At this point in my life, I would rather starve than not write!"

Robin Norwood, author of *Women Who Love Too Much*, told

of a time when she worked in a clinic that served severely ill cancer patients. As she talked with several of them, it turned out that all three had wanted to write. "'I knew from age seven,' said one. 'I knew from age three,' said another. The third said, 'I *always* wanted to write, for as long as I can remember.' But none of them had written *any*thing—it was almost as though they were hoping death would come first, and free them from having to do it! Writing is standing naked—and a lot of people are afraid to do that," she added.

About seven years into the groups, I began wondering: were they merely an escape from my own writing? What was I doing, focusing so much on the work of others—especially *beginner* others? Was my passion for the Zona Rosans just one massive case of caretaking, the ultimate conclusion of my dysfunctional past? As Gloria Steinem said of herself, had I become "co-dependent with the world"? Also, I was a writer with time running out, living inside the trick of creating as though time was malleable, yet knowing all the while it was not. Though I had spent much of my life working toward the goal of becoming an accomplished writer, I had never been especially good at networking or career planning. When, after a few years, people began to stop me on the street, to comment on my generosity, I was uneasy: was this just another massive misuse of my time? Few of my peers, who were beginning to receive those six-figure advances along with huge sums for film rights, were spending *their* time on such activities. Instead, they were holed up in cabins in the North woods, living in luxury in Santa Fe, or had isolated themselves on private islands. Once Pat Conroy had asked jokingly at a party, "When are you going to stop writing that poetry, and write something that makes money?" Poetry had always been the crème de la crème of literature to me, as luxurious as cut flowers in January and first editions of books in hardcover, as well as being as satisfying as needlepoint. Had Zona Rosa become just another pretty embroidery, a surface activity, in my quest?

Sometimes I wondered what I was doing, still in Georgia, where I had begun. When Roseanne told Barbara Walters of going back to Utah to visit the mental hospital she had been put in at age seventeen by her parents, her story resonated for me: "I go up to these two patients shufflin' down the hall, 'n say, 'I was here seventeen years ago, 'n now I make a million dollars a year!' This nurse who's with 'em tries to cut in, but I go, 'I'm not talkin' to you—I'm talkin' to *them*!'" When Barbara Walters asked whether she thought anything was really wrong with her back then, Roseanne looked pensive for a moment. "Yeah—I was in *Utah*!"

Was I still in my own private Utah? I had spent a month at Yaddo, an artists and writers retreat where most of the other writers were from New York, or at the least, the Northeast. One of the artists was John Kelly, a performance artist who performed in exquisite drag, often clad in Todd Oldham gowns. Watching a video of his incredible and subtle act, I felt a resonance: was I, too, in the wrong place or wrong body? I came home to say to Zane that I knew what was wrong with me: I had been meant to live my life in New York, but instead had spent it in the Deep South, which in turn had distorted my personality and made me the person I was. It was not the first time I had had such a feeling, but it was one I had put to the side as responsibilities mushroomed and life upped the ante.

When I started the first Zona Rosa group, I was at the tag end of what could have been called a self-destructive time—a period of heavy drinking, random sexual encounters, and general indulgence; in other words, a period of total disillusionment with everything I had been brought up to believe, with only writing and pure pleasure left to me as a source.

Instead, I felt at the height of personal power. I had lived out my belief that freedom, for women, lay in sexual choice and in economic independence. At a cost few might choose—I had moved from suburban comfort to living in a small flat, without support or a spouse—I had proved my points. I could live without a man, and I could support myself. I had just received the paperback money for *Fatal Flowers*, more money than I had ever had in the bank at one time; my choice of lovers was both delicious and casual. But life was about to give me fresh instructions in humility. In fact, if the period to follow had been a book, it could have been called *Dislocation, or a Life Out of Alignment.* Privately, I thought of it as my Twelve Years of Suffering, or, as a radio commentator termed such involuntary periods of personal growth, "enlightenment at gunpoint."

For one thing, the imperatives of motherhood sprang up again, full-fleshed, as two of my three adult children began experiencing chronic difficulties, the sink hole of our family heritage of addiction and madness sucking them in, for a time, as inexorably as quicksand. For another, I fell in love with Zane, a handsome younger man who, for a number of years, until he put a stop to it, brought Daddy's alcoholism—and my long-repressed love for him—to life again.

During those years, I also watched *The Hurricane Season*—the book into which I had most poured my heart and soul, and which I considered my best piece of writing—fall through the cracks of few reviews and no ads, despite an initial starred review in *Publishers Weekly* and the appreciation of my peers. It was also published at a time when I most needed the cash, having spent much money and energy on hospitals, clinics, and the general picking up of pieces. But no matter how much I had needed the success, I hadn't been able to bring myself to write in a less controversial way. "Women in Germany don't *have* these kinds of conflicts," a young woman editor in Hamburg said to me of my novel about a woman torn between her life as an artist and as a mother to children very much like my own. Erica Jong wrote me supportively, "I'm not surprised the *Times* didn't review it. . . . [It's] too blood and guts, too real. . . . You'll never be politically correct, thank the Goddess!" But despite her and my readers' support, what followed were the moments when I felt like St. Thomas Aquinas on his deathbed—"All that I have written now seems to me like so much straw." Or as Madonna put it in her song "Let's Get Unconscious," words are basically useless, especially sentences.

Miraculously, things in my family smoothed out, got better; slowly, a kind of healing took place. Zane stopped drinking, and the two children found a way to live with what they had been given, even with a degree of happiness. A grandson was born to one daughter, healing family chasms; my other daughter, long a high achiever in the field of science, found herself writing, too. In my work, I felt the kind of internal shifting, akin to that of geographical plates in the psyche, that meant I was going on to newer and deeper levels in my writing. The tide had gone out, and now it was coming back in again.

But it was partly the Zona Rosans—my commitment to them, the regularity of our meetings—that kept me going. When my fat healthy grandson died of crib death only three months after his birth, Nurse Pat, who had been with many in their grief, agreed with my assessment that however short his life had been, it had had meaning: "Sometimes it doesn't take long to do what we came here to do," she said, adding that "now you have a friend in high places"—words that I was able to pass on to my daughter to soothe her in her even deeper pain. And when I broke my ankle a year later, necessitating four months in a cast and three surgeries, it was the Zona Rosans who brought me groceries, took me to doctor's appointments, and made me laugh.

Whatever the crises in my own life, the Zona Rosans surged around me, a warm and soothing wave; if saltwater is the medium of witches, then we could have been called a coven. Because of what had become my need of *them*, there were few occasions when I canceled our meetings. When the groups had been meeting for a dozen years, I accepted a semester-long job as visiting writer at a small college in Massachusetts; instead of taking time off, I flew home each month to conduct combined meetings (in addition to leading a Zona Rosa in the working-class town where I was teaching). While I had seen Zona Rosans through their difficulties, they had seen me through mine, an empathetic audience to both my successes and my failures.

Instead of the distraction (and possible moral weakness) I had feared, Zona Rosa had become my support group, giving me the strength and courage I needed to go on. As I raved on about criteria, standards of excellence, and being true to one's own voice, I was speaking to myself, an evangelist shoring up her own beliefs. During the moments when I lost faith, doubting what I considered my life's calling, the sound of my own rhetoric—confessing to those doubts, yet declaring the glories of art—convinced me afresh. When I quoted from the South African novelist Nadine Gordimer, "We should write as though we are already dead," or shared Einstein's words from his deathbed, "There is only one important question: is the universe friendly?" I was speaking as much to myself as to them. Mentioning Carlyle's comment that "genius is merely attention to detail," I was describing my own belief in the sanctity of craft. As I read Flannery O'Connor's statement, "The man in the violent situation reveals those qualities least dispensable in his personality, those qualities which are all he will have to take into eternity with him," I was restating my commitment to risk. When I cited Rebecca West's observation, "Before Wordsworth, daffodils were merely weeds," or quoted the poet Louise Bogan, "I cannot believe that the inscrutable universe turns on an axis of suffering; surely the strange beauty of the world must somehow rest on pure joy," I was sharing my own belief in it, while hoping to inspire and support theirs.

I had also become the Zona Rosans' defender in dealing with the conflicts that I knew still existed for them, despite media messages to the contrary. "Is the message then, that some women do . . . crave the time honored-bonds and behavior that tie the heart of the family? That they are willing to stretch themselves apart to keep the family image and reality together?" journalist

L. Peat O'Neil asked in disbelief in a review in *Belles Lettres* of Susan Cheever's *A Woman's Life: The Story of an Ordinary American and Her Extraordinary Generation.* As I read, I felt my hackles rise. I knew such women (and men) existed; I met them during every meeting of Zona Rosa. Indeed I was one of them. Though I may not have been Gustave Flaubert, I could honestly say, as he said of his creation Emma Bovary, that Susan . . . Latrelle . . . Joan . . . Charlotte . . . any one of them is *moi.* Pat Conroy said after one meeting with the group, "What is so beautiful about these women is that they are dealing with all kinds of life experiences—breast cancer, trouble with children, the death of a spouse—yet still, they want and love literature, even want to create it."

Despite what appeared to be their conservatism, the Zona Rosans had also fostered the risk-taking part of me—the part that wants to learn to ride horses at age fifty-seven, even though I had feared them as a child; to travel in a foreign country alone, to take up a new language; or even jump out of an airplane. Though I had always done such things, now it was almost as if I was doing it *for* them—or else how could I expect them to take the risks I advised in their writing? (When Melinda got on a plane on an hour's notice to appear for the first time on a national TV talk show, her gutsiness paralleled exactly the risks she had begun to take in her novel in progress.) As I watched them develop and move off on their own, they also taught me lessons in letting go (lessons that I sorely needed in dealing with my real-life children). At first, watching my chicks spread wings, I wanted to maintain control, direct their progress. It took time for me to accept that a student's growing confidence and separation from me was a sign of the group's success.

But most of us stayed for reasons beyond career. For the writers in Zona Rosa—at least, *my* kind of writers—writing means far more than the arbitrary act of putting black squiggles—already abstract, at a remove—onto white paper. Nor is the goal the glory we imagine possible for doing so. For us, it is a vision quest in which language is merely the tool.

Writing is not the flesh, but it is the flesh made word. It heals, empowers; it organizes, beautifies. It represents the desire to make one's life count for more than the mundane, to share whatever flights of joy or moments of pain one has experienced before they melt away, disappearing into the beyond like a hummingbird's flight.

I was now near the age Mother had been when she killed herself; as I told the Zona Rosans, I sometimes feared what I might feel as I passed that birthday. But I also had the one thing Mother never had. The women in Zona Rosa were mothers and daughters, too, and sometimes within the group, we mothered one another; at other times, we became the pampered daughters. And in the group with the men and the women, we created whole families.

Reading M. F. K. Fisher's description of eating gingerbread in Dijon I suddenly thought of Mother—how she had loved to cook, especially such desserts as gingerbread with lemon sauce, or a hot fudge shortcake. No matter how poor we were, she always kept on hand the ingredients to make from scratch the sugary deserts we adored. I recalled the eggs, the sugar, the flour— "One, two, three cake," she called it, mixed it, then poured it into the greased and floured cake tin, then the fudge sauce— cocoa, butter, and sugar cooked over the burner in a saucepan. If Mother had been a Zona Rosan, would she have brought one of those desserts? Would we have been asking for her recipes, then listening intently as her manuscript was read aloud?

Coming across Ruby's scrawled recipe for coconut cake, one of Lenore's illustrated poems, or Courtenay's drawings of the group of us, gives me a feeling of warmth, of deep connectedness. As an aspiring writer I had dreamed that writing would lift me, as if by magic, out of rural Georgia and into a world in which beauty, intellect, and creativity were honored—to New

York or Paris, and places beyond my imagining. Indeed, some of that *has* happened. But if I had received what I dreamed of—an early success, with enough money to do nothing but write and otherwise pleasure myself—would I ever have experienced this sense of belonging?

As the child of pain and grief, I repressed my desire for love and trust, but once again the universe had provided. "What has not been brought to consciousnessness will be made manifest as fate," wrote Carl Jung. For me, this statement has been borne out in a positive way.

Indeed, my experience has led me to wonder whether the alcoholism and depression of some of our more successful—and thus, affluent—writers has been exacerbated by the isolation of writing and nothing else. Through the Zona Rosans, I had learned the healing power of gratitude. (I had noticed that for them, too, gratitude was frequently the step that took them beyond the bêtes noires of the writer's life—envy, competitiveness, and striving. Like me, by the time they had gotten to it, all the rest had fallen away.)

For finally, I had to admit it, teaching had saved me: from my potential narcissism, even the creeping dark of a life without limits. (As anyone who's closed down a disco at 3 A.M. knows, what's left when the music and the gel lights go off and the fluorescent ones come on is just the sad sweepings of trash and grime.) Here, close at hand, rather than in an exotic setting, I had found an enclave of, if not soulmates, then companions in the search for truth and beauty. I thought I had craved a life of solitude, even isolation, but instead I found a family. Ultimately, teaching has been as healing for me as my writing.

It seems appropriate that they who have traveled with me into the Pink Zone should become the subject of my art as well, in homage to what they have given me and to the twin themes of my life. I am the one who has been blessed. Because of them, I am ready to confess to my love of teaching, even if it means sometimes wishing I was a frog again.

< APPENDIX A >

Exorcises from Zona Rosa:
Starting to Write Now, Over, or Late

There are no writing blocks, only feeling blocks.

"Three things about the border are known: It's real, it doesn't exist, it's on all the black maps," writes the western author, James Galvin. In Zona Rosa, we believe that the border is inside ourselves, and that we can get there from here. These exercises, or "exorcises," are designed to release new materials, resolve writing blocks, unleash new energy, and move us permanently out of the role of victim.

Some of the exorcises are to be done sequentially, on a week-by-week basis; others are to be written at random, whenever the writer finds that subject appealing. Few take over fifteen minutes; none are to be judged as finished pieces of writing, though the images and experiences evoked are likely to provide sources for poems, stories, essays, and memoirs. Some members of Zona Rosa have published finished pieces of writing that have begun in this manner.

The best way to do the exorcises is in a notebook, which will become, over time, a personal reference and source book; the notebook is also the place for self-talk, analysis of one's own process as a writer, and the development of a personal criteria of what constitutes a good piece of writing.

Another important part of this process is sharing the results within the group (or, if that's not possible, with one other person); having your most personal thoughts and feelings heard completes the loop, giving a feeling of closure and a sense of the worthiness of your unique subject matter. Within Zona Rosa, we operate with a confidentiality/anonymity agreement, but after a while, many members find their fears have dissipated and are comfortable sharing such materials even in print.

WHAT ARE MY WILDEST FANTASIES ABOUT MY WRITING? What dreams come to mind when thinking of yourself as a writer? Write a paragraph describing them, no matter how far-fetched you consider them to be. These dreams may well come true, but cannot unless we begin. Once these fantasies are brought to consciousness and dissipated, we are freed to go on with our writing in a matter-of-fact way. Part two of this exorcise is to List Your Passions, which will always provide the best subjects for your writing. As you make this list, also note the forms you see these subjects taking; for example, a poem, a story, or a novel.

PIECES OF WRITING I HAVE LOVED. What were your favorite childhood books? What did you love reading as an adult? All of us have read novels we never wanted to end, or poems that provided a delicious shock of recognition. The special qualities of these works are often the ones we would like to emulate in our own writing. But first we must learn to recognize those qualities; it is in this manner that we develop a criteria for what we consider a good piece of writing. By asking ourselves what we like about them, then copying actual paragraphs or stanzas into our notebooks, we become more conscious of how the author constructed them.

"Do you have to write to live?" the poet Maria Rainier Rilke wrote to an aspiring writer in *Letters to a Young Poet.* In *The Path of Least Resistance,* Robert Fritz says that we make fundamental, then primary and secondary, choices that determine the course of our lives. WHAT IS MY FUNDAMENTAL CHOICE IN REGARD TO MY WRITING? WHAT ARE MY PRIMARY AND SECONDARY CHOICES? What am I willing to risk? How much of a player do I want to be? Whether you choose a commitment at the level of a Rilke or Gordimer, or simply wish to preserve family memories or try your hand at a romance novel, there is no right or wrong way: the main thing is a conscious awareness of what writing means in your life, and of the place you are willing to give it. (But please note: in Zona Rosa, those of us who start small sometimes move on to deeper themes.)

YOU. What is more fascinating to us than ourselves? Yet many of us feel inhibited from writing about what we consider to be the mundane, or even dramatic, events of our lives. Think of your life as though it were a piece of natural linen marked by nubby, brightly colored random threads: it is the threads' very random quality that gives the cloth its beauty. What are the memories and images that immediately come to mind when you think back over the years? Unless we are deaf, dumb, and have amnesia, all of us have all the raw materials we need for writing inside us—feelings, fantasies, dreams at night, experiences, ideas, memories, and the world around us. Using a "you" point of view, free-associate about these aspects of your life, no matter how insignificant, silly, or melodramatic they seem to you. Don't worry about putting them down in chronological order; free-associate until you run out, connecting sentences with an "and" chain device; that is, connecting each thought with an *and, then,* or *but.* The more of the raw materials you include, the more dimension your piece will have.

WHAT I HAVE DONE TO SURVIVE. The women of San Cristobal, Mexico, call getting married "committing suicide"; millions of women in Africa have submitted to genital mutilation in order to fulfill a cultural ideal. Our experiences may not have been as extreme, but all of us—women and men—have done what we felt we have had to do to survive. Now, in our writing, we have a choice; the first step in exercising that choice is acknowledging that we have distorted and dislocated ourselves in order to survive in the past, to fit into relationships or society. A fun version of the same question: *New Woman* magazine conducted a competition in which they asked readers to write on "The Dumbest Thing I Ever Did for Love." What is the dumbest thing *you* ever did for love?

DESCRIBE THE MOMENT OF YOUR FIRST PAIN. "Your first pain, you carry it with you like a lodestone in your breast, because all tenderness comes from there," Jane Bowles wrote in *Two Serious Ladies.* All of us have scars, whether physical or psychological. Now we can put such moments to use in our writing, using it as a source of empathy for ourselves and our characters. A further development of this difficult but useful exorcise is to describe ONE OR MORE OF THE MOMENTS I THOUGHT MY LIFE HAD ENDED.

TRIANGULATED PARENTS. For most of us, the images we carry in our head of the parents of our childhood have inordinate power to affect us in our adult lives, especially if we came from dysfunctional families. A simple cure for this is to WRITE ABOUT YOUR PARENTS AS THOUGH YOU'RE ALL THE SAME AGE, and as though you're all children. A visualization in which I imagined my alcoholic father, my suicidal mother, and I playing together in a sunny field of flowers, all of us about three years old, healed many old wounds and added to my ability to empathize with similar characters in my writing.

PAINT A PICTURE WITH WORDS OF YOUR CRITICAL VOICE. Another way of putting this is, "Who have I given my power to?" Almost all of us hold inside us a vision of the monster who tells us we can't do it. Describe this monster in all her/his negativity. Does the voice sound like someone from your past, or worse, the present? After you describe her, talk back to her. Now that the critical voice has lost her power through confrontation, describe THE SWEETHEART INSIDE YOU—the loving mother/friend who stands by, telling you that yes, you *can* do it. List some of these positive messages, and stick them on your mirror or refrigerator.

WHAT DO I GAIN BY NOT DOING WHAT I WANT? Too often, the psyche suggests powerful payoffs for not taking the risk of writing—relatives who don't get angry, rejection that doesn't have to be faced, no struggles with craft (not to speak of more time to watch TV), and, more important, the evasion of our own feelings. What are the worst things that can happen if we write? By confronting these demons on paper, we take away their power.

GIVEN THE REALITIES OF MY LIFE, HOW CAN I BEST FACILITATE MY WRITING? We all have things we think we have to do. But sometimes we don't have to do those things at all. What small increments of time exist that you have not previously considered? What distractions can you reduce or eliminate? What is your best time, biologically, for writing? Twenty percent of our effort creates 80 percent of our success, says Robert Fritz, author of *Creating*.

WHO IS MY IDEAL READER? We all hold in mind an ideal reader, and often she (or he) is someone very much like ourselves. Getting to know her intimately gives us someone to write to, makes our writing an act of love and communication.

SHOCK YOURSELF. The writer Jack Grapes says he knows he's doing something right when he shocks himself. Authors as diverse as Erica Jong and James Dickey have recommended writing to the edge of the ludicrous. In my own writing I've found that often the idea or image that first felt too wild to put onto paper is the very one with which readers will identify, possibly because if one person has experienced something, others have also: the subjective *is* the universal. Robert Fritz says most of us think we must have a worldview, but we don't have to—the fewer preconceived notions we hold, the more creative we are. But how can we shake up our thinking in order to put ourselves in touch with what art critic Robert Hughes termed "the shock of the new"? How can we loosen perceptions, get into quirkiness, move beneath the level of cliché? By habitually giving ourselves small "shocks" and positive stresses—from driving cross-country alone to finding a new way to work, or talking to a stranger in a public place, or daring to speak the language in a foreign country, even though you know your accent is non-existent. Brainstorm ways to shock yourself on a daily basis.

"Before Wordsworth, daffodils were called weeds," noted Rebecca West. In his book *The Art of Fiction*, John Gardner states that in good writing, "We taste the fictional gazpacho, smell the fictional hyacinths." We experience life through the senses; and all of us, every day, are surrounded by images, objects that can bring our subjects alive. WHAT ORDINARY IMAGES CAN I USE TO BRING MY WRITING TO LIFE?

Some authors use a consistent image that becomes heightened through repetition: John Irving's bear appears not only in his popular novel *The World According to Garp*, but in his other novels as well. In *Brief Lives,* Anita Brookner repeats the image of a bright lemon-yellow couch to imply the frivolity of one of her two women characters. WHAT ARE MY RECURRING IMAGES? On a broader scale, WHAT IS MY IMAGE OF MY LIFE? One Zona Rosan saw her life as a dance, another as a menu with a choice of exotic foods. Others have seen themselves as a caged bird, or Lawrence of Arabia, trudging an endless desert. While these images may change with time, visualizing them and putting them on paper helps us see clearly where we are now, and where we might be going. I once saw myself as a person split into male and female, the male with a perpetual suitcase in hand; the female meditating, mentally pregnant with her next project. Although I had this image more than thirty years ago, it has become the real picture of my life as a writer—sometimes on the move, seeking new experiences; sometimes meditative, and solitary.

WHAT PART SYNCHRONICITY PLAYS IN MY WRITING. Carl Jung and others have written of the part that synchronicity plays in our lives, and the even larger part it plays in the lives of creative people. When our minds and spirits are primed, what we need for our writing seems to come to us effortlessly. This has to do with a receptive spirit, and with noticing. The gifts of serendipity come to those who are ready to receive. This exorcise helps us to make *noticing* a part of everyday life.

WHAT PART SHAME PLAYS IN MY WRITING. Most of us feel a transient sense of shame as we begin to expose ourselves—our ideas and feelings—in writing. Anxiety is a natural accompaniment to our first attempts at writing in an honest way. In fact, the basic choice seems to be secret-sharing or shame. Yet through secret sharing, we release the energy that has been used in the service of keeping secrets. WHAT PART MY BODY PLAYS IN MY WRITING is a second part of this free association: writing is a physical act, a sculpting of language, and we react to it in physical ways. Some writers pace, some drink coffee, some chew pencils, some feel sexually aroused. "Writing is sexual—a kind of sexuality. Whatever problem one has in sexuality, one has in writing as well," believes Russell Lockheart, a psychologist at Washington State University. An awareness and acceptance of these reactions facilitates us in the creative process. In fact, When I First Felt at Home in My Body is a good third part to this exorcise: as children, there were times when we felt totally unconscious in our pleasure and play: this delicious freedom from self-consciousness is one of our goals in writing.

WRITE POSITIVELY ABOUT A PERSON OR SITUATION ABOUT WHICH YOU USUALLY FEEL NEGATIVELY. OR BETTER YET, ONE YOU FEAR. Reframing thinking: what psychologists call reframing thinking is a useful life tool, adding flexibility and adventure to our journey. What pushes our buttons almost always says more about us than the other person or situation. In writing, reframing thinking is essential in aiding us in seeing different points of view, and in character development. So if you don't like snakes, or women who wear dark eye pencil, imagine that you have an absolute passion for them.

HOW DO I USE DENIAL IN MY LIFE? HOW CAN I USE IT IN MY WRITING? In psychology and 12-step circles, denial has gotten a bad rap. Sometimes it's what helps us survive until we can move up to the next step in getting on with our lives. And often denial—or sublimation—is a source for fiction. We paint what we couldn't stand in another light, and often this results in good stories.

WHAT DOES MY ENVY TELL ME ABOUT MYSELF? The gift of envy: envy is one of the bêtes noires of the writer's life; in fact, some talented people actually choose not to write or seek publication because of the pain of this unpopular emotion. But, used correctly, envy is a gift, leading us to new heights of accomplishment by telling us what is important to us in writing and life. Ideally, envy confronted leads us to honor what is unique in us, and to choose mastery over competition.

Style begins for writers when we start using our own work as a precedent. A signature evolves with our awareness of what is good about our writing, and what needs work. Of her prize-winning first novel, *Dreams of Sleep*, Josephine Humphries said that she didn't know how to make transitions, so she simply juxtaposed the chapters on the two women characters, a modern southern woman and her black maid. "The flaw that defines the beauty of . . . art is unduplicatable, even by the artist," wrote the diarist and composer Ned Rorem. "Improvement makes straight roads, but the crooked roads without improvements are the roads of genius," said the great poet William Blake. WHAT ARE MY STRENGTHS AS A WRITER, WHAT ARE MY WEAKNESSES? And how can I use both? Have you noticed how the characters in the novels and films you like best often seem larger than life, their weirdnesses, their flaws, even their tendencies toward the socially unacceptable, emphasized? Most of us, most of the time, try to seem "normal" in order to fit in. But ask yourself: What quirks and eccentricities, usually concealed, can I use to bring life to my writing?

WHAT IS MY ANGUISHED QUESTION? Wallace Stegner wrote, "Behind every work of fiction is an anguished question." What is your anguished question? Most writers write of consistent themes thoughout a lifetime. What are your burning themes?

WRITING ABOUT THE THING I MOST DON'T WANT TO WRITE
ABOUT. "Where your wound is, your strength will be," the poet
Robert Bly said. "The sweetest voices are those that come from
hell," said Franz Kafka. "Write hard and clear about what hurts,"
recommended Hemingway. And truly, facing the excruciating
through writing is the creative alternative to a Prozac life. If we
could only use one exorcise in Zona Rosa, this would be the one:
the breakthroughs members experience, the incredible releases
of energy when we no longer feel the need to tamp down the
previously unspeakable, is truly miraculous; as is the new sense
of self-acceptance and worth experienced in sharing this exorcise
with the group. Remember, there are no taboo feelings or experiences in literature. Those who are initially reluctant might first
write about WHY I DON'T WANT TO WRITE ABOUT THE THING I
MOST DON'T WANT TO WRITE ABOUT.

< APPENDIX B >

Further Notes from Zona Rosa

Revision revises us.

In the beginning . . .

Keep your options open, let your intentions flow.

When Melinda first came to the group, she aspired to writing some funny essays for *Cosmopolitan.* But then she began bringing in the serious stories of a young girl much like she had been, growing up in Brooklyn with parents who had survived the death camps. It quickly became evident to the group—and to Melinda—that what she was doing was beginning a literary novel.

Courtenay had already written one novel as part of an M.F.A. thesis before joining Zona Rosa. But she wasn't satisfied—her book was tight, contrived, written to please an academic committee. "Let the chaos flow," I advised, and Courtenay began the thousand-plus pages of a book much closer to her heart, the story of a woman going through a midlife crisis much like her own. It was from those pages that she would select and choose the many resonant and marvelous passages that would make up her finished manuscript.

In a previous incarnation, Jana had been a vocalist in the punk rock band of which her husband had been manager. When she first came to Zona Rosa, she had a bit of a book in hand, describing those experiences. But then the exorcises began to rock her, and she was writing honestly for the first time about her mother's intent to abort her, her father's emotional abuse and his suicide, and the rape that had shaped her college years. Her essays—a couple of which were published—ran parallel to a period of great personal growth in her life—she started a business, made a major move, started a support group for survivors of dysfunctional families. It was several years before Jana got back to her original story—but by then she had learned so much more about writing and herself that the book resonated with the depth and dimension that had been missing from her first draft.

Indeed, there are many examples of Zona Rosans who came into the group to write the Great American Novel and ended up writing literary poetry, or vice versa. The point is, don't limit yourself too early in the game. Ideas happen for many of us when meaning and the right image mentally collide—but that means coming up with a lot of images, or as one Zona Rosan said, "kissing a lot of word-frogs." Write a lot, and see what happens.

Counter to the acquisitive, goal-oriented acculturation that says we should make every minute count—the one that taps into our addiction to money and sudden fame, telling us that if it won't make us rich or quickly known, it's not worth doing—this extravagant use of time is one in which writers, especially beginning writers, need to indulge.

"The mind is very powerful, and never loses its creative force. It never sleeps. Every instant it is creating. . . . There are no idle thoughts," states *A Course in Miracles*. "All thinking produces form at some level. . . . The abilities that you possess are only shadows of your real strength." And we can make use of this truth.

Think *content and form*, rather than form and content. By writing a great deal, we uncover our basic themes, and usually the forms they should take. Indeed, without content our writing is nothing. Writing is a spiritual journal, paralleling the journey of life, and as in life, until death, we only finish individual pieces, never the journey itself.

"What is happiness to the artist is too rarefied to be considered happiness by the average man," the Spanish philosopher Santayana wrote in *The Sense of Beauty*. Because few around you are likely to understand your undertaking at first, it is important that you be clear about your motivations. Here are some questions to ask yourself as you begin:

WHY DO I WRITE?

WHAT REWARDS WILL I GAIN?

WHAT WILL BE REQUIRED OF ME IN TERMS OF TIME & ENERGY?

IF I HAVE WRITTEN BEFORE, WHAT ARE MY STRENGTHS & MY WEAKNESSES?

WHAT ARE MY NATURAL FORMS?

WHAT ARE MY NATURAL THEMES?

WHAT WRITING STYLES AND THEMES AM I DRAWN TOWARD?

And above all:

WHAT ARE MY PASSIONS?

As someone wise once said, "It's always easier to ride a horse in the direction it's going."

Thus, in the beginning. . . .

At a memoir-writing workshop in Iowa, I began a list on the chalkboard, injecting a few comments along the way, to show the process one might go through during the years it often takes to finish a long prose work:

LET THE CHAOS FLOW—WRITE A LOT

READ WHAT YOU HAVE WRITTEN—GO THROUGH
FOR THEMES

CHOOSE THE BEST, OR MOST RESONANT, PARTS
(THE ONES THAT VIBRATE WHEN YOU READ THEM)

"Set aside the rest for possible inclusion later, in this or another work. Think about these cuts like egg whites in a recipe
that only calls, at the moment, for the yolks."

PLAY AROUND WITH STRUCTURE

MAKE PRELIMINARY DECISIONS ABOUT FORM

"Consider structure. What form seems to rise organically
out of the material? Play around with sequence, points of view,
voice. Remember that something must happen, even if only
internally."

REARRANGE SEQUENCE

BEGIN THE FIRST DRAFT

"Stay flexible and open to the new ideas you'll have along the
way. You'll probably need to develop a tracking device for these.
The one I developed for myself was tacking the notes onto the
wall, glueing the pages into a long trailing snake that I could
look up and check out as I typed."

REREAD: MAKE CORRECTIONS AND ADDITIONS:
REWRITE

REREAD: MAKE CORRECTIONS AND ADDITIONS:
REWRITE

"Be sure that you're telling your readers everything they need
to know—but that you haven't told them more than they need to
know."

REREAD: MAKE CORRECTIONS AND ADDITIONS: REWRITE

"Think *unity*. Should anything be added? Should anything be cut?"

WRITE FINAL DRAFT, FROM BEGINNING TO END

"Here, you will find yourself having fun, hurtling toward the finish line."

CHECK FACTS

WRITE FOR PERMISSIONS, IF NECESSARY

MAKE FINAL CORRECTIONS AND ADDITIONS

CREATE A TABLE OF CONTENTS

BE SURE THE PAGES ARE NUMBERED CORRECTLY

By the time I had gotten to the end of the list, the group was laughing, amazed that I expected them to envision the whole process in advance:

TITLE YOUR BOOK

ADD EPIGRAPHS

WRITE DEDICATION AND ACKNOWLEDGMENTS

Yet I was merely modeling *visualization*, a process that I, rock climbers, surgeons, and others use to keep ourselves on track. In fact, I added, it might be good for them to picture themselves holding a finished 400-page manuscript in their hands. I asked them to imagine how good that might feel: "The only possible thing I can think to compare it with is holding your newborn baby in your hands—and they weigh about the same thing!"

"Actually," I said, beginning another list on the board, "you

will also constantly find yourself considering and reconsider-
ing . . ."

CONTENT AND FORM
UNITY
STRUCTURE
CHARACTER
SUBTEXT
TIME & PLACE
POINT OF VIEW
TENSE
VOICE & TONE
IMAGERY
SIGNIFICANT DETAILS
TRANSITIONS
FLASH FORWARDS & FLASHBACKS
STYLE & SYNTAX
LANGUAGE
PUNCTUATION
SCENE & CHAPTER BREAKS
CODAS
EXTERNAL MATERIALS, SUCH AS LETTERS,
     DIARY EXCERPTS, LINES FROM SONGS

". . . and so on."

For a poetry workshop during the same week, I jotted down
a simplified version of the process I had ultimately devised for
myself, following how I write a poem from beginning to end
(though the list can also be used for writing prose). It was the
same one I had written on the board for fifth-graders while
working in the schools. But Jalaine said that when she first saw
this page, she had an immediate breakthrough, finishing her
complex poems for the first time:

Revision

To carve an Indian, take away everything that is not the Indian.

1. Reread first draft.
2. Paraphrase unity of poem (or story): what is it about?
3. Underline best parts.
4. Rewrite, using only underlined parts.
5. What is the natural rhythm of the lines?
   Should meter be consistent?
   Should stanzas be used to separate thoughts? (or paragraphs, in prose?)
6. Are the lines in the best possible order?
7. Is there any extraneous material?
8. Does anything need to be added for clarity?
9. Are the images as clear, concrete, and appropriate as possible?
10. Eliminate, except in special cases, abstract nouns; excessive modifiers; clichés; and unnecssary language (such as "very," "so," "some," and "sometimes").

My lists were simplifications, cartoons of a complex activity. But like many simplifications, they also expressed a truth, breaking down and demystifying what, at first, could seem an overwhelming task. Emotionally and intellectually, I told them, the process of completing a writing project might feel something like this:

TRUDGING THE SAHARA, AND OTHER PROBLEMS OF THE CREATIVE LIFE

How a writing project begins: —
How it grows:

IDEA

First notes
Further notes

Evolution of
themes, structure,
characterizations,
subtext
EXCITEMENT!

Developing a criteria for style:
        Images: connecting the dots
        Images as metaphors for theme(s)
        Creating a virtual reality
Further development of structure/theme:
        Buildup, plateau, resolution (yes, it's a lot like sex!)

THE GRIND: Actual day-to-day writing
             Filling in the blank spaces facilitated by
             notes and *more* notes
             (*This* is the long-term relationship)

PROBLEM AREAS: Transitions, dialogue
                 What to use, what to cut
                 Syntax, word choice, and so on

EMOTIONAL FATIGUE
ANXIETY

Keep in mind all the above and how they relate and re-relate:
a mosaic or weaving in which every part must work.

KEEPING ON, KEEPING ON, DESPITE THE PROBLEMS
BREAKING DOWN BLOCKS, WORKING THROUGH OBSTACLES

Defining and redefining:
Toward the conclusion of the project, writing speeds ahead:
the themes have been clearly defined and resolved. Writing
skills, in one's chosen style, have accelerated.

RESOLUTION & COMPLETION
(here, send yourself flowers!)

In reality, much of this will be happening simultaneously. But
an awareness that each step is an organic one keeps us
from discouragement. We hold in our sights:

THE BOOK!
(poem)
(story)
(essay, etc.)

Make Writing Your Pleasure Craft

In Savannah, folks like to get out on the water on weekends, and sail or even drift a bit. Carolyn has written some of her best poems about the hours she spends on the water, sailing and not thinking about writing at all. Peggy sold her house in Atlanta after becoming interested in Native American lore and hiked with the Cherokees for three months, one of the few Caucasians to follow the Trail of Tears on the Cherokees' 100th anniversary trek. Her four grown children thought she was crazy at the time, but now they've become accustomed to the fact that Mom is likely to follow her bliss. Peggy now lives on a sailboat docked in Savannah, and goes home to it every night after her job in a hospital office: "I'm just in ecstasy—so excited and happy about my life that sometimes I can't even sleep!" Naturally, Peggy has plenty to write about: when she came to Zona Rosa a year ago, the stories simply poured forth, even though she hadn't written before.

A couple of years ago, *New Woman* magazine surveyed married couples, and found that the marriages that endure are those in which the couples have the most fun. It's the same thing with writing, or anything else that we wish to make a discipline (or become a disciple of). We are more likely to keep doing something when that something is fun. This is especially true in the years that we are developing our basic skills; as in learning to play the piano or speaking a foreign language, the pleasure increases as our skills develop. You have to keep at it long enough to generate involvement. Then you can say, as Susan, a college professor writing her third novel, said, "I would rush home to work on it as though I was meeting a lover!"

NO GUTS, NO STORY is a slogan I keep tacked over my desk to inspire me to take risks in my writing. Even before Teresa, who had more need for courage than most in writing of her struggles with multiple personality disorder, shared with me this text from a greeting card she had seen, I had stuck up the original version, NO GUTS, NO GLORY. Even Benedictine monks include military imagery in their daily readings; and there are others that work as well. "Get down and do push-ups!" Zane, as a platoon sergeant, would say to his young charges when they got stuck during a test. Within moments, they would come up with a correct answer. Of course, you, too, will get stuck along the way; it's a good idea to come up in advance with your own form of push-ups, whether it's going for a long walk, working in your garden, trying a new recipe, or even vacuuming the house. (In *House & Garden*, in a piece called "The Art of Sucking Up," fashion designer Isaac Mizrahi avowed his love of vacuuming, calling it "more of a purge than anything.") I was single while finishing *Fatal Flowers*, and all I did besides write was go out dancing (and inadvertently research what I didn't yet know was to be my next book, *Sleeping with Soldiers*).

Just as there are no bad dogs, there is no bad writing, only writing in which the problems haven't been solved yet. If I thought that every time I sat down to write I had to produce something publishable, I would feel paralyzed with fear. And so will you. In fact, most of the writers I know have developed devices for demystifying what they do. Philip Roth said that he once wrote 800 pages to get the first line of a book. Poet Dana Wildsmith writes letters each morning to get started. (Among the people to whom she writes are authors whose works she has read and admired; Dana says she has made a number of writing friends this way.)

Pat Conroy works in longhand, a tedious process that slows production, but gives him the feeling of making a book the old-fashioned way. He overwrote *Beach Music* by a good 400 pages, then cut them at the end under the guidance of his editor, Nan Talese, reducing the manuscript to a mere thousand pages!

When John Berendt came to Savannah to hang out for seven years, the word around town was that he was just another Savannah eccentric who *said* he was writing a book. But at Zona Rosa we knew differently: John had visited the group to read from his manuscript in progress, and we had seen the voluminous and carefully filled three-hole notebooks he had packed with draft after draft of *Midnight in the Garden of Good and Evil.*

Joyce Maynard calls her writing "typing," as in "I just go out to my study and start typing." As I mentioned, I have an acronym stuck up over my desk: JUST, for Just You Start Typing. Doing this breaks through my resistance every time.

To further demystify the act of writing, KEEP NOTEBOOKS. It's no accident that my daughter Laura had written the first draft of a novel by age seventeen, or that all three of my children write poems as easily as they brush their teeth: our house has always been filled with journals—every family member kept them (and probably read each other's, despite hiding places throughout the house!)—books, and people in the art of writing. In chapter 6, I described my four-notebook method for tracking my own thoughts, feelings, ideas, and goals. Use my method, or devise your own—but do keep notebooks. They are your source material.

Most important, keep a WRITING NOTEBOOK. Date the first page, and list your writing goals. In your writing notebook, talk to yourself about your writing. Analyze your own process. Give yourself suggestions for improvement. Consider your strengths and weaknesses as a writer as you become aware of them, and give yourself suggestions for either overcoming or bypassing them.

In this notebook, DEVELOP A CRITERIA for what you like and don't like in a piece of writing. (When a student tells me that one thing she likes about my workshop is that I don't try to make her write like me, I consider this a high compliment, as it shows that I have achieved my goal of facilitating each person in developing her own criteria.)

Copy and analyze passages from poems, stories, and novels you like. Before I began *The Hurricane Season,* I read novels for six months, writing a "report" on each one—what I liked and didn't like—in my writing notebook. Remember: no writer writes in a vacuum; we all learn from one another. This is the place to look at how others have done it.

I keep a separate notebook with a flowered-fabric cover for quotes that inspire or amuse me, as well as keeping some written in large letters, among the images and clippings, on the bulletin board above my desk. Among those hanging there now are:

LIFE IS A PARACHUTE VOYAGE AND NOT WHAT WE WOULD THINK.
—Huidobro

A WRITER IS SOMEONE FOR WHOM WRITING IS MORE DIFFICULT THAN IT IS FOR OTHER PEOPLE.
—Thomas Mann

MY ONLY JOB IS TO BE TALENTED; THAT IS, TO UNDERSTAND HOW TO DISTINGUISH IMPORTANT TESTIMONY FROM (THE) UNIMPORTANT.
—Chekhov

SUGAR-COATED BABY BORN TO CHOCOHOLIC MOTHER.
(Tabloid headline)

Your writing notebook might be a good place for these, too.

I also buy cheap white posterboard at the supermarket and on it I list the parts—chapters, poems, essays—of a major work in progress in bright felt-tip marker: checking each part as I complete it gives me a feeling of satisfaction, and reinforces my belief that I can complete the rest.

In addition, I stack a special shelf with the books I love most. When I need inspiration, I pull one out and read a few paragraphs or stanzas, then go back to my desk refreshed.

Pat Conroy says that though he writes prose, he reads poetry every day; in fact, he draws words from the poems and finds a place for them in his prose. Because poetry is such a demanding and concise literary form, reading good poetry—whether one intends to write it or not—is good for every writer.

The short story writer Raymond Carver kept a sign above his desk, NO CHEAP TRICKS, which he amended to NO ~~CHEAP~~ TRICKS. As you progress in skill, your notebook is a good place to list your own cheap tricks. Among mine are "coagulating," or gathering, similar material into one place in order to avoid redundancy, then choosing the one best way to say it. Admittedly this is easier to do with a computer, but I recall doing the same thing by cut-and-paste method back in my manual typewriter days. I would cut a first-draft manuscript into pieces, making little piles on the rug of the paragraphs and sections that went together, then I would glue them in order, selecting only the best parts (maybe making outlines by topic in high school *had* had an effect!). I did this with poetry, too, cutting out alternate images and laying them atop the stanzas, then reading them aloud into a cassette recorder in order to see which read best. I would glue the yellow second sheets end on end into one long page, which I draped across my bed, so I could look at all the parts at once.

Your writing notebook is also the place to work out problems in writing, a place to give yourself pep talks, like a good coach. When I first began writing poetry, and heard about meter, I thought I would go mad—how could I ever conquer it, or contain my most passionate ideas within such limitations? Now, years—and hundreds of poems—later, I consider my ability to devise an organic—and metered—structure for each poem I write to be one of my strengths. While writing *Fatal Flowers* I struck another brick wall: dialogue. Again, I worked at ways to create and use dialogue in my own way—for example, giving a narrative paragraph energy by beginning it with a pungent quote—and today I feel comfortable with my use of this literary element. In addition, I have learned, wherever I am, to *listen*; indeed, overheard conversation and bits of speech often end up in my journal for further use.

On the other hand, when anyone compliments an aspect of your writing, write that down, too. If no one else does it, compliment yourself!

In your notebook, VISUALIZE your finished product, and the qualities you wish it to have. "I want my novel to be so delicious, you would eat it off a sore leg," Courtenay wrote, using a southern saying, which even if somewhat revolting, got the point across. "I want this book to have style and verve," I jotted as I began *Sleeping with Soldiers*. One of my more ethereal early goals for my writing was "to bridge the gap between immediacy and depth." It is one that still holds for me today.

Those Peanuts—or Even Continents—of Styrofoam,
and How to Ferret Them Out

The two biggest obstacles to writing well, aside from lack of perseverance, are failure to develop a criteria for a good piece of writing and resisting the act of revision. In fact, this willingness to make whatever changes that are to the betterment of the manuscript may be the sign of the true professional. Revision revises us; indeed, it is possibly the most character-enhancing task the writer undertakes.

But the sting can be taken out of even this exercise in self-denial: rather than seeing what you write as engraved in stone, be willing to play around with your work. Consider whether or not each part contributes to the whole—if it needn't be there, it probably shouldn't be, no matter how wonderful. But this doesn't mean it won't be appropriate for your next project—keep the rejected darlings in file folders, ready to be brought out at the first opportunity, when they may more fully come into their own. Keep your old drafts, too—no telling when you may want to look over them for that one phrase you thought you had lost. (Of course, you will also want to have them on hand in case universities come looking to buy your papers as the years go on!) And if you think small changes don't matter that much, just think what fifteen extra pounds in the wrong place can do to a beautiful woman!

But the real test comes if a major change is needed: when I turned in the final manuscript for *Sleeping with Soldiers* to my editor Jennifer Josephy, three years after I had signed the contract with her, she was pleased—except with one chapter. "This seems to slow down the whole," she said, speaking of a 70-page section. In a flash, I saw what she meant. "Let's take it out then," I said, cutting in a matter of seconds what it had taken me three months to write. Indeed, when I sent what I considered to be the final draft of this book off to my writer friend Carol Polsgrove, she called within days to suggest a major structural change, one that would mean including the same materials, but reordering them. Envisioning the work such a restructuring would mean, I at first resisted what she was saying. Then I realized she might be right, and the next day I began.

The point is not to determine the theme, the structure, or anything else, too early. The theme, I told the memoir-writing workshop in Iowa, will emerge naturally and organically from the material, as will a structure. I asked each member to come up with a "log line," as it's called in the movies, or a simple paraphrase to describe the theme of his or her memoir. Rene's was simple, and was contained in her title, *I Married a Bloody*

Yank. Bob came up with "a boy's coming to terms with his eth-
nicity." His story was of gowing up Czech and Bohemian in
the middle of the cornfields of Iowa. Because his grandfather
had been a baker who made wonderful Czech pastries, which
the young Robert loved, he later became a gourmet cook. I suggested food might also be a major theme in his book. Margarett's theme was not quite so easily discernible. In her first
story of growing up in a blue-collar neighborhood in industrial
Cambridge, Masschusetts, she tells a horrendous tale of being
pulled and held beneath the water by a boy she thought she
liked. In the second, she described her teenage observations of
what she saw as her mother's enslaved life as the subservient wife
of the neighborhood druggist; and her own efforts to free herself from being pulled under as her mother had been. "*I* see it
clearly," I said to her as she looked at me, puzzled. "Here is a
young woman, trying to save herself from being pulled down
by life."

PET, or Paraphrase Every Time

Paraphrasing is useful at any stage of the game. When you are
stuck and having a hard time finding the way to say what you
mean, write a paraphase of the stanza, the paragraph, or a whole
section. Then ask yourself whether what you have written expresses the paraphrase, or if not, how can it best do so?

My sister, Anne, a poet, believes in this method so much that
she came up with the acronym PET, or Paraphrase Every Time.
Before that, she often had gotten stuck, wondering what belonged in her poem and what didn't, but when she started beginning each new draft with a rough paraphrase, written in the mar-
gin, she found herself choosing more easily among images,
selecting the ones that exactly fit her meaning.

I knew I would be able to begin and complete *The Hurricane
Season* when I was able to put a simple three-word outline, each
followed by a series of phrases describing possible scenes, on my

bulletin board: *Narcissism, Denial,* and *Acceptance.* These were the three words I used to describe the path my character Easter O'Brian would follow through more than 400 pages.

"Take the greatest unknown, and say it in the simplest way," an artist friend said to me once, not knowing that he was giving me the gift of a lifetime.

Along the way, deal with EXTERNAL AND INTERNAL IMPEDIMENTS.

We all have them and we all have to deal with them. Rather than living in ivory towers, many writers have more complicated lives than most. But it is possible to WRITE THROUGH THE PAIN. Pat Conroy's brother committed suicide, just as Pat was completing *Beach Music.* I have often written around and through major life tragedies, and have found the process of anger, denial, bargaining, and acceptance to be accelerated by writing regularly, especially in my journals. Julie Cameron, author of *The Artist's Way,* says in her *Morning Pages Journal,* "We are tempted, always, to reverse cause and effect: 'I was too crabby to write . . . ,' instead of, 'I didn't write . . . so I am crabby.'" Indeed, there may be no one who needs to write more on a regular basis, and only in the notebooks if that is all one can accomplish at the time, than a woman caretaking a dying husband, or a woman who has lost her child—or a woman who is losing her sanity.

Yet dealing with EXTERNAL IMPEDIMENTS is often the easier matter. Carol Polsgove, a single mother and full-time college professor, goes to bed at eight in order to get up at four-thirty to finish her book. While writing her third novel, *Looking for Mr. Goodbar,* Judith Rossner was also a single mother who rose early to write before going to her job as a secretary in a methadone clinic.

Until we have learned to shrivel them with lack of attention, and/or confrontation, the INTERNAL IMPEDIMENTS will raise their ugly heads. As long as we pay pay homage to them, the six Fears, as discussed in chapter 4, will thrive—the Fear of Retribution, the Fear of People, the Fear of Failure, the Fear of Shame, the Fear of Success, the Fear of Chaos. The best way to subdue them is to do the work anyway.

An exorcise suggested by Tessa Albert Warschaw, in her book, *Rich Is Better*, might help you understand the why of your fears: list the things you were permitted to do, required to do, and forbidden to do as a child, she suggests; then make a similar list of what you permit yourself to do, require yourself to do, and forbid yourself to do as an adult. Most of us find that the two sets of lists are remarkably similar.

On the other hand, REFUSE JUDGMENT. In Zona Rosa, everyone loved it when Mary, age seventy and a devout Catholic, shared her fantasy of a fling with her dream man, Anthony Hopkins. Not liking a character or what he or she does, thinks, or feels is not a good basis for criticism, if it is true to the human experience (and if someone has thought to write about it, it surely must be).

Which leads to the next principle: THE PERSONAL (AND THE SPECIFIC) LEADS TO THE UNIVERSAL, rather than the other way around. Think of a book you never wanted to end: wasn't there something about the protagonist you identified with, no matter how different your lives might really have been? Whatever is within the realm of human, or even imaginary, experience, is appropriate to literature. At least two writers, James Dickey and Erica Jong, have advised that we write to the edge of ludicrousness, to write the very thing we thought we couldn't. I have learned that whenever I think, *I can't write that—that's too outrageous/too shocking/too honest*, that very line or image becomes the one about which people come up to me and say, "I had that very same experience, I've just never heard anyone express it before."

GET HELP IF YOU NEED IT. Edna, a grocery store stock clerk, was embarrassed by her lack of formal education. But she wanted to write her true-life story of twice being an unwed teenage mother, being held prisoner during her pregnancies, and then forced to give her babies up for adoption. When I read it as written, in her own simple language, her tale brought her, and others in the group, to tears. Grammar and syntax were not Edna's forte, but with the help of Susan, a grammarian, and the others, she received gentle coaching in these matters. Grammar could even be funny, we found. Everyone tittered as Susan advised Peggy that the friend she had described in her tender memoir had "hanged—not hung—himself; though he very well might have been *hung!*" When Melinda at last finished her novel, *The Mark of Eve*, she asked Danielle, who makes her living as a freelance copy editor, and June, who we felt was an "ideal reader"—both intelligent and receptive to her story—to give the manuscript a careful reading before she sent it to agents.

In Zona Rosa, WE READ EXORCISES AND MANUSCRIPTS ALOUD. Often, I read so the authors can hear how their work sounds. But this is something you can do at home, either with a trusted writing friend or into a cassette recorder, a method I frequently used while learning to write poetry. Some Zona Rosans have found writing buddies, good friends with whom they can sit and write, then read back to one another. Susan and Carolyn, for example, have made a ritual of renting the same mountain cabin for a weekend during the Christmas holidays, while they have time off from teaching. "We walk and drink and eat and write and read our manuscripts to one another," says Susan. "It's wonderful!"

On the other hand, BE CAREFUL TO WHOM YOU READ (OR SHOW) YOUR WRITING. A spouse, a sister, a professor, or a close friend might not be the best person. Watch out for that sinking feeling that comes from sharing with someone who does not share your goals, indeed, may even feel threatened by them. Margarett told me about feeling dashed by a much-lauded author she had had a conference with: "'You're too intense; you need to step back from your work,' she told me. I felt devastated and went away not knowing what she meant." She seemed relieved when I suggested it sounded very much like saying why don't you have brown eyes instead of blue—not very useful advice at all! If you're writing what you hope will communicate to a wide audience, it may not pay to read it to someone who reads only literary journals and *The New York Review of Books*, as wonderful as those publications may be. While considering titles for this book, I picked up the telephone to call Nell, a close friend, then put it down again, realizing that she reads mostly scholarly tomes, and had hated one of my favorite novels, *Anywhere But Here* by Mona Simpson. While Nell and I might be friends, we might not be on the same wavelength as far as this book is concerned.

SUPPORT, STIMULATION, and STANDARDS OF EXCELLENCE are the three attitudes that make Zona Rosa work. Make sure that you receive all three in any writing group in which you participate and in any discussion of your work. Insist that your strenghs be supported, your weaknesses, while you are still conquering them, be treated with respect. Remember that what is commonly called criticism can be positive, and experienced as support.

Finally, keep in mind that writing and publishing are two different processes. The writing is a spiritual journey, paralleling our journey through life. Through it, we become part of the secret world of artists and writers, and enter a perpetual church of the arts, which, if we let it, will ward off the envy, competitiveness, and the other bugaboos of the creative life, leaving us grateful on a daily basis. Don't trouble yourself with the second until you have done the first, and have done it well. As Courtenay said, coining another acronym that has stood the test of time for the Zona Rosans, FIF, or Finish It First. Folks who do otherwise—no matter how talented they may be—tend to fall away long before the first process is completed. But that's another book, perhaps best read when you have done your heart's work and hold your completed manuscript in hand.

< APPENDIX C >

And Even a Few Recipes

Over the years, the food we consumed to keep us going while discussing writing in Zona Rosa has become a highly anticipated aspect of each meeting. Indeed, it was largely because of the refreshments we enjoyed that we labeled ourselves "The Goddesses of Excess."

For a while we had a list, with volunteers agreeing to supply refreshments for a certain month. But that didn't last long: either the ones who had agreed would forget on her month, or others would bring food anyway, overwhelming my small kitchen. So we fell back into the old way—with me preparing maybe one thing, and others bringing what they wished and when they wished. Some of the Zona Rosans liked to cook, others didn't— Susan had an almost allergic reaction to the word *recipe*, and Carolyn and Abbie had an aversion to it, too ("You expect *me* to make coffee?" Abbie asked one day when I asked her to do so in a pinch. "Why, chile, I ain't *never* learned to do that!"). But Susan would do her share by bringing the prerequisite half-liters of white wine, and Abbie knew just where to buy the Coca-Colas in the small curvaceous classic glass bottles.

Seeing how chintzy I was—I used paper napkins in the coffee pot instead of filters, and never had paper towels on hand— Tyler, who had more reasons for frugality than most, brought me a pack of the filters, drawling in her thick Buckhead accent,

"Hyah! Ah know they're just *too* ostentatious. But use them anyway!" When I made a low-fat cheese to mix with basil and garlic by draining nonfat yogurt in a sieve, I explained to June that I lined the sieve with a Handi-Wipe instead of cheese-cloth. "Ooh!" she said, wrinkling her nose, until I explained that I meant a *new* Handi-Wipe, not one I had used in the kitchen sink.

Indeed, we were all experts, it seemed, at making do. Grated Parmesan cheese from a round cardboard cylinder, mixed with low-fat mayonnaise, grated onion, Texas Pete or Tabasco, was a popular spread for crackers, or could be mixed with canned arti-choke hearts, baked, and served warm, becoming a mysterious dish for which newcomers always asked the recipe. Marna dumped readymade chili sauce and canned tiny shrimp over a hunk of cream cheese, and it tasted just fine (as everyone down South knows, cream cheese is simply a palette on which other flavors are deposited, from pepper jelly to Pickapeppa or Jezebel sauce—a wicked mixture of pineapple preserves, hot mustard, apple jelly, and horseradish). As was fitting for a group called Zona Rosa, jalapeno peppers and Tex-Mex snacks played an inordinate role in our noshing. Sometimes we ordered pizza in from Godfather's, or bought a bucket of Kentucky Fried Chicken or a big bowl of shrimp salad from Cary Hilliard's, a local seafood restaurant. Peggy, who lived on a sailboat and held two jobs, had little time to cook, but always seemed to have friends in the right places, such as the male cook whose dense raspberry chocolate mousse cake she brought one day. Latrelle would bring a hunk of sharp cheddar, also known in the South as "rat cheese," and a box of Ritz Crackers; Ruby would supply Mallomars, Fig Newtons, chocolate-covered graham crackers, or vanilla wafers with marshmallows stuck between them—the same simple treats she had enjoyed as a child, back in South Car-olina in the 1920s. Everyone depended on my having at least one bag of Pepperidge Farm Chocolate Chunk with Pecan cook-ies on hand. Like my Grandmother Carroll had throughout her life, Joan loved "sweet things," and her fashionably petite figure was a contradiction to an otherwise pure life.

However some of us might diet for the the rest of the month, we all seemed to suspend counting calories and fat grams on this particular day, just as we suspended disbelief in reading one another's manuscripts. Judy had even self-published a book, *D.I.E.T. (DID I EAT THAT?)*, describing her loss of 135 pounds. But on Zona Rosa days, mortification of the flesh was left behind. A small bow might be made in the direction of "light" ingredients (the amount of cream cheese we consumed would have been criminal, had some of us not started using the low-fat variety). But the recipes themselves remained sinful. On the day Clare, lean and elegant, brought her Southern Comfort Cake, she had just run a marathon, arriving a bit late for the group. "I don't eat that stuff," she declared, explaining her fitness while handing over the recipe for the cake that made the rest of us drool.

When Melinda, a superb cook, suspended her weight-loss goals to prepare yet another treat for us, we were grateful; after all, would we have faulted Julia Child for supplying the kinds of treats that made her plump? Melinda introduced us to southern variations of the Jewish foods she had adored as a child growing up in Brooklyn; an inventive cook, she took liberties with tradition, as when she served us "blintze muffins—something that only a writer could come up with. But their smell while baking is sexier than pheromones!" Nor was she above preparing southern ingredients Yiddish-style. She said that her Vidalia onion pie, which couldn't be richer if she tried, was actually the creation of her mother-in-law, Esther, "a nice Jewish lady from Brighton Beach who just happens to love okra, grits, and Vidalia onions, but not boiled peanuts."

In fact, many of us used the food we served on Zona Rosa days to tap into the sense memories that gave us ideas for our writing. Danielle smeared cream cheese on canned brown bread, which recalled the sandwiches my mother had made of canned date-nut bread and cream cheese; she also brought cream cheese and olive sandwiches, just like the ones I had had as a child. Danielle was my daughter's age, and when I said I wanted to make popovers but lacked the proper pan, we reminisced over memories of the popovers her daddy, the cook in the house, had made for her around the same time I had been making them for my kids—"hollow, with a big hole in the middle for butter and jam." Courtenay enjoyed the ladylike sandwiches, undoubtedly reminiscent of the ones she had enjoyed at her women's or garden club, that I made by layering butter, watercress, and a ground chicken and walnut salad on whole wheat bread, which I then cut into triangles.

One day, as we sat with paper plates perched on our knees, Debbie regaled us with stories of the Mardi Gras King cake that had been part of the celebration each year when she had been a girl growing up in New Orleans; in fact, her sister still sent her one annually. "The surprise was to see who would get the piece with the ring in it." But the memories the cake had tapped were not only happy ones; the next month, the pastry appeared in a poignant story that she had not been able to fully recall before.

When I was a child, Grandmother Carroll made coconut cakes, grating the coconut herself on a hand grater for however many hours it took; to this day, I can remember the sweet sugary taste of coconut along with a rich yellow cake melting in my mouth. But Delta gave me the recipe for a Kitty Brown cake that was equally delicious and used ingredients off the supermarket shelf. And when Maxine gave me a recipe for a candy called White Trash on the very day we had been discussing whether the use of the phrase "white trash" was descriptive or condescending in a story set in a trailer park, the name alone made it too good to pass up.

At Christmas each year, Courtenay supplied a big box of fat Georgia pecan halves, which I toasted with butter and salt, or saved for pecan pie or pralines. Since pralines could only be successfully made at home in warm weather, I kept the pecans in the freezer until late spring.

MELINDA'S BLINTZE MUFFINS

12 ounces cottage cheese (any kind, even low fat)
2 eggs, lightly beaten
½ cup flour
½ teaspoon baking powder
7 tablespoons sugar
2 tablespoons melted butter
Pinch of salt

Combine ingredients. Spray tartlet pans or muffin tins with Pam (or grease them). Fill almost to the top. Bake small tartlets at 350 degrees for 20–30 minutes (until puffed and lightly browned around the edges). Larger muffins will take longer. The muffins freeze well, and can be microwaved out of the freezer.

HER MOTHER-IN-LAW'S VIDALIA ONION PIE

1 cup saltine crackers, crushed
¼ cup melted butter
2 large Vidalia onions, thinly sliced
2 tablespoons butter
¾ cup milk
2 eggs, lightly beaten
¾ teaspoon salt
Pepper
¼ cup grated cheddar cheese

Mix crumbs and melted butter in a 9-inch pie plate; press firmly to form bottom crust. Cook onions in 2 tablespoons butter until soft. Place on top of prepared crumbs. Top with milk-egg mixture. Sprinkle cheese on top. Bake for 30 minutes at 350 degrees. Let cool a bit before serving.

For individual pies, spray the cups of a deep muffin tin generously with Pam. Divide the cracker-crumb butter mixture evenly among the cups, pressing down firmly. Top with onions, then milk-egg mixture and cheese. Allow about 20 minutes baking time. Remove carefully from muffin cups.

ZONA ROSA QUICHE

1 8- or 9-inch pie crust
½ pound sharp cheddar, grated
2 small firm tomatoes, diced
1 7-ounce can of jalapeno peppers, drained
4 eggs, well beaten

Preheat the oven to 350 degrees. Sprinkle cheese in pie shell, cover with tomato and peppers. Pour eggs over. Bake for 30–40 minutes. Serve at room temperature.

JANA'S OLIVE–CREAM CHEESE APPETIZER

1 sheet cracker bread (available at some markets) or soft
    flour tortillas
2 8-ounce packages cream cheese
1 7-ounce can of jalapeno peppers, well drained
Small black and green olives, chopped or sliced
(pimento-stuffed olives for the center of the rolls)

Mix cream cheese, peppers, and chopped or sliced olives. Spread on cracker bread or tortillas. Place a row of stuffed olives down the middle. Roll each strip tightly. Wrap in plastic wrap and refrigerate for 2 hours. Slice into circles. Serve alone or with salsa.

ONETHA'S CREAM CHEESE POUND CAKE

3 sticks butter
1 8-ounce package cream cheese
3 cups sugar
Dash of salt
1½ teaspoons vanilla (or almond extract to taste)
6 large eggs
3 cups sifted cake flour (best results with Softasilk)

Cream butter, cream cheese, and sugar until light and fluffy. Add salt and vanilla or almond extract, and beat well. Add eggs, one at a time; beat well after each addition. Stir in flour. Spoon mixture into greased tube pan and bake at 325 degrees for about 1½ hours. (For loaf cakes, divide equally between three greased (Pam) loaf pans. Bake at 325 degrees for 1 hour, 10–15 minutes.)

CLARE'S SOUTHERN COMFORT CAKE

Glaze:
4 tablespoons butter or margarine
⅛ cup water
½ cup granulated sugar
¼ cup Southern Comfort

Cake:
1 box (18¼ ounces) Duncan Hines Yellow Cake Mix with Pudding
1 package (3¼ ounces) instant vanilla pudding mix
4 eggs
½ cup cold water
½ cup oil
½ cup Southern Comfort

To make glaze, melt butter in a saucepan. Sir in water and sugar. Boil 3 minutes, stirring constantly. Remove from the heat and stir in Southern Comfort.

Combine cake ingredients in a large bowl and beat at medium speed for 2 minutes. Pour into a greased and floured 10-inch tube or 12-cup Bundt pan. Bake at 325 degrees for 1 hour. Set on a rack to cool. Invert on serving plate. Prick top immediately; drizzle and brush half of glaze evenly over top and sides. Reserve remaining glaze. After cake has cooled, reheat glaze and brush it evenly over cake. Just before serving, sift 1 tablespoon powdered sugar over cake.

KITTY BROWN CAKE

1st day: mix together 2 packages (or 12 ounces) frozen coconut, 1 8-ounce carton sour cream, 2 cups sugar, 1 teaspoon vanilla. Refrigerate overnight.

2nd day: Prepare Deluxe Duncan Hines Yellow or Butter-Flavored Cake Mix. When baked, let cool and split into 4 layers. Spread all but 1 cup of sour cream mixture between the layers. Blend the remaining cup of the mixture with 1½ cups whipped cream. Spread on tops and sides. Refrigerate for three days in an airtight container before serving.

ROSEMARY'S SOUTHERN PECAN PIE

¼ cup butter
1 cup brown sugar
¼ teaspoon salt
1 cup dark Karo syrup
3 eggs, beaten
1 teaspoon vanilla (or a little Jack Daniels' Black Label)
1½ cups pecan halves
1 9-inch pie shell (frozen is fine)

Cream butter and sugar together until fluffy; add next 4 ingredients. Sprinkle pecans on bottom of pie shell; pour the filling over the pecans. Bake at 450 degrees for 10 minutes, reduce temperature to 350 degrees and bake 35 minutes longer. Outer edge of filling should be set, center slightly soft, when knife inserted in center comes out clean.

RUBY'S SWEET POTATO PIE

2 sticks butter
1 cup mashed sweet potatoes
3 cups sugar
1 small can evaporated milk
3 eggs
1 teaspoon vanilla

Whip potatoes and butter while potatoes are hot. Then add the other things. Pour into a pie shell and bake at 325 degrees.

SAVANNAH PECAN PRALINES

¾ cup white sugar
¾ cup light brown sugar
½ cup evaporated milk

Heat, stirring, until a bit dropped from a spoon into a glass of water forms a soft ball. Add 1 teaspoon vanilla and 1 tablespoon butter or margarine. Remove from the heat. Beat until the mixture begins to thicken; add 1 cup pecan halves. Drop quickly onto waxed paper. Let set to harden.

(Don't try this on a day that is the least bit steamy or moist.)

MAXINE'S WHITE TRASH

1 box Golden Grahams cereal (all but 2 cups)
16 ounces lightly salted peanuts
24 ounces white chocolate

Mix cereal and peanuts in a large bowl. Melt chocolate in the microwave. Pour over dry mixture on waxed paper. Let cool and break into pieces.

For information on Zona Rosa workshops, please contact Rosemary Daniell at:

Zona Røsa
P.O. Box 1472
Savannah, Georgia 31402

E-Mail: MyZonaRosa@aol.com